PHYSICS
AND ITS FIFTH
DIMENSION:
SOCIETY

PHYSICS AND ITS FIFTH DIMENSION: SOCIETY

DIETRICH SCHROEER
University of North Carolina, Chapel Hill

ADDISON-WESLEY PUBLISHING COMPANY
Reading, Massachusetts · Menlo Park, California
London · Amsterdam · Don Mills, Ontario · Sydney

This book is in the
ADDISON-WESLEY SERIES IN PHYSICS

Consulting Editor
David Lazarus

ISBN 0-201-06767-6
LMNOPQRS-AL-8987654

PREFACE

This book is the outcome of a one-semester course dealing with the science-society interaction, a course which I have presented several times since 1969 in the Physics Department of the University of North Carolina at Chapel Hill. While the approach toward science in this course was fairly general, the examples chosen to illustrate this interaction were taken primarily from the area of physics—partly for reasons of "one-upmanship," since I at least know a little about that field.

The intention of the course was to let liberal-arts students face science on their own terms rather than on terms chosen by scientists. For this reason, and to make the course as comfortable for them as possible, the main theme was the relevance of physics rather than physics itself. There was, for example, no mathematics (I wrote down five equations during the semester and apologized five times), and the grades for the course were based primarily on term papers with topics chosen by the students themselves.

Classroom procedure differed considerably from that in the usual physics courses. Without equations to write on the board and discuss, the lectures had to be essentially written in advance (in fact in the earliest version of this course the lectures were more "read" than "given"). Each 40-minute lecture was then followed by a discussion period of similar length. In stimulating the discussion, questions like those at the end of the chapters in this book proved helpful, although it was generally easy to involve the students in debates. This book then consists of these lectures as modified by such discussions.

There were three main threads running through these lectures. (a) There was just enough of the science of physics to give the students a feeling for what it was all about. This was presented mainly through demonstrations such as the spiraling of electrons in a magnetic field or a search by scintillation counter for a radioactive "hot spot" in a phantom thyroid gland. The amount of physics included did tend to shrink as the course developed. (b) There was an attempt to place physics in a historical and social context in an effort to illuminate history itself. (c) Finally and most importantly, there was a continuing examination of the impact of physics on other sciences like geology and botany, on humanistic disciplines like philosophy and literature, and on social activities like war and politics.

It is difficult to acknowledge all the contributions made to this book by the students in the course and by the many fellow faculty members and friends who have had to suffer through my seemingly eternal involvement in it. Ed Ludwig provided inspiration for starting the course. Among the people who made some very specific helpful comments were David Lazarus, Allan Franklin, Roger H. Stuewer, Kenneth W. Ford; and the typist-proofreaders Cathy and Robert C. Nininger, Jr. Waldo E. Haisley and Charles D. Spencer very critically read all the manuscript for both content and English. Thank you very much for all of your help. The responsibility for all errors and false conclusions is of course my own. Finally, whatever good there is in this book I would like to dedicate to my wife Bunny, whose sacrifices gave me the time and will power to do the work.

Chapel Hill, North Carolina   D. S.
January 1972

ACKNOWLEDGMENTS

The author wishes to thank the following publishers for their cooperation in allowing him to reprint the material appearing on the pages listed below.

Pages 10, 11, 22. From F. R. Leavis and M. Yudkin, *Two Cultures? The Significance of C. P. Snow* (New York: Pantheon Books, a division of Random House, Inc.), pp. 28, 30, 34, 46–48. Copyright © 1962 by Random House, Inc. Reprinted by permission.

Pages 20–22. From Sir J. Stamp, *Science of Social Adjustment* (London: Macmillan). Copyright © 1937 by Macmillan. Reprinted by permission of St. Martin's Press, Inc., The Macmillan Company of Canada, and Macmillan, London and Basingstoke.

Pages 53–55. From A. Pannekoek, *A History of Astronomy* (London: Allen & Unwin Ltd.), pp. 31, 39, 42–45. Copyright © 1961 by Allen & Unwin, Ltd. Reprinted by permission.

Pages 60, 94–98. From S. L. Jaki, *The Relevance of Physics* (Chicago: The University of Chicago Press), pp. 71, 72, 75, 145, 375–377. Copyright © 1966 by The University of Chicago Press. Reprinted by permission.

Pages 62–64, 68–70. From S. Sambursky, *The Physical World of the Greeks* (New York: Collier Books), pp. 44, 61–63, 117, 258–260. Copyright © 1962 by Macmillan; reprinted by their permission and that of Routledge & Kegan Paul, Ltd.

Pages 64–66. From G. Gamow, *Biography of Physics* (New York: Harper & Row, Publishers, Inc.), pp. 12, 15–16. Copyright © 1961 by Harper & Row. Reprinted by permission.

Pages 73, 78, 80–82, 84, 85. From Gerhard Szczesny, *The Case Against Bertolt Brecht*, translated by Alexander Gode (New York: Frederick Ungar Publishing Co., Inc.) Copyright © 1969 by Frederick Ungar Publishing Co., Inc. Reprinted by permission.

Page 83. From *Introduction to Contemporary Civilization in the West*, Vol. I, 2nd edition (New York: Columbia University Press). Copyright © 1957 by Columbia University Press. Reprinted by permission.

Pages 91, 92. From J. D. Bernal, *The Social Function of Science* (Cambridge, Mass.: The M.I.T. Press), p. 167. Copyright © 1967 by The M.I.T. Press. Reprinted with their permission and that of Routledge & Kegan Paul, Ltd.

Page 110. From J. W. von Goethe, *Faust*, translated by C. F. MacIntyre (New York: New Directions Publishing Corporation). Copyright © 1949 by New Directions Publishing Corporation. Reprinted by permission.

Pages 111–112. From S. L. Jaki, "Goethe and the Physicists," *The American Journal of Physics*, **37**, 195–203 (1969). Reprinted by permission.

Pages 145–150. From A. Burroughs, *Art Criticism from a Laboratory* (Westport, Conn.: Greenwood Press), pp. 93–96. Copyright © 1965 by the Greenwood Press, Inc. Reprinted by permission.

Page 168. From J. Updike, "Cosmic Gall," *Telephone Poles and Other Poems* (New York: Random House, Inc.) Originally published in *The New Yorker*, Dec. 17, 1960. Reprinted by permission of Random House, Inc.

Pages 178, 180, 186. From W. Haftman, *Painting in the Twentieth Century*, Vol. I (New York: Praeger Publishers, Inc.), pp. 117, 253. Copyright © 1965 by Praeger Publishers, Inc. Reprinted with their permission and that of Lund Humphries Publishers, Ltd., London.

Pages 180, 181. From Joshua C. Taylor, *Futurism* (New York: The Museum of Modern Art). Copyright © 1961 by The Museum of Modern Art. Reprinted by permission.

Pages 193–195, 199. From P. Frank, *Einstein: His Life and Times* (New York: Alfred A. Knopf). Copyright © 1957 by Alfred A. Knopf. Reprinted by permission of Random House, Inc.

Pages 195, 196. From D. Fleming and B. Bailyn, Eds., *The Intellectual Migration* (Cambridge, Mass.: The Belknap Press of Harvard University Press), p. 203. Copyright © 1969 by the Harvard University Press. Reprinted by their permission and that of Hans Bethe. From J. Stark and A. V. Hill, in *Nature*, February 24, 1934. Reprinted by permission.

Pages 213, 214. From N. P. Davis, *Lawrence and Oppenheimer* (New York: Simon and Schuster). Copyright © 1968 by Simon and Schuster. Reprinted by permission.

Page 224. From David Irving, *The German Atom Bomb* (New York: Simon and Schuster). Copyright © 1967 by Simon and Schuster. Reprinted with their permission and that of William Kimber & Co., Ltd., London.

Pages 227, 228. From Alice Kimball Smith, "Behind the Decision to use the Atomic Bomb: Chicago 1944–45," *Bulletin of the Atomic Scientists,* **14,** 288–312 (1958). Copyright © 1958 by the Educational Foundation for Nuclear Science. Reprinted by permission of *Science and Public Affairs, the Bulletin of the Atomic Scientists.*

Pages 245, 246. From P. Brown, *American Martyrs to Science Through the Roentgen Rays* (Springfield, Ill.: Charles C. Thomas, Publisher), pp. 101–1040. Copyright © 1936 by Charles C. Thomas, Publisher. Reprinted by permission.

Pages 247, 248. From P. Alexander, *Atomic Radiation and Life* (Baltimore: Penguin Books, 1965), pp. 110 and 145. Copyright © Peter Alexander, 1957, 1965. Reprinted by permission of Penguin Books Ltd.

Pages 275–278. From C. P. Curtis, *The Oppenheimer Case—The Trial of a Security System* (New York: Simon and Schuster), pp. 24, 38, 153–154, 184, 235, 243. Copyright © 1955 by Simon and Schuster. Reprinted by permission of Choate, Hall, & Stewart, executors of the estate of Charles P. Curtis.

Page 291. From L. C. L. Yuan, Ed., *Nature of Matter: Purposes of High-Energy Physics* (Upton, L.I. Brookhaven National Laboratory, 1965), pp. 15, 17, 27. Reprinted by permission.

Pages 296, 297. From E. Ashby, *Technology and the Academics* (London: Macmillan), pp. 10, 34, 36–37. Copyright © 1958 by Macmillan. Reprinted by permission of St. Martin's Press, Inc., The Macmillan Company of Canada, and Macmillan, London and Basingstoke.

Pages 300, 301. From *Physics: Survey and Outlook—A Report on the Present State of U.S. Physics and Its Requirements for Future Growth,* Publication 1295, Physics Survey Committee, National Academy of Sciences National Research Council, Washington, D.C., 1966, pp. 48–59. Reprinted by permission.

Pages 302, 303. From *Final Report of the Review Panel on Special Laboratories* (Cambridge, Mass.: The M.I.T. Press), pp. 20–21. Copyright © 1969 by The M.I.T. Press. Reprinted by permission.

Pages 306, 307. From Edmond Rostand, *Cyrano de Bergerac,* Hooker Translation (New York: Holt, Rinehart & Winston), pp. 123–125. Copyright © 1923 by Holt, Rinehart & Winston, Inc. Copyright © 1951 by Doris C. Hooker. Reprinted by permission of Holt, Rinehart & Winston, Inc.

Page 313. From Leonard Wibberley, *The Mouse on the Moon* (New York: Bantam Books JC136), p. 112. Copyright © 1958 by William Morrow and Company, Inc. Reprinted by permission.

Page 357. From a letter to the Editor by Lincoln P. Brower, *American Scientist* **58,** 618 (Nov.–Dec. 1970). Reprinted by permission.

CONTENTS

ix

INTRODUCTION

PURPOSE OF THE BOOK

It seems clear that science is doing things to our lives right now and will do much more in the future. Science, particularly through technology, may ultimately control and determine not only our lives but our very being as well. The discoverers of the knowledge from which this vast influence derives are the scientists, and perhaps they should also be the ones to develop the guidelines for the use of science. But actually it is others who will—the lawyers, TV commentators, and politicians. Consequently these other people must become acquainted with science; they must understand it well enough to control it rather than be controlled by it. Somehow scientists and nonscientists must converse to provide this understanding.

My personal involvement in the material presented here reflects the present soul-searching among scientists in general as they are being forced by economic and other pressures to face the question whether science is the future Saviour of Society or just an overpriced Sacred Cow which is taking money away from more worthy causes. Any satisfactory answer to this question must rest on an understanding of the way science and society interact. This book is therefore an attempt at a conversation to provide this understanding.

I have chosen to limit myself primarily to topics from physics—largely because it is the branch of science with which I am most familiar. This limitation has the added advantage that it permits the selection of a more comprehensive set of examples within the bounds of manageability, as well as allowing a more consistent viewpoint in presentation. Hopefully, this limitation does not detract seriously from the generality at which I have aimed.

THE APPROACH

Included in the discussion are such diverse topics as: "the Ralph Nader of ancient Greece," "the average lifespan in the 16th century," "the Declaration of Independence," "a sudden rise in the suicide rate among young people in Europe after 1774," "the melting of the polar icecap through energy pollution," "the unemployment of physicists," "secrecy and the Atomic Energy Commission," and "the social responsibility of scientists." The common thread which connects these topics is, of course, that they all are aspects of the science-society interaction. The general approach used in this book will be to outline and delineate certain useful categories of this interaction, followed by a presentation of specific examples (including the above) with discussion of how they fit into these categories.

The four categories I have found most useful for this purpose may be labeled as the *cultural, technological, social,* and *disciplinary* aspects of the science-society interaction. Each of them permits one to grasp a sizable aspect of this interaction by grouping together many seemingly unrelated examples.

By the word *cultural* I mean primarily the aspect of science as a culture traditionally opposed by or contrasted with something which can be called the humanistic culture. The most recent description of this conflict is in C. P. Snow's book *The Two Cultures,* but such a contrast can be traced back through history. In a deeper sense the contrast is between two modes of looking at the world, between viewing it as a mechanical device or as an organismic whole.

The *technological* impact of science on society has to do with changes in the quantity and the quality of life due to technological advances induced by science. By the quantity of life I mean such things as a longer lifespan, better health and more food; by the quality of life I mean more intangible things like the joy of living and human happiness. This interaction between science and society is probably the one most visible, and until recently it has been fairly favorable. It must be understood in order to appreciate many of the recent concerns about potentially harmful consequences of science.

The *social* impact of science is really a more concrete aspect of the concern with the "quality of life." It is a question of priorities. How much is science doing for us? How much support does it deserve? Do we fly to the moon, build high-energy accelerators, or build housing for the poor? I will review some criteria which may be used to evaluate the contributions of science to society as a whole and then apply these criteria to various examples in the past and the present.

The *disciplinary* aspect of this interaction has to do with what science as a discipline has to offer toward the solution of problems. Here the concept of science as a discipline aiming toward a public consensus on knowledge allows a distinction between the contributions that scientists can make toward a decision as experts in a field and the contributions they can make as laymen. The idea of the social responsibility of scientists is closely related to this view of science.

For each example presented and discussed in terms of these categories, there is then a list of references. The "prime references" are those books or articles that provided me with the basic outlook for each chapter. The "interesting reading" consists of material related to the topic but not necessarily specific to the content of the chapter. The questions at the end of each chapter are intended to stimulate thought and discussion and are not intended to have definite "right" answers.

A NOTE OF CAUTION

The material presented in this book should be approached with a healthy amount of skepticism. I obviously am not expert in all of these topics. I have tried to present what appeared to me a consensus of viewpoint among the authorities, but such a consensus can be only as definitive as the amount of material I have read and understood. And the conclusions are often quite personal. To give a few specific examples of places where there are hints of a personal bias: in Chapter 6 at least one of the references that I like (Farrington's *Science and Politics in the Ancient World*) has been labeled as Marxist in orientation; in contrast, Chapters 8, 16, and 21 may contain too much cold-war rhetoric. Since the references are not meant to be complete, but rather are intended to indicate what material was helpful or interesting to me personally, this is a problem which is ultimately resolvable only by independent reading—and through exercise of skepticism.

1 | THE TWO CULTURES

The opposite of a correct statement is a false statement. But the opposite of a profound truth may well be another profound truth.

Niels Bohr

This chapter is based on the book *The Two Cultures* by C. P. Snow and on various reviews and criticisms of his viewpoint of the problems facing our society. The dichotomy discussed here, which can be characterized as a conflict between two modes of thought, is one aspect of the interaction between science and society.

INTRODUCTION

In 1959 Sir C. P. Snow's *The Two Cultures* was published. In this book he expressed his feeling that there is a definite polarization of society into two components: a scientific culture and an intellectual culture. In the scientific culture he included both scientists and technologists; in the intellectual culture he included the whole of the humanities, or those endeavors that aim to form a Complete Man. He then complained that these two cultures are too isolated from each other, and that this isolation is a threat to society.

The response to *The Two Cultures* was immense. There were innumerable book reviews and commentaries—some favorable, some not so favorable, and a few scathingly hostile. The main objections centered around taking this culture gap too seriously. These two cultures may be just the extremes of a very broad spectrum of intellectual attitudes. Indeed, the proper approach toward this problem may perhaps best be represented by the sign "Culture versus Agriculture" displayed during a basketball game between an A & T college and a school oriented toward the liberal arts. Yet the very magnitude of the reaction to this book suggests that it touched on a very raw nerve. And this concept of a cultural polarization does turn out to be a useful one insofar as it indicates a contrast in modes of thought which has characterized many trends in the development of the science-society interaction.

In this chapter we shall therefore begin by discussing some of the characteristic distinctions of these two cultures. For our purposes, the most relevant distinction will, in fact, be the contrast in their modes of thought. And this contrast will then be used throughout the remainder of this book as a "tiepoint" for understanding the attitudes involved in this *cultural* interaction.

THE TWO CULTURES OF C. P. SNOW

The use of the words scientists and nonscientists in the Introduction already hinted at a cultural dichotomy. Specifically, there appear to exist two intellectual subdivisions of people in the world, two distinct cultures. According to Snow, there is the scientific culture, with the physical scientists as an exteme, and there is the intellectual culture, with the literary figures as its aristocrats. This is a contrast with an honorable history, and some of our present conflicts plaguing our society, such as the campus rebellion, are in a broad sense derivatives of it.

One may be somewhat unhappy with this particular way of describing our social polarization. I for one intend to call one of these the humanistic culture, since scientists can also be intellectuals. Yet there does seem to exist now a significant cultural dichotomy; whatever they may be called, there are two cultures with very different spheres of influence. The effect of the scientific culture, through the technological and scientific developments of the industrial and scientific revolutions, is open, visible, and clear. Our whole way of life is permeated and controlled by the consumer plenty, the social mobility due to automobiles, and the communications possibilities of TV and telephone. The influence of the humanistic culture is somewhat more subtle; but through control of the contents of TV, newspapers, cinema, and books, it is equally pervasive.

Fig. 1.1 Computer composition with lines (1964) is a fusion of the two cultures. (Copyright © 1965 by A. Michael Noll. Reproduced by permission.)

There is a difference between these two cultures in outlook on life. Scientists tend to look at the present and to the future with confidence. Characteristic of this optimism is Lord Rutherford's comment about the 1930s, "This is the heroic age of science!" as well as the statement by physics Nobel prize winner Isodor I. Rabi that

> Science inspires us with a feeling of hopefulness and infinite possibility . . . the human spirit applied in the tradition of science will find a way toward the objective. Science shows that it is possible to foresee and to plan. . . . (Ref. 1.11, p. 30.)

While scientists can be religious, their future-oriented attitude makes them less able to accept an uncontrollable *fate*; they instinctively reject pessimism. In exchange for their precise ways of thinking, they become somewhat impatient and even to an extent shallow. And their concreteness is achieved at the expense of imagination.

The humanistic culture, on the other hand, has a great deal of imagination but deals perhaps too much with the past. The humanists look at man; and since the human condition seems to have changed relatively little over the ages, they ask "Why look to the future?" In a way this looking toward the past tends to make the humanists too realistic, too ready to accept things as they are, too slow to change. Snow uses the word traditional in connection with the humanistic culture, implying thereby some of the stability of a status quo. A literary or art movement has arrived . . . when it has a name. But by that time it is already well-crystallized and stationary, ergo no longer a movement.

Basically, of course, it is not bad that there are two cultures in our society. Two points of view always contain richer possibilities than one; two cultures are always in a position to contribute to each other. Unfortunately, a breakdown in communications has led to a hostile polarization, which in turn has led to an impoverishment of both cultures due to a lack of crossfeeding. The lack of common images has oversharpened the contrast of scientific precision with humanistic imagination.

In the resultant hostility, the scientists see the humanists as being failures because they have not solved the world's basic problems, but rather appear to be always saying either "This is how it has always been" or "The way we used to do it was better." Of course, even the scientific culture sometimes has difficulty resisting the theme "Those were the good old days." But basically the scientific culture believes that there were no good old days, that only the rich or the humanists want to go back to them. So the scientific culture sees the humanists somewhat as wishful ostriches. On the other hand, the humanists see the losses due to the technological revolution, some of them very real. The population explosion leads to overcrowding so that there is no retreat from one's neighbor; the air stinks from technological pollution; the atom bomb is like the Sword of Damocles; the good things in life seem to be vanishing. The humanists see no sense of social responsibility in the scientists and consider them reprehensible for this lack.

At the risk of appearing presumptuous, let me summarize this split and its relevance by using myself as a microsample of the scientific culture. The key words are probably imagination-realism and past-future. I have not the touch, not the imagination. I see the consequences of real things, but not the multifaceted aspects of subtle things. My preference is history books over D. H. Lawrence. Plays-within-plays, like *Kiss Me Kate* or Ingmar Bergman's movies, appeal to me, because there the basic plot is presented several times in slightly different guises. I found the lecturing in the course on which this book is based very hard. In a typical science lecture, the same theories are examined over and over, but always from a slightly different angle; many different problems are solved to illustrate a single principle. But in these lectures, as in much of literature, many relatively independent tales had to be told which only finally made up a whole. It is the creation of this impression, through all the right words, the ringing words, that is difficult for me.

CRITICISMS OF THE TWO CULTURES

We have presented the theory of two cultures which Snow readvanced in 1959. We will shortly extend it by a parallel description of two existing and opposing modes of thought. But it might be worthwhile to first indicate the nature of the enormous reaction to the publication of *The Two Cultures*. Many valid questions were raised about Snow's theory. For example, are these social subsets homogeneous enough to be called cultures? There is, after all, some question as to how much the basic scientists and the applied engineers mix. But they do seem to make up one distinct culture; at least they can communicate since they speak the same language, and they certainly don't ignore each other. Another suggestion which has been made is that society is actually controlled by yet a third culture made up of sociologists, political scientists, economists, and politicians—all those people who are concerned with how human beings are living or have lived as a part of society. And furthermore, considering how technological our society has become, is not in fact the scientific culture right now totally dominant?

Since the reviews and commentaries frequently illustrated Snow's thesis in revealing the writer's prejudices, a few quotations will demonstrate that there is indeed a cultural gap. A. C. B. Lovell, the director of the Jodrell-Bank radiotelescope in England, reacted to Snow by stating that the free world was behind the Russians in science and needed more money to keep up with them (the necessity to keep up with the Russians was taken for granted). Lovell's version of a unified culture had a scientific tinge to it:

> The restoration of a unified culture which might give us a basis from which to handle the problem is being hindered by the new crisis in the universities.... I am impatient with those who oppose from within the scientific revolution in the universities. (Ref. 1.5a.)

There seems to be an intrinsic lack of appreciation by scientists of the two sides of the problem; even C. P. Snow shows enough leaning toward the scientific culture so that he cannot be considered impartial. The scientific culture seems to be saying that it is the most important, since it is remaking the world.

The reactions of the other culture to Snow's book likewise illustrate this cultural split. The greatest modern British literary critic, F. R. Leavis, responded to *The Two Cultures* in such style that Leavis' publisher, prior to printing the criticisms, asked Snow whether he would respond by suing. Some quotations from Leavis' review indicate how difficult it would be to bring the two cultures together:

> *The Two Cultures* exhibits an utter lack of intellectual distinction and an embarrassing vulgarity of style.... (Ref. 1.2, p. 30.)

> But the argument of Snow's Rede lecture is at an immensely *lower* conceptual level, and incomparably more loose and inconsequent, than any I myself, a literary person, should permit in a group discussion I was conducting, let alone a pupil's essay.... (Ref. 1.2, p. 34.)

> The judgement I have to come out with is that not only is he not a genius; he is intellectually as undistinguished as it is possible to be.... He is a portent in that, being in himself negligible, he has become for a vast public on both sides of the Atlantic a mastermind and a sage.... He doesn't know what he means, and doesn't know he doesn't know.... (Ref. 1.2, p. 28.)

> But of history, of the nature of civilization and the history of its recent developments, of the human history of the Industrial Revolution, of the human significances entailed in that revolution, of literature, of the nature of that kind of collaborative human creativity of which literature is the type, it is hardly an

exaggeration to say that Snow exposes complacently a complete ignorance. . . . (Ref. 1.2, p. 28.)

It is pleasant to think of Snow contemplating, daily perhaps, the intellectual depth, complexity and articulation (of the scientific edifice) in all their beauty. But there is a prior human achievement of collaborative creation, a more basic work of the mind of man (and more than the mind), one without which the triumphant erection of the scientific edifice would not have been possible: that is, the creation of the human world, including language. It is one we cannot rest on as something done in the past. It lives in the living creative response to change in the present. (Ref. 1.2, pp. 47–48.)

It is as though the humanistic culture is saying that it is the most important since it understands people and human experience.

THE HISTORICAL DICHOTOMY

This book will try to show that this cultural split is only a modern version of a conflict which is very old and has continuously affected the culture of the Western world, and that this conflict is between two different modes of thought as much as between two different cultures. One mode of thought, which might be associated with the scientific culture, looks at the universe as something machinelike which can be understood by taking it apart and studying the pieces separately. This examination of details is typical of scientific studies where each phenomenon gives one clue about the whole. In the opposing mode of thought, which is primarily associated with the humanistic culture, nature is looked at as an organism; here the overall picture is thought to be the significant one. In this mode of thought the whole is greater than the sum of its parts, man is something more than just a collection of atoms, and nature takes on a personality of its own.

Later chapters will try to show that the Aristotelian attitude toward science, the scientific impact on the Age of Enlightenment, the emotions of the Romantic Period, and the modern protests against technology can all be better understood as part of a long-standing opposition of these two modes of thought and of these two components of society.

REFERENCES

Prime references

1.1 C. P. Snow, *The Two Cultures and a Second Look*, New York: Mentor MT916, 1963.

1.2 F. R. Leavis and M. Yudkin, *Two Cultures? The Significance of C. P. Snow*, New York: Pantheon Books, a division of Random House Inc., 1962.

Interesting reading

1.3 M. Green, *The Shabby Curate of Poetry*, London: Longmans, Green & Co., Ltd., 1964.

1.4 L. Trilling, "A Comment on the Leavis-Snow Controversy," in *Commentary* **33**, 461 (1962).

1.5 Miscellaneous comments in *Encounter*: (a) **13** (#2), 67–73 (1959); (b) **13** (#3), 61 (1959); (c) **18** (#2), 87 (1962); (d) **18** (#5), 37 (1962).

1.6 J. Barzun, *Science; The Glorious Entertainment*, New York: Harper & Row, 1964; Chapter 2, "One Culture, Not Two," pp. 9–30.

1.7 T. Roszak, *The Making of a Counter Culture*, Garden City, N.Y.: Doubleday & Co., Anchor Book A697; Chapters 1 and 2, "Technocracy's Children" and "An Invasion of Centaurs," pp. 1–83.

1.8 J. Bronowski, *Science and Human Values*, New York: Harper & Row, Harper Torchbook TB505G, 1965; "The Abacus and the Rose," pp. 79–119.

1.9 Various novels by C. P. Snow, such as *The Search, The Affair, New Men*, and *The Masters*.

1.10 R. B. Lindsay, *The Role of Science in Civilization*, New York: Harper & Row, 1963; Chapter 3, "Science and the Humanities," pp. 37–73.

1.11 I. I. Rabi, "Faith in Science," *Atlantic Monthly* **187** 28–30 (January 1951).

1.12 M. Nicolson, "Science and Literature," *The American Journal of Physics* **33**, 175 (1965); a bibliography.

1.13 M. H. Nicolson, *Science and the Imagination*, Ithaca, N.Y.: Cornell University Press, 1956; a variety of articles on such topics as the effect of the telescope on Milton's imagination.

1.14 W. H. Davenport, "Resource Letter TLA-1 on Technology, Literature and Art Since World War Two," *American Journal of Physics* **38**, 407 (1970).

QUESTIONS FOR DISCUSSION

1. Is the evidence for the existence of two cultures convincing?

2. Science and technology seem to be remaking the world. Should the members of the scientific culture therefore be in complete control as philosopher kings?

3. Into what cultural category do legislators fit? Housewives? . . . ?

4. Can an understanding of the *other* culture be helpful? That is, why do universities have humanities course requirements for engineers and science course requirements for poets?

5. Leavis complains about Snow's interchangeable use of the words "literary culture" and "traditional culture." What is the difference between these?

6. Yudkin feels that reading Dickens, listening to Mozart, or seeing a Titian is a rewarding experience, while learning the meaning of acceleration is merely acquiring a piece of factual information (Ref. 1.2). Is this a reasonable statement?

7. Yudkin believes that the appreciation of European art requires no specialization, while the understanding of scientific procedure demands at least an undergraduate science course (Ref. 1.2). Is this true? Isn't our feeling for the Jefferson Aeroplane and the Fifth Dimension predicated on all the education we receive just by living in this decade?

2 | THE WORLD WE HAVE LOST

Come Lammas—eve at night shall she be fourteen.
Wm. Shakespeare: *Romeo and Juliet*
... the average age of these Elizabethan and Jacobean brides was something like 24 ...

P. Laslett

This chapter outlines the impact of science, through technology, on both the quantity and the quality of life.

INTRODUCTION

The most visible interaction of science with society is through technology. There is, of course, a difference between science and technology, a difference which will be examined more carefully in Chapter 4; yet they have become so strongly coupled that it often becomes difficult to separate them. As a result of this *technological* interaction, there has come about since the Industrial Revolution a tremendous change in both the quantity and the quality of life—a change in both such objective variables as the average human lifespan, nutrition, and health, and such subjective variables as human happiness.

This impact of technology has become such a pervasive part of our society that it has led to a wide range of critical reactions. Many people feel that technology is improving the quantity of life at the expense of the quality: instead of the clean country air of the past there is now the pollution of the industrial cities; nuclear annihilation is threatening; traditions and family life are being disrupted; in fact, the "good life" of Plato is disappearing. There is the modern complaint that man is suffering spiritual anguish in our culture, an anguish evidenced by the arid wasteland of TV, the starvation in the midst of plenty, the student revolt against the dehumanization of the monster universities, and all the current involvement in the fight against technological pollution.

Considering the enormity of these complaints, any discussion about science and society clearly must consider this particular interaction. This chapter is intended to lay the foundation for its use in later analyses. Here we will try to separate the effects of the technological interaction on the quantity from those on the quality of life. Examples will be cited to show that the quantity of life has indeed been improving, and that most of the antitechnological complaints are actually about changes in the quality of life.

THE QUANTITY OF LIFE

The most easily measurable aspect of the quantity of life is probably the length of time that the average person lives. This can be measured by such indexes as the infant mortality rate, the average lifespan, and the life expectancy as a function of age. Since the concept of a national census is relatively new, data related to changes in even these simple measures is not easy to obtain. Fortunately considerable effort has recently been invested in obtaining such information by tracing births, marriages, and deaths in old parish registers. It is now possible to carry out statistical comparisons between the present and the times before the Industrial Revolution.

The most clear-cut statistics deal with the length of life. Figure 2.1 presents an index related to this variable. It shows a plot of the percent of the female population surviving to various ages in York (England) in 1600, in Wales in 1910, and in the United States in 1967. The differences are obvious. Note particularly that in 1600 a "lady" had a four times larger chance of surviving to age 40 than did the average woman. Similar information is contained in the life expectancies shown in Table 2.1, in which England, Wales, and Germany in the 1690s are compared with Egypt in 1936–38, the United Kingdom in 1951, and the United States in 1900 and 1967. Again the improvement in the quantity of life is clear. Interestingly enough, the

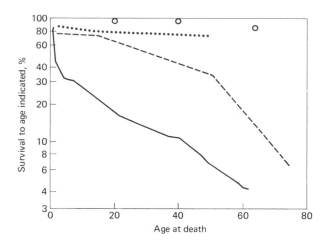

Fig. 2.1 The survival rate in percent to various ages: for York townswomen (solid line) and aristocratic ladies (dashed line) in 1600, for Welsh women born in 1910 (dotted line) and for U. S. women in 1967 (circles). (Data from Refs. 2.3 and 2.4.)

Table 2.1
Life expectancy for various nations at different time. (Data taken from p. 93 of Ref. 2.2 and p. 53 of Ref. 2.4.)

At age	England and Wales 1690s both sexes	Breslau 1690s both sexes	Egypt 1936–38 males	U.K. 1951 males	U.S. 1900 males white/colored	U.S. 1967 males white/colored
0	32	27.54	42.9	65.8	48.2/32.5	70.5/61.1
10		40.25	46.86	58.7	42.2/35.1	62.4/54.2
20		33.93	39.77	49.1	—	52.9/44.8
30		27.64	32.96	39.7	27.7/23.1	43.5/36.3
40		22.05	26.12	30.5	—	34.3/28.3
50		17.05	19.42	21.7	—	25.7/21.1
60		12.33	13.29	14.3	—	18.1/15.3
65		—	—	—	11.5/10.4	14.8/12.7
70		7.74	8.6	7.9	—	11.9/11.1

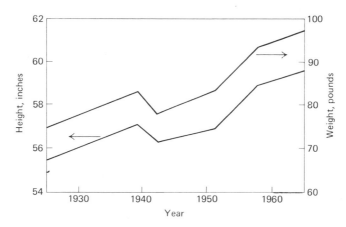

Fig. 2.2   The trend of increasing height and weight of boys (at age 13) in Moscow was temporarily reversed by the famine of World War II. (Data from Ref. 2.1.)

further life expectancy, once old age has been reached, was almost the same in 1690 as it is in the 20th century, suggesting that there may be a physiologically predetermined lifespan which technology has not yet been able to modify. In part, these improvements in the life expectancy are due to a vast decrease in infant mortality, from typically 20% in the 17th century to about 2% now in the U. S. (which is actually not one of the leading countries in this statistic).

These data on life expectancy and infant mortality speak for themselves; clearly our technological improvements in sanitation, hygiene, and medicine have paid off. But there are more subtle impacts on human physiology, about which there is neither as much data nor as widespread agreement. These involve the general health and well-being of the average population. One might ask, for example, how widespread starvation was in the preindustrial Western world. While there is some evidence of agricultural crises, they appear to have occurred only infrequently and then in only very restricted areas. There are, however, indications that the general level of health and strength has significantly improved. Such physiological indexes as height and age of puberty seem to be strongly related to health and

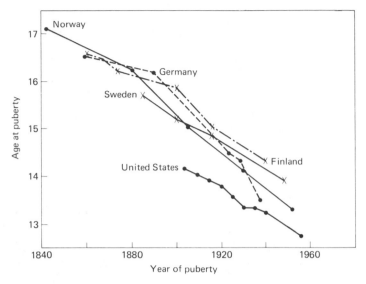

Fig. 2.3 Age at puberty versus date in various European countries and the United States. (Data from Ref. 2.1.)

Table 2.2
Mean age at first marriage in 17th-century Canterbury.
(Data taken from p. 83 of Ref. 2.2.)

	Mean age of brides	Mean age of bridegrooms
All applicants for licences, Diocese of Canterbury, 1619–60 (1082 brides, 1070 bridegrooms)	23.95	26.87
Gentry only amongst Canterbury applicants (84 brides, 84 bridegrooms)	21.66	26.54
Marriages of nobles, from about 1600 to about 1625 (325 brides, 313 bridegrooms)	19.39	24.28
Marriages of nobles, from about 1625 to about 1650 (510 brides, 403 bridegrooms)	20.67	25.99

nutrition. Figure 2.2, for example, demonstrates that malnutrition during World War II retarded growth in the height and weight of boys in Moscow; and Fig. 2.3 illustrates the effect of a century of technological improvements in health on the age of puberty in Europe and the United States. In turn, the age of puberty is correlated with the age of first marriage. Table 2.2 shows the mean ages of brides and bridegrooms of various social stratas in 17th-century Canterbury—ages which compare with a contemporary marriage age of about 20 for U.S. females. The marriage of Romeo and Juliet at 14 was obviously not typical of their time. In any case, the overall impression is that health in general has indeed improved since 1600.

THE QUALITY OF LIFE

However, the data just cited are not particularly relevant to the issue of technologically induced changes in the quality of life. The fact that the quantity has gone up does not imply that the quality has gone up as well. Healthier people may be more alert and capable, but they also may be enjoying life less because of some technological degradation of the whole social milieu. The question about quality is much harder to answer than the one about the quantity of life because it is not readily quantifiable and hence involves subtle value judgments.

Discussions about the quality of life usually have two aspects. One is a worry about the pleasure of living, the other is about the relative satisfactions and costs of various technological improvements: the comforts of air conditioning versus the consequent dangers of thermal pollution, the convenience of the automobile versus the softening of man's physical condition through lack of exercise, the improved availability of physical conveniences which relieve drudgery versus the consequent competitive rat race of keeping up with the Joneses, the ability to see and do more things versus the resulting loss of depth in the appreciation of life. Such concerns are not new; they have a tradition which can be traced back to the ancient Greeks. The critical question is whether the present-day concerns about the degradation of life are different from, and more justified, than the older complaints. This is a question to which we will return in later chapters. But to put these concerns in a historical perspective, it might be interesting at this point to present a few excerpts from a book written in 1673 entitled *The Grand Concerns of England* (as quoted in Ref. 2.5, pp. 22–28). This book examines the various effects on England, and on English society, of the introduction of carriages. The conclusions are that both the quantity (economy) and the quality of life were being degraded.

These Coaches and Caravans are one of the greatest mischiefs that hath hapned of late years to the Kingdom, mischievous to the Publick, destructive to Trade, and prejudicial to Lands.

First, by destroying the Breed of good Horses, the Strength of the Nation, and making Men careless of attaining to good Horseman-ship, a thing so useful and commendable in a Gentleman.

Secondly, by hindring the Breed of Watermen, who are the Nursery for Seamen, and they the Bulwark of the Kingdom.

Thirdly, by lessening of his Majesties Revenues.

For the first of these; Stage-Coaches prevent the breed of good Horses, destroy those that are bred, and effeminate his Majesties Subjects, who having used themselves to travel in them, have neither attained skill themselves, nor bred up their Children to good Horsemanship, whereby they are rendred uncapable of serving their Countrey on Horseback, if occasion should require and call for the same; for, hereby they become weary and listless when they ride a few miles, and unwilling to get on Horseback; not able to endure Frost, Snow, or Rain, or to lodg in the Fields; and what reason, save only their using themselves so tenderly, and their riding in these Stage-Coaches, can be given for this their inability?

What encouragement hath any Man to breed Horses whilst these Coaches are continued? There is such a lazy habit of body upon Men, that they, to indulge themselves, save their fine Cloaths; and keep themselves clean and dry, will ride lolling in one of them, and endure all the Inconveniences of that manner of travelling rather than ride on Horseback; So that if any Man should continue his Breed, he must be one that is a great lover of them, and resolve to keep and please his own fancy with them; otherwise most certainly he (as most Breeders already have done) will give over his breeding.

The author deplores the ruining of the 1673 version of the roadside stand, namely the watermen. And what is worse, the government is losing taxes:

> It prejudiceth his Majesty in his Revenue of Excise: for now four or five travel in a Coach together, and twenty or thirty in a Caravan, Gentlemen and Ladies, without any Servants, consume little Drink on the Road, ... But if Travellers would, as formerly they did, Travel on Horseback, then no Persons of Quality would ride without their Servants: And it is they that occasion the Consumption of Beer and Ale on the Roads, and soo would advance his Majesties Revenue.

The secondary industries are also being depressed:

> These Coaches and Caravans are destructive to the Trade and Manufactories of the Kingdom, have impoverished and ruined many thousands of Families, whose subsistence depended upon the Manufacturing of Wool, and Leather, two of the staple Commodities of the Kingdom: For, before these Coaches were set up, Travellers rode on Horseback, and men had Boots, Spurs, Saddles, Bridles, Sadle-clothes, and good riding Suits, Coats and Cloaks, Stockings and Hats.

Not only is travel by coach ruining the country, not only is it more expensive, but it is less comfortable and convenient:

> Travelling in these Coaches can neither prove advantagious to Men's Health or Business: For, what advantage is it to man's Health, to be called out of their Beds into these Coaches, an hour before day in the morning, to be hurried in them from place to place, till one hour, two, or three within night. What addition is this to men's Health or Business, to ride all day with strangers, oftimes sick, ancient, diseased Persons or Young Children crying; to whose humours they are obliged to be subject, forced to bear with, and many times are poysoned with their nasty scents and cripled by the crowd of the Boxes and Bundles. Is it for a Mans Health to travel with tired Jades ...

And finally, morals are also being degraded:

> For passage to London being so easie, gentlemen came to London
> oftner than they need, and their Ladies either with them, or hav-
> ing the Conveniences of these Coaches, quickly follow them. And
> when they are there, they must be in the Mode, have all the new
> Fashions, buy all their Cloaths there and go to Plays, Balls and
> Treats, where they get such a habit of Jollity, and a love to Gayety
> and Pleasure, that nothing afterwards in the Countrey will serve
> them, if ever they should fix their minds to live there again; But
> they must have all from London, whatever it costs.

This example is not meant to deride all criticisms of technology. There
certainly exist enough examples of bad effects on man and his environment due to technology. But some care must obviously be taken before
accepting a particular criticism.

The second concern with changes in the quality of life has to do
with the technological impact on man as something more than a mere
animal, as a being with a soul. And here I shall let writers and philosophers speak, since this is among their legitimate concerns. First,
the philosopher E. M. Adams:

> One may well ask whether our naturalistic culture makes for
> wretchedness of the human spirit. There are many indications
> that it does. (Ref. 2.8, p. 52.)

Secondly, literary critic F. R. Leavis:

> ... [I see] the vision of our imminent tomorrow in today's
> America; the energy, the triumphant technology, the produc-
> tivity, the high standard of living and the life-impoverishment—
> the human emptiness; emptiness and boredom craving alcohol—
> of one kind or another. Who will assert that the average member
> of a modern society is more fully human, or more alive, than a
> Bushman, an Indian peasant, or a member of one of those poign-
> antly surviving primitive peoples, with their marvellous art
> and skills and vital intelligence. (Ref. 1.2, p. 46.)

Finally, the writer D. H. Lawrence, who has given some very depressing descriptions of the impact of the coal and steel industry in Britain:

> The fault lay there ... in those evil electric lights and diabolical
> rattlings of engines. There, in the world of the mechanical

greedy.... It was producing a new race of mankind, overconscious in the money and social and political side, on the spontaneous, intuitive side dead, but dead. (Ref. 2.9, pp. 205–206.)

SUMMARY

While technology is not science, the two are very closely related. Therefore, when in subsequent chapters we are looking for the impact of science on society, we will have to consider this technological interaction. The quantity of life does seem to have been measurably improved by technology. The effect on the quality of life is harder to determine because it involves subjective value judgments. The particular concerns reflect in a sense the two cultures: the scientific culture appears to be more interested in the changes in the quantity of life, while the humanistic culture worries primarily about the quality of life. The frequent complaints about the degradation and dehumanization of human beings mirror these interests. So in considering this interaction in subsequent chapters, we will pay attention not only to the nature of this technological interaction but also to the validity of the complaints about the loss of the good life.

REFERENCES

Prime reference

2.1 J. M. Tanner, "Earlier Maturation in Man," *Scientific American* **218** (#1), 21–27 (January 1968).

Interesting reading

2.2 P. Laslett, *The World We Have Lost*, London: Methuen and Co., Ltd., 1965.

2.3 U. M. Cowgill, "The People of York, 1538–1812," *Scientific American* **222** (#1), 104–112 (January 1970).

2.4 U. S. Bureau of the Census, *Statistical Abstract Of the U. S. 1969* (90th Edition), Washington, D. C., 1969.

2.5 Sir J. Stamp, *The Science of Social Adjustment*, London: Macmillan, 1937.

2.6 T. Veblen, *The Theory of the Leisure Class*, New York: The Modern Library, 1934.

2.7 L. Mumford, *The Myth of the Machine*, Vol. 1. *Technics and Human Development*, Vol. 2. *The Pentagon of Power*, New York: Harcourt, Brace and World, 1967.

2.8 E. M. Adams, *The Personalist* **49** (#1), 37 (Winter 1968).

2.9 D. H. Lawrence, *Lady Chatterley's Lover*, New York: Grove Press, Evergreen Black Book B9, 1962.

2.10 A. Huxley, *Brave New World* and G. Orwell, *1984*, any one of many editions; two views of our technological future.

QUESTIONS FOR DISCUSSION

1. Is the technological impact of science primarily on the quantity or on the quality of life?

2. What credit, and what responsibility, should science get for this technological impact?

3. What might happen if ever automation creates a large class of people with total leisure, a situation which would be in stark contradiction to the Puritan Ethic?

4. Were there ever "good old days"?

5. Is Leavis right when he says that a Bushman is as alive as the average member of a modern society?

3 | THE GROWTH OF SCIENCE

How are you, baby?
Why, don't you know,
You're only so big,
And there's still room to grow.

Nursery rhyme

An attempt is made to show that the magnitude of the Western scientific effort has been growing exponentially since about 1700, threatening to swallow all of society's efforts. Possible criteria for evaluating the social priority of science (the Weinberg criteria) are presented and are used in an analysis of the origin of the unemployment crisis in the scientific community of the early 1970s.

INTRODUCTION

Derek J. de Solla Price used the above nursery rhyme to introduce his book *Little Science, Big Science* (Ref. 3.1). His theme was that science has been growing at an exponential rate since about 1700, and that it must reach saturation some time in the not-too-distant future. Since he wrote this book in 1961, science has continued to expand tremendously; however, it appears that since the middle of the 1960s saturation has begun to set in. The self-evident is finally becoming clear: science is only one of many possible efforts by society and must undergo a social priority analysis along with all other possibilities. It may no longer be true that "there's still room to grow."

This chapter will expand on this growth theme and will support the contention that this growth forces us to develop a set of priorities for science. Any approach toward analyzing the merits of science as a social activity must include the evaluation of the *social* interaction of science and society. The *Weinberg criteria* will be proposed specifically to help in such an evaluation. They will be used in later chapters whenever a priority analysis is needed for some specific scientific and/or technological activity. But first it will be shown how the absence in the past of any external evaluation of science has contributed to the overproduction of scientific manpower in the late 1960s and early 1970s.

THE GROWTH OF SCIENCE

The great physicist Isaac Newton once made the remark "If I have seen farther, it is by standing on the shoulders of giants." It is characteristic of science that at any given moment 80 to 90% of those preceding giants are still alive. Science is a thoroughly contemporary activity; it has been growing so rapidly that by the time one scientist dies, many more have been trained to replace him. By now about three percent of the total gross national product (GNP) in the United States is devoted to research and development (R&D); about $3 billion (1/10th) of this goes into basic science (Ref. 3.4). This makes it Big Science, not only compared to its size in the past, but even compared to our total economy. In fact, it is now so big that we have to worry about the consequences of a continued growth of science in the future.

The size of science seems to obey an exponential (geometric) growth law (like the algae in a culture), with a doubling period of about 15 years. It is not too easy to find statistics on the size of science that have been collected for a long enough period of time to demonstrate convincingly this continuing exponential growth. But since the accomplishments of scientists tend to be judged by their output, it may be at least plausible to use the number of scientific publications as a measure of this size. Obviously changes may have occurred over the years in the quality of the papers, and in the number of pages per journal, but these are hopefully small perturbations on the overall trends. In Fig. 3.1, therefore, the number of scientific journals founded since 1650 is plotted as a function of founding date. The dashed line, which represents a doubling in number every 15 years, is in good

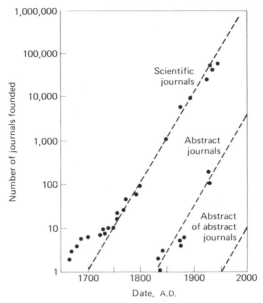

Fig. 3.1 The number of scientific journals founded as a function of time. The dashed lines represent a doubling every 15 years. (Data from Ref. 3.1.)

agreement with the data points, except in the very beginning. The number of journals still in existence exceeds 30,000. At the rate of 100 pages per month for each journal, this amounts to the equivalent of about 300 books per day of 300 pages each. To keep up with this information explosion, abstract journals are published. These are publications which present summaries of articles in regular journals; one reads these abstracts to decide what journal articles deserve a more detailed study. Interestingly enough, the number of these abstract journals is also doubling every 15 years, as shown in Fig. 3.1. The ratio of journals to abstract journals is about 300 to 1; it is as though such a "condensation" factor of 300 is desirable. This suggests that since there are now more than 300 abstract journals, these too are due for a further condensation. And indeed there now exist "current content journals" which publish nothing but the titles of regularly appearing articles. In the sense that a title is a summary of an abstract, these are abstract-of-abstract journals. The information explosion is clearly a serious problem.

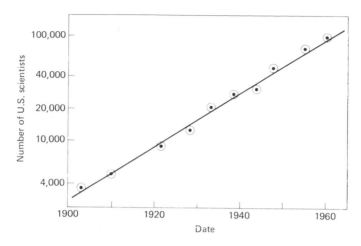

Fig. 3.2   Number of men cited in *American Men of Science*. (Data from Ref. 3.1).

Not only is the output of scientists growing, but also the number of scientists. Figure 3.2 shows the number of scientists in the United States over the period 1900 to 1960 (taken from *American Men of Science*). The doubling period of 13.5 years is in good agreement with the 15 years extracted from the publications data. Note that this compares with a doubling period of about 50 years for the general population of the United States.

Once this number of 15 years is taken as representative of this exponential growth, it is easy to show that at any given moment more than 85% of all the scientists who ever lived are still alive. If there were N scientists active when a certain scientist started his career at age 25, then at his death at 70 (three doubling periods later) there will be $8N$ active scientists. Essentially all the N scientists active before him will be dead, while the $8N$ who became active after him will still be alive. So he will be survived by about $8N/(N+8N) = 89\%$ of all scientists who ever lived.

PROBLEMS DUE TO THE SIZE OF SCIENCE

The tremendous expansion in science raises the question of "quality control." Not only is there an explosion in the sheer quantity of in-

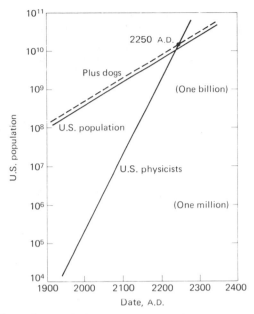

Fig. 3.3   The U.S. population and number of U.S. physicists as a function of time. Doubling rates are taken respectively as 50 years and 15 years.

formation acquired; there may also be a dropping off in the average quality, as less capable individuals may be inducted into the sciences. References 3.1 and 3.5 concern themselves with this more-or-less predictable trend.

However, the 15-year doubling period in the scientific effort portends a far more serious problem. This growth obviously cannot go on forever because it will simply exhaust the available supply of manpower. Figure 3.3 shows an extrapolation into the future of both the U.S. population and the U.S. physicists (just to pick a specific subset of scientists), with doubling periods of 50 years and 15 years respectively. This plot suggests that by the year 2250, there will be one physicist for every man, woman, and child—in fact, for every dog as well. Since dogs would probably make poor physicists, something has to give before then. This obviously nonsensical extrapolation clearly shows that science cannot, and will not, continue to grow at its past rate. Some saturation will inevitably set in; the only question is how, when, and at what level this saturation will occur. At best this coming transition will be a smooth one; at worst it will induce violent oscillations in the magnitude of scientific effort. And there is some evidence that this transition has begun, as I will discuss below.

SOCIAL PRIORITIES OF SCIENCE

Since science is beginning to absorb such a sizable portion of society's efforts, and since there are various crises over resources and their allocation now taking place inside the scientific community, it is becoming apparent that we must begin to evaluate the social impact of science to a much greater extent than in the past. The old-style justification for the support of science, as given below by Harvey Brooks, is beginning to sound slightly hollow:

> The rate of incorporation of technical people into our society is limited primarily by supply rather than demand, and this will continue to be so . . . scientific and engineering manpower availability acts as a spur to development, rather than the economy exerting a pull on the manpower supply. (Ref. 3.6, p. 196.)

Questions must be asked. How much is science contributing to society? How much support does it deserve? Do we build high-energy accelerators, fly to the moon, build housing for the poor, or plan for a leisure society? There exist some criteria which may be useful in such an evaluation of the social impact of science.

Alvin Weinberg, Director of the Oak Ridge National Laboratory, has long concerned himself with this sort of question and has suggested some specific criteria which should be examined in deciding how to split the science "pie" among the various scientific disciplines (Ref. 3.2). These criteria may be extended to evaluate the merit of science as one of many possible efforts of society. The first of Weinberg's criteria address themselves to the question: How well can the science be done? This question must be answered from inside the scientific discipline. The second criteria ask: Why should society support this activity? This question must be answered to a large extent from outside the scientific discipline.

The internal criteria have two aspects. (a) Is the field ready for exploitation? (b) Are the scientists in the field really competent? When the National Science Foundation (NSF) acts on a submitted research proposal, it first has the proposed research activity evaluated by several referees who are experts in that specific field. And these are essentially the two questions which the referees consider in their evaluation. In fact, the internal criteria have not infrequently been proposed by scientists as the only relevant concerns in evaluating the sciences. This is implicit in the above quotation from Brooks.

The external criteria are obviously much harder to apply in any evaluation of science. Three further possible questions are those of (c) technological merit, (d) scientific merit, and (e) social merit. If a research project has possibilities toward future applications, and if these applications are potentially very useful, then there can be some evaluation of the possible benefits. In that case the decision reduces simply to a hazy technological guess, which can, however, be based on some quantitative evaluations.

The application of the scientific-merit criterion is even harder. How does one measure the scientific merit of a subsection of a scientific discipline? Weinberg suggests that the viability and contribution of a discipline is related to its contact with other disciplines. If a discipline inspires and is inspired by neighboring disciplines, then it has more scientific merit, and is hence more worthy of consideration and support than another discipline which is very isolated. This criterion has been used to find fault with the very expensive high-energy physics program, insofar as there seems to be no other scientific discipline anxiously awaiting the results obtained from those efforts.

The social merit of scientific efforts is almost impossible to evaluate objectively. How much does a specific project ultimately improve the quality of life in society as a whole? This involves comparing science to such totally disparate fields as the poverty program and art. It involves questions of economics, sociology, politics, and philosophy. And who is qualified to make such comparisons?

A FAILURE IN PRIORITY ANALYSIS

Hopefully these criteria will become clearer as we go on and use them to analyze scientific priorities in later chapters. But it may be instructive to apply the Weinberg criteria to one fairly recent decision of the scientific community, a decision which contains in it the seeds of the present crisis in this community. This example illuminates the origins of the exponential growth of science and also shows the consequences of ignoring the Weinberg criteria.

About 1964 the National Academy of Sciences was asked to project the future needs for scientists and engineers in the various research fields and to project the financial requirements of the nation's scientific activities. The academy projected for most fields at least a doubling in the demand for research activities over the next six years; in the case of physics, the projection was a 15% annual growth rate (Ref. 3.7, Fig. 10). One reason for the projection of such a huge growth rate was the emphasis on internal criteria. Instead of asking how much science is desirable, the panels asked, how many scientists are there and how much money can they reasonably use? Instead of asking how many physicists are needed to do a desirable amount of physics, the Pake panel asked, how many physicists are needed to train a physics-student population which will almost double in six years? The necessity for these students in society was never seriously analyzed. And the fact that the physics-student enrollment was already leveling off, rather than growing exponentially along with the overall college enrollment, was ignored. With the use of some equations with reasonable teacher-student ratios, a need for 12,000 academic physicists was projected for six years later. The amount of appropriate research support, as well as the predicted number of industrial physicists, was then based on this number 12,000. With the same equations, and inserting the physics enrollment which actually occurred, a need for only 7000 to 8000 professors is calculated. But these 12,000 physicists were produced anyhow, and the result is an oversupply of 4000 physicists clogging the job market. (See Ref. 3.8 for some discussions of this crisis.) This disaster could perhaps have been avoided if some thought had been given to the demands for physicists external to the discipline. The whole argument for more physicists was a circular one, in the sense that the question asked was: How many physicists are needed to produce the physicists who are needed to produce . . . ?

SUMMARY

There is sufficient evidence that science has been growing at an exponential rate for a long time, a rate which is far in excess of the growth rate for the general population. This cannot continue forever, and a transition toward a steady-state size is imminent; in fact, this transition may have already arrived. In such a future steady-state situation, priorities must be assigned, and the Weinberg criteria are suggested as a means for evaluating these priorities. The social interaction of science with society can no longer be ignored; the merits of science as only one of many possible activities of society must be analyzed. In fact, the present job-situation crisis in the sciences illustrates the consequences of neglecting the external criteria. Later examples of decision-making on scientific activities will hopefully clarify these criteria and how they are to be applied.

REFERENCES

Prime references

3.1 D. J. de Solla Price, *Little Science, Big Science*, New York: Columbia University Press, 1965.

3.2 A. Weinberg, *Reflections on Big Science*, Cambridge, Mass.: The M.I.T Press, 1967; Chapter 4, "The Choices of Big Science," pp. 65–122.

Interesting reading

3.3 D. J. de Solla Price, *Science Since Babylon*, New Haven, Conn.: Yale University Press, 1961.

3.4 J. P. Martino, "Science and Society in Equilibrium," *Science* **165**, 769–772 (1969).

3.5 C. Herring, "Distill or Drown: The Need for Reviews," *Physics Today* **21** (#9), 27–33 (September 1968).

3.6 H. Brooks, *The Government of Science*, Cambridge, Mass.: The M.I.T Press, 1968; Chapter 7, "The Future Growth of Academic Research: Criteria and Needs," pp. 176–207.

3.7 *Physics: Survey And Outlook—A Report On The Present State Of U.S. Physics And Its Requirements For Future Growth*, Publication 1295, Physics Survey Committee, National Academy of Sciences—National Research Council, Washington, D.C., 1966. Also known as *The Pake Report*.

3.8 See, e.g., A. A. Strassenburg, "Supply and Demand for Physicists," *Physics Today* **23** (#4), 23 (April 1970); W. R. Gruner, "Why There Is a Job Shortage," *Physics Today* **23** (#6), 21–25 (June,

1970); L. Grodzins, "The Manpower Crisis in Physics," *Bulletin of the American Physical Society* **16**, 737 (June 1971).

3.9 P. R. Ehrlich and A. H. Ehrlich, *Population, Resources, Environment: Issues in Human Ecology*, San Francisco: W. H. Freeman and Co., 1970; has more detailed predictions of future growth of the human population.

QUESTIONS FOR DISCUSSION

1. Is the vast increase in scientific activity reflected in the growth of a scientific attitude throughout the population?

2. What might be some reasons why the growth rate of the sciences has been so constant for so long?

3. Since there is some concern about the quality of scientists, should there perhaps be a fixed minimum I.Q. requirement for Ph.D.'s?

4. There is a publish-or-perish syndrome in academia. What can be done to keep the resultant literature explosion under control?

5. How could we use the Weinberg criteria to compare the merits of NASA with those of building a high-speed railway system?

6. Can science be planned?

7. What is a reasonable size of science?

8. To what extent are the scientists themselves responsible for evaluating their activities in this "broader" external context?

4 | THE SCIENTIFIC ESTATE

*Science has become the major establishment in the American Political
System; the only set of institutions for which tax funds are appropriated almost on faith, and under concordants which protect the auton-
omy, if not the cloistered calm, of the laboratory.*

Don K. Price, 1965

. . . tax funds [were] appropriated . . .

Editorial correction to the above, 1972

The disciplinary aspects of the science-society interaction are dis-
cussed using Ziman's public-knowledge definition of science.
This definition is used to analyze some attempts after World War
II to establish organizations to carry out such consensus science.

INTRODUCTION

In this chapter science will be defined in terms of public knowledge
and of achieving a consensus. This definition is not so much concerned
with how and why the individual scientist performs his research;
instead it relates to how scientists interact with each other—how
science is done as an institutionalized activity. This definition will
therefore allow us to better understand the *disciplinary* effect of science on society. To illustrate its usefulness, this definition of science
will be used to analyze some modern attempts by scientists to set up
institutions for carrying out consensus science.

35

THE AMERICAN SCIENTIFIC ESTATE

Daniel S. Greenberg (in Ref. 4.2) has suggested that since the second world war there has arisen an unofficial American scientific estate. According to Greenberg, The University of California, The California Institute of Technology (Caltech), Harvard, and The Massachusetts Institute of Technology (M.I.T.) are its performing centers. Its breeding grounds were the World-War-II research centers; i.e., the Los Alamos Scientific Laboratory and the M.I.T. Radiation Laboratory (of atom bomb and radar fame, respectively—see Chapter 17), and the Bell Telephone Laboratories. The Cosmos Club in Washington is the "invisible college" of the estate, the physicists are its aristocrats, the National Academy of Sciences is its established church, and the President's Science Advisory Committee is its Privy Council. This estate has two branches. The eastern wing is headed by a triumvirate consisting of Jerome B. Wiesner (see Chapters 22 and 24), science advisor to President Kennedy and president of M.I.T.; George B. Kistiakowsky, science advisor to President Eisenhower, professor of chemistry at Harvard, and vice president of the Academy; and Detlev Bronk, past president of Rockefeller University and former president of the Academy. The western branch is headed by Lee DuBridge, another Eisenhower science advisor, who was president of Caltech, and was again science advisor during President Nixon's first two years in office. Isodor I. Rabi (see Chapter 1), yet another advisor to Eisenhower, and emeritus professor of physics at Columbia University, is the estate's "gray eminence"; *Science*, the weekly magazine of the American Association for the Advancement of Science, is its semi-official journal; the National Science Foundation is the Bank (see Chapter 22); Frederick Seitz, former president of the Academy is the Peacemaker; Emmanuel R. Piore, vice president of IBM, is the Chief Trouble Shooter; Harvey Brooks, Dean of Engineering and Applied Physics at Harvard is the Chief Political Theoretician (see Ref. 3.5); and J. Robert Oppenheimer is the tragic hero (see Chapter 21).

This loose grouping of people, with a leadership derived from the Second World War, makes up the scientific community in the United States, a community whose main aim is to promote science, preferably basic science. What is it that makes this community different from other communities like law, religion, philosophy, or even technology?

SCIENCE AS PUBLIC KNOWLEDGE

A major contribution toward understanding the uniqueness of science as a discipline was made by Prof. J. Ziman in his book *Public Knowledge* (Ref. 4.1), in which he suggested that any definition of science must recognize its central concern with achieving a public consensus. In Ziman's view, scientific knowledge is something to which every reasonable person who makes the effort at understanding can subscribe (compare this with the discussions in Ref. 4.3). To clarify this definition (or interpretation) it will be interesting to see how it fits in with other definitions of science. Following this we shall examine how this interpretation has colored individual and collective activities of scientists and how it thereby makes science a unique discipline. In later chapters this interpretation of science will have a particularly strong bearing on the question of the social responsibility of scientists.

Let us begin by comparing this consensus definition of science with some other frequently encountered alternative definitions:

Science is the control of nature.   Historically this has been the most prominent definition of science and dates back to Francis Bacon's *New Atlantis* and *Novum Organum* (compare Chapter 3 or Ref. 4.3). It certainly has provided one of the strongest arguments to justify financial support of scientific research. This control concept is, however, somewhat unsatisfactory; it excludes some fields of science, such as cosmology (the study of the development of the universe), while, on the other hand, it includes product-directed technology. In contrast, the concept of science as a public consensus on knowledge is particularly useful in allowing us to separate pure science from technology and in letting us determine when applied science should no longer be called science.

This distinction of science and technology goes as follows. When an applied scientist is asked to answer a specific question to help in producing or improving a product or process, it is neither the newness nor the usefulness of the answer which decides whether the work is science. Rather, it is the extent to which the answer adds to a consensus on the scientific knowledge in a public way which decides whether it is science. If the investigation ultimately adds only to the private knowledge of the producer, then it is not science. If, on the other hand, the work is published in the public scientific literature, then it is science.

Technology therefore is clearly distinct from science. An engineer is given the assignment to built a better razor. He certainly uses the knowledge accumulated by science, but he is himself not aiming for a consensus. He could design an enormous number of different razors without ever having any assurance that he has hit upon the best possible design. It is, of course, possible to have a consensus on the feasibility of a particular design, as in the case of the atomic bomb (Chapter 17); that might be called a technological consensus. The engineer's final design will, however, be an economic compromise; and both he and his peers know this. There is then no question of a consensus; hence technology is not science.

Science is the study of the material world.   This definition of science is incomplete because it also excludes certain fields, such as mathematical physics, which are very abstract, and probably all of the social sciences, which deal with the social behavior of man rather than with any material aspect of the world. The public-knowledge definition will include any of these disciplines as long as they are aiming for a consensus on the acquired knowledge. A consensus may be more difficult to reach in the social sciences, but it is certainly the ultimate goal.

Science is the experimental method.   Again this definition is unsatisfactory because it excludes certain scientific disciplines. Astronomy in the past did not perform experiments in the sense of varying a parameter under controlled circumstances and then studying the results; astronomy for a long time involved a purely observational technique. Yet astronomy is a science. The public-knowledge definition of science does, however, allow us to understand the significance and importance of the scientific method (experimental method) to science. It is simply an excellent and widely-agreed-upon technique for achieving a consensus. The general model of the scientific method consists of four stages: gathering of data, setting up a hypothesis on the basis of this data, taking more data to check out predictions of the hypothesis, and finally formulating a more-or-less firm theory. Neither the initial data gathering nor the formulation of that first hypothesis is particularly related to a consensus. It is only the next two steps which make science. The hypothesis is subjected to further tests, frequently experimental tests and often tests performed by the peers of the proposer of the first hypothesis. And even if the predictions of the hypothesis are not checked by anyone else, the scientist-proposer knows this could happen, and hence acts as his own devil's advocate. It is this concern to ensure the peers' agreement which distinguishes science from non-science; it is this concern which makes the scientific method so useful and powerful. But this does not make the scientific method identical with science.

Science consists of logical inferences from many observations. This is probably the least acceptable of these definitions. Many of the most brilliant scientific theories were not only based on skimpy data but also came through very intuitive flashes of insight. For these insights, genius was often more necessary than logic. Science does not depend on the origins of a hypothesis; it depends only on the rigorous checks of its predictions.

Needless to say, such a definition of science as a consensus on public knowledge is also imperfect. For example, it puts perhaps too much emphasis on the public activities of scientists, thereby raising the specter of putting Leonardo da Vinci into scientific limbo for the hundred years that passed before his research notebooks were discovered and published. But since he wrote them in mirror-writing code, perhaps he really was unscientific in not wanting the knowledge to become public. The second problem with this definition is that it takes science to be a monolithic organization, consisting of selfless individuals, rather than as a collection of egotistical prima donnas. There are times when scientific theories become so entrenched as paradigms that only a revolution (and death of the old guard) can correct the errors. (See, e.g., Ref. 4.4; and note the total nonacceptance of Velikovsky's geological theories as discussed in Ref. 4.5.) And finally there is the problem that religion also aims for a consensus, and in fact achieves one. The resolution of that difficulty must be in the facts that religion is based on an individual act of faith in some unverifiable data (as for example in past miracles) and that there is no way, except by a new act of faith, to change the religious convictions of a believer (as from Christianity to Buddhism).

SCIENCE AS A DISCIPLINE

The definition of science as a striving after a consensus on public knowledge seems to be a reasonably satisfactory concept which complements well the various alternative definitions that were mentioned. It illuminates particularly the aspects of science as a community of scholars. The individual scientist may be doing his research for reasons very different from trying to achieve a consensus; it is quite possible that he simply looks at nature as a puzzle and considers solving this puzzle an entertaining game. But in his dealings with his peers, the scientist generally conforms to this model and tries to convince rather than persuade.

This public-knowledge definition clearly separates science as a discipline from such studies as law, history, and sociology, and shows what makes it such a distinctive discipline. Law can never be a scientific discipline. Judgments presented in court, by their very nature, do not contain a consensus; if there were a consensus (i.e., if the defendant pleaded guilty), then there would not have to be a trial. A trial judgment, almost by definition, is a matter of judging the data and then giving an opinion on the basis of the limited data available. In a jury trial, a verdict of "not guilty" may only mean a presumption of innocence, not necessarily a proof of innocence. And in financial judgments, a decision must be reached no matter how controversial the evidence may be. It appears that history can be a science only to a limited extent. Insofar as the historical facts are unearthed and the documents are presented, to that extent history is a science. But when the really interesting questions of interpretation arise (e.g.: why did the Second World War start? why did the Greeks have no real science?), then the historian may be scholarly, but not scientific. What about sociology? It attempts to be very scientific with questionnaires and statistical analyses. To the extent that the results of these questionnaires are reproducible, sociology is a science. But the interaction between observer and observed here is often so strong that it is difficult to make the data reproducible for different observers; the questionnaires do not necessarily lead to a consensus. This problem does not make sociology a nonscience; however, it does make it a more difficult science than the "hard" science of physics.

THE POLITICS OF SCIENCE AND PUBLIC CONSENSUS

This achievement-of-a-consensus criterion illuminates the whole disciplinary interaction of the scientific estate with society in general, and with politics in particular. In later chapters it will help to clarify the activities of scientists as scientific advisors, as in recommending the construction of the atomic bomb in World War II; and it will make clearer the way in which government-related scientific institutions have been set up in an attempt to make them as much as possible directed toward consensus research. To illustrate these implications of the consensus definition, we will now analyze the Lindemann-Tizard controversy of World War II as an example of such advisory activities of scientists, and the Atomic Energy Commission and the National Science Foundation as examples of the consensus spirit of the scientific community.

THE LINDEMANN-TIZARD CONTROVERSY

A particularly interesting example of the difference between a consensus and nonconsensus interaction of science and politics is the Lindemann-Tizard controversy in Great Britain during the Second World War (as told by C. P. Snow in Ref. 4.6 from an admittedly pro-Tizard viewpoint). In this example these two approaches toward scientific-political decisions are exemplified by the consensus approach of Sir Tizard toward radar and by the individual decision of Lindemann concerning strategic bombing.

Sir Henry Tizard in 1935 was chairman of a committee for the Scientific Study of Air Defense. This committee decided to push radar as the defense solution for Great Britain. The desire to achieve a consensus on this decision was at first frustrated by the scientist F. A. Lindemann (later Lord Cherwell), who had his own pet projects for air defense. But after Lindemann left the committee, radar became a spectacular success. The ultimate reasons why the radar stations and organizations were ready for the Battle of Britain were not only that the finances were readily available once the committee was wholeheartedly in favor of this approach, but further that Tizard and his committee went to the lower echelons of the British air force and achieved a consensus among the future users concerning its feasibility on the basis of the scientific evidence in favor of radar.

Then Churchill took over as Prime Minister after France was invaded. And with him came Lindemann, as his scientific advisor and personal friend. Due to the past animosities over the radar issue, Tizard then began to lose power, and was finally entirely retired from the war effort as a result of the debate over the value of strategic bombing. The final resolution of that dispute was a case of a non-consensus decision in a field in which scientific knowledge could have lead to a consensus through operations research. This dispute came about because the British military at that time held as an article of faith that strategic bombing of the civilian population would lead to the defeat of an enemy. This was then proposed by Lindemann in 1943, on the basis of a quantitative estimate, as the policy for Great Britain which would most quickly terminate the war. Tizard, however, felt that the estimates were badly mistaken, as they ultimately proved to be, and that extra support for antisubmarine warfare was far more important. If a more general consensus had been attempted, Lindemann's figures would not have stood up among the scientific experts. But the only one who had to be persuaded was Churchill, and he accepted the solitary opinion of Lindemann. The result was an overestimate of the damage by a factor of 10; 500,000 German civilians were killed in these attacks on low-class housing, together with 160,000 U.S. and British airmen; and no significant drop occurred in either production or civilian morale. This false decision was at least in part the result of the absence of any attempt to gain a consensus concerning the quantifiable aspects of the problem.

SCIENTIFIC INSTITUTIONS AFTER WORLD WAR II

Besides the advisory impact of science on politics, another interaction occurs in the establishment of scientific institutions connected with the federal government. An illustration of this is the activity of the scientific community at the end of World War II. After the wartime experience with secret research, and with other political interference in scientific work, scientists responded to the end of the war by trying to "civilianize" the war-induced scientific effort. Attempts were made to reintroduce or to retain the benefits of the scientific consensus approach for the postwar science-government relationship. The primary problem, therefore, became the civilianization of the Atomic Energy Commission (AEC), both to release to the public as much wartime research data as possible and to make future scientific activities in the nuclear field as open as was consistent with national security. The result was a battle in 1945 in Congress between the adherents to the May-Johnson bill (sponsored by the Department of Defense) and the

Federation of Atomic Scientists, who wanted a bill which would not restrict all atomic research to government agencies, immunize the AEC from public review, exclude private enterprise from nuclear power, bottle up atomic information, and impose severe security restrictions on scientists. The Federation of Atomic Scientists strongly opposed the bill and successfully fought it in public hearings. The final AEC bill was due to Senator Brian McMahon, who aligned himself with the atomic scientists. (His is the statement that atomic energy "is too big a matter to leave in the hands of the generals.") In August of 1946 a compromise bill passed, which was, however, not all it might have been. For one thing, the Canadian spy story about losses of atomic secrets broke during the hearings, so that the security clearance requirement remained in the bill. The victory of the scientists was not very clear-cut; much of the research carried out by the AEC is still secret. But the point is illustrated: the scientific community did attempt to make public as much as possible of their wartime and postwar research.

Only after the question of the civilian control of the AEC was settled could the scientists devote their attention to passing legislation specifically directed toward basic research. In late 1944, Vannevar Bush, the wartime czar of American science, proposed a National Research Foundation, which was to be responsible for the primary government-sponsored, long-term, undirected research. Interestingly enough, the social scientists were to be excluded from this program; as the Harvard physicist Edward Purcell (a "graduate" of the MIT Radiation Lab) put it:

> It would be very helpful in some cases to have an economist in there. But in social science you dip into a very broad spectrum of stuff . . . . I have heard arguments between an economist and a physicist, and the physicist says, "Tell us one theorem that you fellows have that isn't trivial that you all agree on." (Ref. 4.2, p. 110.)

A consensus was to be the aim of this foundation, and in the judgment of the physicists, the social sciences could never achieve a scientific consensus on any worthwhile topic.

The process of establishing the National Science Foundation (NSF) took several years. An NSF bill was passed in 1947, but President Truman vetoed it because it would have been too independent of the executive branch. When in 1950 the NSF finally came into being, it did not in any way represent an organizational consensus. The medical scientists, for example, insisted on their own foundation, so the National Institutes of Health were set up, which now have about twice the annual budget of the NSF. The foundation is charged with fulfilling several tasks. Unfortunately, immediately after its establishment, a government economy drive, followed by the Korean War, hampered it in fulfilling all its prescribed goals. While the NSF budget has now grown to one-half billion dollars, this is only on the order of 15% of the total federal expenditures on basic research. Hence, the NSF has been restricted to setting the tone in basic research rather than directing or supervising all the nation's efforts in that area. In later chapters we will go into some of the quantities of big and little science. But clearly the scientists' success in obtaining the type of wide-open funding agency they wanted was limited; they did not gain overall control of science. Actually some of the recent attacks on the Department of Defense have led to the shifting of an additional fraction of the nation's research to the NSF, so perhaps sometime in the future this success may yet come.

CONCLUSIONS

Our fourth approach toward understanding the science-society interaction concerns itself with the disciplinary aspects of science. In this approach we analyze what contribution science as a discipline has made to society and what makes it different from other fields of study. Our guideline in future analyses will be the consensus aspects in the definition of science. This definition of science does indeed point up the uniqueness of science, particularly its separateness from technology. It also clarifies the origins of some present-day organizations of science. In later chapters we will try to use this disciplinary aspect of science to distinguish between the credibility of a scientist when acting in his expert capacity of science advisor and when acting as a citizen who happens to be informed on the scientific or technical aspects of a broad problem. We will also use this definition to support later arguments that "the social responsibility of scientists" may be a meaningless concept.

REFERENCES

Prime reference

4.1 J. Ziman, *Public Knowledge*, Cambridge, England: Cambridge University Press, 1968; Chapters 1, "What is Science," and 2, "Science and Non-Science," pp. 1–29.

Interesting reading

4.2 D. S. Greenberg, *The Politics of Pure Science*, New York: The New American Library, 1967.

4.3 J. Haberer, *Politics and the Community of Science*, New York: Van Nostrand Reinhold Co., 1969; Chapter 3, "The Baconian Community of Science," pp. 29–53, and Chapter 4, "The Cartesian Community of Science," pp. 55–78.

4.4 T. S. Kuhn, *The Structure of Scientific Revolutions*, Chicago: The University of Chicago Press, 1962.

4.5 I. Velikovsky, *Worlds in Collision*, New York: Doubleday, 1950, and R. E. Juergens, "Minds in Chaos: a Recital of the Velikovsky Story," *American Behavioral Scientist* 7 (#1), 1 (September 1963).

4.6 C. P. Snow, *Science and Government: And Appendix*, Cambridge, Mass.: Harvard University Press, 1961.

4.7 W. R. Nelson, Ed., *The Politics of Science*, New York: Oxford University Press, 1967.

4.8 R. E. Lapp, *The New Priesthood*, New York: Harper and Row, 1965.

4.9 J. B. Wiesner, *Where Science and Politics Meet*, New York: McGraw-Hill, 1965; Part III.

4.10 J. L. Penick, Jr., C. W. Pursell, Jr., M. B. Sherwood, and D. C. Swan, Eds., *The Politics of American Science, 1939 to the Present*, Chicago: Rand McNally and Co., 1965.

4.11 M. Thomas (with R. M. Northrop), *Atomic Energy and Congress*, Ann Arbor: University of Michigan Press, 1956.

4.12 R. G. Hewlett and O. E. Anderson, *The New World 1939–1946*, University Park: Pennsylvania State University Press, 1962; concerns the AEC founding.

4.13 V. Bush, *Science: The Endless Frontier*, Washington, D. C.: Government Printing Office, 1945; the influential examination of the postwar future of the new science-government relationship.

4.14 J. D. Watson, *The Double Helix*, New York: Signet Book Q3770, 1969; a very readable description of the unraveling of the DNA structure by Nobel prize winner Watson; it shows that science can be very unrational.

QUESTIONS FOR DISCUSSION

1. Is it meaningful to think of science in terms of an estate?

2. Why is it so difficult to get scientists to accept the consensus definition of science?

3. If science consists of a consensus, can there ever be a scientific revolution?

4. Is a scientist a "scientist" if he works in secret and never publishes any of his data or theories?

5. Can there ever be a consensus about a political issue?

6. Why is it so difficult to obtain a technical consensus about the need for disarmament?

7. Is it appropriate in the light of the consensus definition for a scientist to do secret research for the military? Is it all right to accept money from the Department of Defense to carry out publishable research?

5 | MYTH, COSMOLOGY, AND ASTROLOGY

Indeed it is estimated that there are 10,000 professional astrologers but only 2000 astronomers in the United States.

Robert S. Morison

A survey is presented of the development and the uses of astronomy before classical Greece. Structures such as Stonehenge testify to the existence of astronomical knowledge in connection with religion. The question whether astrology is a science is discussed.

INTRODUCTION

In this chapter we will consider the combination of astronomy and astrology as one of the earliest known examples of the interaction of science with society. We will start with the most ancient times about which we have significant amounts of information, namely the period preceding the ancient Greek civilization (about 4000 B.C. to 600 B.C.). This period includes the time when Egypt and Babylon were at their height of power and saw the development of something resembling a science of astronomy. Interestingly enough, this astronomy ultimately gave rise both to the science of physics and to the pseudoscience of astrology.

This example will serve the purpose of illustrating some of the origins of modern science, as well as the development of science in terms of a consensus. The discussion of astrology will indicate how some topics are by their very nature "unscience." Finally, we will see how certain scientific meteorological and sociological studies have been retarded by their association with astrology.

THE EARLIEST MYTHS AND COSMOLOGIES

The earliest approaches toward science were for the purpose of understanding nature. All the early stories of creation were intended to make understandable the origins of the universe. There exist many of these explanations. The ancient Babylonians had their *Enuma-Elish*, the Greeks had Hesiod's *Theogony*, and there is the Nordic *Edda* with its Götterdämmerung. To us the best-known of these is, of course, the Biblical Genesis:

> In the beginning God created the heaven and the earth.... And God said, Let there be light; and there was light.... And God made the firmament, and divided the waters which were under the firmament from the waters which were above the firmament.... And God said, Let the waters under the heaven be gathered together unto one place, and let the dry land appear.... And God said, Let there be lights in the firmament of the heaven to divide the day from the night; and let them be for signs, and for seasons, and for days, and years.... (Quoted for example in Ref. 5.14, pp. 1–2.)

However, no matter how fanciful these myths were, their cosmologies did have a base in real astronomy.

ASTRONOMY: THE NEED TO TELL TIME

Astronomy became the first of the physical sciences because it provided knowledge which was relevant to the struggle for survival. The stage beyond myths was a step toward a control of nature; by acquiring the capability to tell time, society could become more sophisticated and stable. A knowledge of the time of day determined from the position of the sun allowed organization by making it possible to allocate tasks in such a way that they could be accomplished before dark. Paralleling this was the organization of longer periods of time. The sun is, of course, the most significant time marker because of the seasons; but the moon is much more striking because of its phases, and is a more practical time marker because its period is so short. Consequently, the tendency was for nomads, who were not so dependent on the seasons, to use the moon for timing. The Jewish Midrash, for example, says: "The moon has been created for the counting of days." The moon cults all indicate that the moon was thought to control time—note the werewolf stories and the belief that mood depends on the phase of the moon ("she is going through a phase"). In moon-oriented cultures the time of day starts in the evening. Agricultural people in contrast to nomadic ones were more in need of a solar calendar. They had to prepare for floods, monsoons, snowstorms; and had to plant and harvest in the right seasons.

Both nomadic and agricultural societies ultimately had to couple moon time (months) and solar time (years). This necessity occurred time and time again. For example, the Jewish calendar was first established when the Jewish tribe was in the desert; it was then based on the moon. When the Jews then came to Canaan, they turned into farmers, and the calendar had then to adapt to the solar year. The Passah had originally been a nomadic festival; it was a time when newborn lambs were offered to Jehovah. In Canaan it then merged with the agricultural Massoth festival in which the first harvested sheaves of barley were offered and unleavened bread was made from the first grain. Since one of these festivals was coupled to the year and the other to the moon, there were some difficulties in uniting them. This was finally resolved by letting the phase of the moon determine the day of the festival, but letting the solar year determine the appropriate moon cycle. All the other festivals during the year were then based on this date.

This was the general solution of the moon-sun problem. There were a certain number of months each year whose names distinguished between planting months and harvesting months, and in some cases there were insignificant and hence unnamed months. (For example, the Romans originally had only 10 months through December, with January and February unnamed since no agriculture takes place then.) Every so often an additional month would be added to bring the year back into agreement with the seasons. The Arabs, for example, initially adopted this system of interlocuting a month every few years. A certain tribe of priests was then responsible for deciding when this extra month was necessary. However, Mohammed ultimately forbade this system, both to break the power of this tribe

Fig. 5.1 A view of the ancient astronomical monument Stonehenge, taken from the southwest. (Photograph by Jon H. Gardey.)

and to separate Islam more sharply from the Jewish religion. So the Mohammedan calender year now has 12 lunar months (i.e., 354 days) and runs through all the seasons in 33 years. This is an example of a petrified Bedouin (nomad) tradition.

STONEHENGE

Once priestly castes arose, they began to investigate the motion of the planets and stars in much greater detail, thus beginning the science of astronomy. The knowledge was, however, not made public, but rather was kept secret for the greater power of the priesthood. There is much evidence of bodies of astronomical knowledge, even among peoples with no written tradition. One of the more recently discovered astronomical "cultures" is associated with megalithic structures such as Stonehenge (Fig. 5.1), a religious shrine which has surprisingly turned out to be an astronomical observatory as well (Refs. 5.3 and 5.4).

Between 1900 and 1600 B.C., the old Britons erected an enormous structure about 100 miles southwest of London. It is imposing, even in its present "decayed" state, since it includes not only an outer ring of 56 evenly spaced holes, but also an inner ring of very heavy rocks (weighing up to 50 tons each) with crosspieces, as well as miscellaneous other holes and heavy gateways near the center of the building. For a long time Stonehenge was thought to have been a religious temple. More recently, investigations have shown that it, as well as many other structures in England and in Europe, is also a very precise indicator of season-related astronomical events which is even thought to have been useful in predicting eclipses. By looking through various sequences of apertures, an observer could view the sun and moon rises at the beginning of the four seasons. The 56 holes on the perimeter seem to be correlated with the 56-year cycle in lunar eclipses.

So Stonehenge, and other similar structures, were probably the gathering place of the people when the priests called them together to celebrate such events as midsummer and the new year. Some of the festival customs of Europe, as well as our Thanksgiving and Mardi Gras, date from these seasonal celebrations (Ref. 5.5). In the British Isles, for example, the Beltane fires are ignited at midsummer on top of mountains; this may be a remembrance of the times when the news of the midsummer eve had to be quickly communicated from places like Stonehenge. In some places in Europe, burning brands in the form of wheels with notches were thrown into the air at such seasonal festivals, presumably in an effort to influence the length of the day. And one can certainly picture the power accruing to the priests who were able to predict the occurrence of an eclipse. Stonehenge represents astronomy with a social purpose. Astronomy here was both an ornament for religious activities and a necessity for agriculture; here was knowledge for the purpose of controlling both nature and society.

EGYPTIAN ASTRONOMY

Once power became associated with astronomy, religions inevitably developed which incorporated astronomical aspects. Ancient Egypt illustrates this quite well. To the Egyptians the seasons were (and still are) all-important; through the floods of the Nile, all life was governed by the seasonal configurations of the stars; the new year and midsummer had to be know very precisely. Consequently the sun, moon, and stars were very thoroughly studied until they gradually acquired individual personalities and names. The dawn (preparing for the sun) was called Isis; the morning sun, Storus; the noon sun, Amen Rá; the evening sun, Atmu; and the sun (when set), Osiris. Such stars and constellations as the Great Bear, Orion, the Pleiades, and Sirius were recognized and named. All the Egyptian astronomical ideas and gods are surprisingly deeply embedded in our present culture. The Rosicrucians, the Shriners, and the Free Masons all use rituals involving these mythical names and ideas. As another example, Mozart's opera *The Magic Flute* invokes many of these characters, like Osiris.

The Egyptian religions reflected astronomical concerns. The temples of deities, as well as the pyramids, tend to be pointed toward sun-risings or sunsets at new year or midsummer (Ref. 5.6). Most of Egypt ran on a summer year because the Nile rose at midsummer; in contrast, Babylon ran on a spring year since the Tigris and Euphrates flooded in the spring, and their temple orientations reflect these interests. Since the star Sirius rose for the first time each year in synchronization with the Nile floods, there are even some Isis temples oriented to observe this first rise.

With religion so closely related to the everyday operation of the Egyptian society, frequent power struggles ensued between the priesthood and the secular authorities. Two examples might illustrate this. At one point the priesthood had set the year at 360 days, and then resisted changes in this tradition. When finally the 365-day calendar was adopted, each subsequent Egyptian king had to make a vow before the priests of Isis at Memphis not to add either days or months at some later time. Then in the 15th century B.C. the Theban priests tried to wipe out the worship of the solar disk. They persuaded Thotmes III to build a shrine to the Theban sun god Amen Rá across the fairway of the chief temple to the solar disk at Karnak, blocking the view critical in the worship proceedings. In turn, 150 years later Amenhotep IV (Ikhnaton) tried to reduce this priestly power by favoring the cults and priests of cities in the north, by entering into diplomatic relations with Asia and Babylon, by proscribing the worship of Amen, and ultimately by leaving Thebes and adopting the solar disk Aten as his personal god. Through its predictive power in this agricultural society, astronomy became involved in political power struggles.

BABYLON AND ASSYRIAN ASTROLOGY

In the Mesopotamian plain of Persia, between the rivers Tigris and Euphrates, civilizations had been developing in parallel with those in Egypt. In the "Old Babylonian" period (ca. 1800–1600 B.C.), the priesthood also possessed an astronomy to predict the seasons; they too had to determine the length of the year and to decide when to interject an additional month. A document concerning such an interlocution from the 18th century B.C. states:

> Thus Hammurabi speaks: Since the year is not good, the next month must be noted as a second Ululu [i.e. the sixth month must be repeated]. Instead of delivering the tithes to Babylon on the 25th of Tishritu [the seventh month], have them delivered on the 25th of Ululu II. (As quoted in Ref. 5.1, p. 31.)

The court could not stay hungry; a month's delay in food delivery had to be avoided.

Then about 800 B.C., the Assyrians from the northern part of the Tigris conquered the area. Since they were warriors rather than agriculturalists, the calendar then was no longer the only motive for observing the stars. Astronomy was joined by astrology; the stars were thought to directly influence the course of events here on earth. And,

Fig. 5.2   Mickey Mouse as the Sorcerer's Apprentice. (© Walt Disney Productions.)

as indicated in the introductory quotation, astrology is still very much with us. To us, a magician is like Mickey Mouse (Fig. 5.2) in the "Sorcerer's Apprentice" (in Walt Disney's *Fantasia*), with a black hat (like the night sky) sprinkled with stars (from which to read our fate). We have our horoscopes and our newspaper astrologers. This *is* the age of Aquarius. All thanks to the Assyrians.

Assyrian astrology was actually quite formalized, and it was oriented primarily toward predictions on a national level. It was during the Hellenistic era that astrology came also to foretell the fate of individuals. In Assyrian astrology different months, constellations, and areas in the sky were associated with the four regions of the country. The moon and the planets were pointers which foretold the future for these regions. Since the moon is so variable, it was considered to have an enormous influence:

> When the Moon and Sun are seen with one another on the 16th day, king to king will send hostility. The king will be besieged in his palace for the space of a month. The feet of the enemy will be against the land; the enemy will march triumphantly in his land. . . . When it is seen on the 16th day ⌊of the 4th month⌋ it is lucky for Subartu ⌊the north⌋, evil for Akkad ⌊Babylon⌋ and Amurru ⌊the Western Desert, Syria⌋.

When a halo surrounds the moon and Jupiter stands within it, the king will be besieged. The halo was interrupted; it does not point to evil. . . . (As quoted in Ref. 5.1, pp. 42–43.)

Eclipses were, of course, regarded as very important omens. They were predicted and used as symbols of the future:

When an eclipse happens and stands on the second side [of the night], the gods will have mercy on the land. When the moon is dark in Simannu [3rd month], after a year Ramanu [the storm god] will inundate. When the moon is eclipsed in Simannu there will be flood and the produce of the waters of the land will be abundant . . . .

On the 14th an eclipse will take place; it is evil for Elam [Eastern mountains] and Amurra [the Western desert], lucky for the king my lord; let the king, my lord, rest happy. . . . The great gods who dwell in the city of the king, my lord, overcast the sky and did not permit to see the eclipse, so let the king know that this eclipse is not directed against the king, my lord, nor his land. Let the king rejoice . . . . (As quoted in Ref. 5.1, pp. 44–45.)

In these predictions, the planets, since they wander among the fixed stars, have special significance. In fact, their names often tell their character: Jupiter was the planet of Marduk (god of Babylon) and hence lucky; red Mars was the planet of the god of pestilence and hence evil:

When the star of Marduk appears at the beginning of the year, in that year corn will be prosperous . . . . When a planet [Mercury] approaches star Li [Aldebaran] the king of Elam [the eastern mountains] will die . . . .

When Venus grows dim and disappears in Abu there will be slaughter in Elam. When Venus appears in Abu from the first to the thirtieth day, there will be rain, and the crops of the land will prosper. (As quoted in Ref. 5.1, p. 39.)

IS ASTROLOGY A SCIENCE?

Astrology is hard to accept in any rational way, since it demands the belief that the momentary configuration of celestial bodies at a person's birth has an effect on his fate for the rest of his life. There has never, for example, been any statistical evidence to support the association of the sign of Libra with artistic ability or of Mars with criminal tendencies (Ref. 5.7, p. 84). The scientific revulsion against astrology is particularly strong because it claims to predict events— just as science does in the scientific method. The internal contradictions inherent in astrology already show that astrology cannot be a science. Among these contradictions is the fact that over the last 2000 and more years the signs of the Zodiac have changed by one month, so that now the astrological names and characteristics are associated with different parts of the sky. Furthermore, the Indian-Chinese Zodiac is different from the Assyrian Zodiac. And finally, modern technology is in a position to modify a person's natural birthdate through induced labor and Caesarean deliveries. So even the most formal astrological predictions can never approach a consensus as a function of time and nationality and medicine.

BLOCKED MATRICES

Actually celestial bodies do in fact influence earthly events in many scientifically validated ways (Ref. 5.7). It has been found that rainfall is on the average higher after the full and the new moon than otherwise. There are 11-year cycles related to sunspots in the Nile water level and in seismic shock activity; plants and animals sense tides even when far away from the ocean; man's blood changes at sunrise, independent of physical activity; police records indicate a higher crime rate at the full moon; and the health of babies depends on the season of birth. Much of this data may be explainable on the basis of changes in the cosmic ray intensity, in very high sensitivity of organisms to changes in the earth's magnetic field, etc. Yet scientists have in the past been reluctant to perform studies of such matters simply because they so closely resemble astrology. Not only is this field too attractive to quacks, but there is an automatic prejudice which springs up in scientists on reading of such work. The point is that resemblance to a pseudoscience can make it more difficult to obtain consensus in a science. A similar situation obtains in scientific investigations into extrasensory perception (ESP), where it is not only difficult to obtain reproducible data, but where there exist similar automatic prejudices (Ref. 5.8).

SUMMARY

The earliest attempts at a physical science took place when astronomy developed beyond the stage of pure myth-making because agricultural society required information about the starts of the seasons. This knowledge was accumulated by the priesthood, which thereby acquired even greater power. This greater power led to astronomy-oriented religions, not only in Egypt and Babylon, but even in England. Inevitably there were then power struggles between religious astronomy and the secular authorities.

To what extent was this ancient astronomy a science? The stars by automatic repetition of their configurations provided a ready-made laboratory for observations. Astronomy was then science in the sense that verifiable predictions could be made. But when the priest-scientists withheld their knowledge from the general public, except to make pronouncement for the purpose of acquiring religious power, they were violating the public-knowledge criterion. It was then very easy for astronomy to be perverted into astrology, where everyone could use the same data-input to draw very disparate and equally unprovable conclusions, and where the objective is personal revelation rather than consensus.

REFERENCES

Prime references

5.1 A. Pannekoek, *A History of Astronomy*, London: George Allen and Unwin, 1961; Chapters 1–4, "Life and the Stars," "Agriculture and the Calender," "Old Babylonian Sky-Lore," "Assyrian Astrology," pp. 19–47.

5.2 J. L. E. Dreyer, *A History of Astronomy from Thales to Kepler*, New York: Dover Publication Co., 1953; the Introduction.

Interesting reading

5.3 G. S. Hawkins, *Stonehenge Decoded*, New York: Doubleday, or Dell Publ. Co., (Paperback), 1965.

5.4 R. Müller, *Der Himmel über dem Menschen der Steinzeit*, Berlin: Springer Verlag, 1970; and A. Thom, *Megalithic Sites in Britain*, Oxford: Clarendon Press, 1967.

5.5 J. C. Frazer, *The Golden Bough*, any one of many editions; has accounts of many European festivals and traditions.

5.6 J. N. Lockyer, *The Dawn of Astronomy*, New York: Macmillan Co., 1897.

5.7 M. Gauquelin, *The Cosmic Clocks*, London: Peter Owen, 1969; celestial objects do influence events on earth.

5.8 G. Schmeidler, Ed., *Extrasensory Perception*, New York: Atherton Press, 1969; tells of attempts to make ESP a science.

5.9 M. K. Munitz, Ed., *Theories of the Universe*, Glencoe, Ill.: Free Press, 1957; T. Jacobsen, *"Enuma-Elish—The Babylonian Genesis,"* pp. 8–20.

5.10 B. Malinowsky, *Magic, Science and Religion*, New York: Doubleday Anchor Book A23, 1948.

5.11 R. S. Morison, "Science and Social Attitudes," *Science* **165**, 150 (1969); the introductory quotation is on page 151 of this reference.

5.12 G. Sarton, *A History of Science*, Vol. 1, New York: Wiley Science Editions, 1952; detailed discussion of Babylonian and Egyptian "science," pp. 1–99.

5.13 O. Neugebauer, *The Exact Sciences in Antiquity*, New York: Harper Torchbooks, 1962.

5.14 W. C. Dampier and M. Dampier, *Readings in the Literature of Science*, New York: Harper Torchbook TB512, 1959.

QUESTIONS FOR DISCUSSION

1. Why does man require myths when he doesn't understand something?

2. Is science a replacement for myth? Is science our religion?

3. Is it a coincidence that the story in Genesis resembles other ancient myths?

4. If someone had offered the ancient Egyptian priests a modern textbook in astronomy, that might have been their reactions?

5. Why was there no industrial revolution in Babylon?

6. Could the "Sorcerer's Apprentice" be made into a modern parable—a parable in which the apprentice is society and the magic broom is technology?

7. Can the study of ESP ever be a science?

6 | THE FAILURE OF GREEK SCIENCE

For the seventeenth-century founders of mechanistic physics there was the "divus Archimedes" as a supreme symbol, whereas the defenders of the traditional organismic physics waged their battle from behind the protective authority of "the Philosopher" [Aristotle].

Stanley L. Jaki

The conflict between the views of the universe of Aristotle and Archimedes is the precursor of all the subsequent clashes between the "two cultures." The limited success of the ancient Greeks in developing a real science is analyzed.

INTRODUCTION

Much of our cultural background in the West is derived from the Greeks, from that almost mythical period from 600 B.C. to 150 A.D. Our literature, philosophy, logic, and art are so strongly influenced by the Golden Age of Greece in Athens that it is hard to carry out a dispassionate analysis of these contributions. In the same way, the Greek attempt at science has also had a profound influence on our modern science.

I find myself somewhat unsympathetic toward this attempt. To me it appears that Greek science, initially well on the way toward blooming, was ultimately distorted and twisted to be a handmaiden to overall philosophical considerations.

The word "failure" in the title of this chapter, as applied to Greek science, must be put into context. When I first read the *Odyssey* as a young boy, it left me with the deep impression that the Greeks were heroic. My labeling Greek science as a failure is probably only my way of saying that the Greeks were not as heroic in their scientific accomplishments as in other activities. Worse still is the way in which Greek science coupled to our time. When Greek writings were reintroduced into Western civilization in the Middle Ages, it was the Aristotelian view of science, together with all of its teleological and philosophical arguments, which became entrenched through scholasticism. This view was taken so seriously that the link between philosophy and science finally became a drag on the further development of science during the Renaissance. Moreover, the Aristotelian organismic approach to nature has proved to be so persuasive that it is still with us today and provides the basis for many of the attitudes taken up by the humanistic culture.

In this chapter we will briefly outline the development of Greek science, with emphasis on the two alternate characteristic modes of thought which arose. Then some possible reasons for the relative failure of Greek science will be analyzed in terms of the four science-society interactions presented earlier.

THE RISE OF GREEK SCIENCE

As indicated in the last chapter, before the Greek developments, science was mostly mythical. Astronomy did exist, though it was closely identified with astrology. There were some recorded observations of natural phenomena and there was some technology developed for agriculture and construction. But rationale was lacking; there were no broad hypotheses, no overall principles, no general body of scientific thought. It was the Greeks who developed such a scientific approach.

Greece too had its myths. Hesiod tells of Cronos, of the elder gods who first populated the earth, and of the births of the newer gods from the mysterious marriage of Heaven and Earth. But there slowly developed attempts to relate the figures of the gods to more universal ideas: Eros became the God of Love in general; Erebus and Tartarus began to stand for the Chaos and the Night which existed before the earth, sky, and air came into being. There developed an attempt to make a physical picture, to develop a physical sequence of the earth's creation, to change the gods from unbelievable creatures to representatives of states of being. These were the first steps out of myth into reality. It was with the next steps that modern science became inevitable, perhaps even in spite of the Greeks. These next steps were the development of two trends of thought about science. One of these was the Pythagoras-Archimedes sequence which was quite promising, but unfortunately too secretive and mechanistic. The other was a sequence leading to Aristotle, which became entangled in philosophy because of its organismic approach.

THE PYTHAGOREAN APPROACH TOWARD SCIENCE

The geometrician Pythagoras characterized the breakthrough toward Greek scientific thought by connecting numbers with sensory perceptions. He lived in the 6th century B.C. and is said to have traveled extensively through Egypt and Persia. What he picked up in the way of mathematics during these travels influenced him greatly and directed him and his disciples for the next 200 years at his school in southern Italy. Pythagoras thought and lived numbers, as reported centuries later by Aristotle:

> Evidently then, these thinkers also consider that number is the principle both as matter for things and as forming both their modifications and their permanent states, and hold that the elements of number are the even and the odd, and that of these the latter is limited, and the former is unlimited; and that the One precedes both of these (for it is both even and odd); and number from the One; and that the whole heaven, as has been said, is numbers. (*Metaphysics*, as quoted in Ref. 6.1, p. 44.)

The real accomplishment of the Pythagorean school was to make quantitative order out of the physical chaos of nature. This breakthrough started with music, when the connection between string length and musical notes began to be explored. The observed quantitatively simple relationship between something as physical as the length of a string and something so aesthetic as the resulting harmony was tremendously appealing to these mathematicians. The next step was to extend numbers to other phenomena, and the stars were the most likely candidates for such numerical studies. It was reported that "They infer that there is a certain arithmetical proportion for the other planets as well, and that the movement of the heavens is harmonious." "The harmony of the spheres" refers to the notion that the planetary orbits, like the strings of a musical instrument, have harmonious ratios in their lengths. The notion even included the idea that the heavenly spheres constantly emit music, that the stars in their courses make sounds, since we have been hearing these sounds all our lives, we are no longer conscious of them. Leibnitz once said "Music is the arithmetic of the soul, which counts without its being aware of it."

The cosmology which finally resulted from this concern with numbers was far from perfect. For the later Pythagoreans the world was made up of four elements: earth, water, air, and fire; the universe had a spherical earth traveling around in a circle once every 24 hours (instead of rotating); there was an invisible central fire, with the sun reflecting light from it; and in order to have exactly 10 major bodies in the universe, there was stipulated an antiearth, visible only from the back of the earth. However, although these ideas now seem somewhat silly, they at least had potential for expansion and even room for proof and disproof. Since there were no strong philosophic ideas connected with it, other than that of numbers, this could lead to the heliocentric theory where the earth rotates about the sun, and could thus promote, rather than retard, the future scientific progress of astronomy.

Why did this promising start in science fail? In part it was because the Pythagorean school was a secretive organization. Its members vowed not to reveal any of the accumulated knowledge; in fact, most of what we know about this school comes through commentators such as Aristotle. And, in time, an element of mysticism entered, possibly engendered by this secretiveness. Finally, through Plato and Socrates, during the period 429–347 B.C., numbers became separated into pure and impure numbers. Impure numbers were then preferable to bare reality, pure numbers preferable to the impure, with the philosophy of numbers regarded still more highly:

What is the science of calculation or measurement used in building or commerce, when we compare it with the philosophy in geometry and exact reckoning? The arts and sciences which are animated by the true philosophy are infinitely superior in accuracy and truth to measures and numbers. (Plato, *Philebus*, as quoted in Ref. 6.1, p. 61.)

And philosophy alone is best. As a result of this viewpoint, the whole Pythagorean concept was diverted, and quantitative experimentation was held in contempt. Astronomy was bearable only because experimentation was unnecessary; general numerical experiments were not acceptable. As Plato had Socrates say in the seventh book of the *Republic*:

> I cannot think of any study as making the mind look upwards, except one which has to do with unseen reality. . . . These intricate traceries in the sky are, no doubt, the loveliest and most perfect of material things, but still part of the visible world, and therefore they fall far short of the true realities—the real relative velocities, in the world of pure number and all perfect geometrical figures, of the movements which carry round the bodies involved in them. These, you will agree, can be conceived by reason and thought, not seen by the eye. . . . You are thinking of those worthy musicians who tease and torture the strings, racking them on the pegs. . . . They are just like the astronomers—intent upon the numerical properties embodied in these audible consonances: they do not rise to the level of formulating problems and inquiring which numbers are inherently consonant and which are not, and for what reasons. (As quoted in Ref. 6.1, pp. 62–63.)

The Pythagorean attitude did not go down without a struggle. Aristarchus of Samos (310–230 B.C.) had the earth going around the sun and determined the relative distance of the sun and the moon; and Eratosthenes (275–195 B.C.) determined the earth's diameter. And then there was that practicing physicist Archimedes, who was both a Greek Ralph Nader and a military consultant. In 275 B.C. he detected a fake gold crown for King Hiero of Syracuse:

> At the appointed time [the maker of the gold crown] delivered to the King's satisfaction an exquisitely finished piece of handiwork, and it appeared that in weight the crown corresponded precisely to what the gold had weighed. But afterwards a charge was made that gold had been abstracted and an equivalent weight of silver had been added in the manufacture of the crown. Hiero,

thinking it an outrage that he had been tricked, and yet not knowing how to detect the theft, requested Archimedes to consider
the matter. The latter, while the case was still on his mind, happened to go to the bath, and on getting into a tub observed that
the more his body sank into it the more water ran out over the
tub. As this pointed out the way to explain the case in question,
without a moment's delay and transported with joy, he jumped
out of the tub and rushed home naked, crying in a loud voice
that he had found what he was seeking: for as he ran he shouted
repeatedly 'eureka, eureka!' (Vitruvius *On Architecture*, as quoted
in Ref. 6.4, p. 12.)

By comparing the weight of the gold crown when submerged in water
with that of equivalent masses of gold and of silver, Archimedes found
that indeed the "consumer" had been cheated.

Later Archimedes played the role of military consultant when he
almost singlehandedly defended Syracuse against the Romans from
214 to 212 B.C.:

When, therefore, the Romans assaulted them by sea and land,
the Syracusans were stricken dumb with terror; they thought
that nothing could withstand so furious an onset by such forces.
But Archimedes began to ply his engines, and shot against the
land forces of the assailants all sorts of missiles and immense
masses of stones, which came down with incredible din and
speed; nothing whatever could ward off their weight, but they
knocked down in heaps those who stood in their way, and threw
their ranks into confusion. At the same time huge beams were
suddenly projected over the ships from the walls, which sank
some of them with great weights plunging down from on high;
others were seized at the prow by iron claws, or beaks like the
beaks of cranes, drawn straight up into the air, and then plunged
stern foremost into the depths, or were turned round and round
by means of enginery within the city, and dashed upon the steep
cliffs that jutted out beneath the wall of the city, with great
destruction of the fighting men on board, who perished in the
wrecks. Frequently, too, a ship would be lifted out of the water
into mid-air, whirled hither and thither as it hung there, a dread-
ful spectacle, until its crew had been thrown out and hurled in

all directions, when it would fall empty upon the walls, or slip away from the clutch that had held it. . . .

Then, in a council of war, it was decided to come up under the walls while it was still night, if they could; for the ropes which Archimedes used in his engines, since they imported great impetus to the missiles cast, would, they thought, send them flying over their heads, but would be ineffective at close quarters, where there was no space for the cast. Archimedes, however, as it seemed, had long before prepared for such an emergency engines with a range adapted to any interval and missiles of short flight, and through many small and contiguous openings in the wall, short-range engines called "scorpions" could be brought to bear on objects close at hand without being seen by the enemy. When, therefore, the Romans came up under the walls, thinking themselves unnoticed, once more they encountered a great storm of missiles; huge stones came tumbling down upon them almost perpendicularly, and the wall shot out arrows at them from every point; they therefore retired. And here again, when they were some distance off, missiles darted forth and fell upon them; many of their ships, too, were dashed together, and they could not retaliate in any way upon their foes. For Archimedes had built most of his engines close behind the wall, and the Romans seemed to be fighting against the gods, now that countless mischiefs were poured out upon them from an invisible source. However, Marcellus made his escape, and jesting with his own artificers and engineers, "Let us stop," said he, "fighting against this geometrical Briareus. . . ." (Plutarch, *Life of Marcellus*, as quoted in Ref. 6.4, pp. 15–16.)

When Sycracuse finally fell through treachery, Archimedes was killed by one of the conquering soldiers. At that time scientists were not yet considered part of the booty.

This approach toward nature, this connecting of physical phenomena with numbers, was a profitable one. But it ultimately failed, presumably because there were no continuous schools of such thought to counteract the philosophies of Plato and Aristotle. And this should not be too surprising. No school of thought about nature which includes the provisions of secrecy can be successful. By the definition of science as a consensus on public knowledge, this kind of approach is not viable; indeed, it basically isn't even science.

ARISTOTLE ON NATURE

The Pythagorean mode of quantitative thinking can be contrasted with the organismic mode of Aristotle. Aristotle (384–322 B.C.), famous as the tutor of Alexander the Great, is important as the intellectual heir of Plato. Socrates and Plato had modified the Pythagorean philosophy of numbers into the notion of an idea underlying the reality: the sun is real, but the circle which it represents is ideal and perfect. Soon reality became subservient to the ideal.

Consequently, Aristotle in his scientific studies (he was an excellent observer of nature) emphasized the *why* rather than the *how*. For him everything became teleological; everything in the cosmos was the result of previous planning. In this picture scientists should approach their problems like students of architecture who, from the details of a house, learn the functions assigned by the builder to the various parts. This organismic approach may be productive in scientific fields like botany and biology, where living entities are involved; but taking the whole universe to be an organism is not satisfactory.

Aristotle thought in terms of natural motions, things seeking their own levels, and the dialectic of opposites. To Aristotle the stars and their circular motions were perfect. After all, straight-line motion would lead to infinity; yet the universe is finite, therefore only circular motion can be continuous and immortal and hence perfect. This means the stars are divine and the earth is base. It is this divinity of the stars which ultimately hampered attempts to move the earth away from the center of the universe, and hence haunted the Renaissance. And we are still teleological (Aristotelian) when we ascribe a purpose to nature, as when we say that "water seeks its own level" or "the organism adjusts to its environment." The other Aristotelian concept was that of extreme opposites. There are up-down, light-heavy, dry-wet, and warm-cold with all intermediates made up of combinations of these extremes. In the early 19th century, Goethe, for example, tried to use a dark-light antithesis to explain the whole range of colors. But these contrasts do not lend themselves to quantitative discussions. In fact, Aristotle did try to be quantitative when talking about falling objects. He abstracted a general law of motion from his experience with motion in a resistive medium:

> If a certain weight move a certain distance in a certain time, a greater weight will move the same distance in a shorter time, and the proportion which the weights bear to one another, the times too will bear to one another, e.g. if the halfweight covers a distance in x, the whole weight will cover it in $x/2$. (*DeCaelo*, as quoted in Ref. 6.1, p. 117.)

All Aristotle had to do was drop one 10-pound brick and one 1-pound brick from the top of the nearest building and he could have seen them arrive at about the same time, not one in one-tenth the time of the other. But Aristotle was so enamored of the imperfectness of the earth that he could not picture the absence of friction; hence to him all motion ("locomotion") required a *mover* to keep things going, except in circular motion, which is natural.

Aristotle left behind him a philosophy which dominated Greek thought. It was this philosophy which survived through the Middle Ages to be adopted as the medieval philosophy of the science of Christianity and which both helped and harmed the rise of modern science.

REASONS FOR THE ULTIMATE FAILURE OF GREEK SCIENCE: A SUMMARY

In a positive sense the Greeks took science out of the myth stage. But it never progressed further and, in fact, became entangled with philosophy. Why did the organismic view of Aristotle, rather than the quantitative views of Archimedes, become the epitome of Greek science? Possible answers run the whole gamut of the four science-society interactions.

a) There was a feeling of fate, of teleology.
b) There were no independent universities, insofar as science was always a part of a philosophic school.
c) There was a dearth of experimentation, a dislike of artificiality.
d) And there was an absence of technology coupled with the existence of slavery.

In a sense, the concept of teleology introduces a very early version of the division between the two cultures. The mode of thought of the modern humanistic culture may perhaps be characterized as viewing the universe as one vast organism in which everything has a purpose. This requires the "big picture," and it asks the question why rather than how. The Greek equivalent of the scientific culture is then represented by Archimedes, who was willing to ask how, who was willing to consider details, to dissect nature, and to talk in quantitative terms.

Closely related to this problem was the lack of universities (in the best sense of totally undirected inquiry) in the Golden Age of Greece. Science was always tied to a school: the Pythagorean school, the Aristotelian school, etc. It was bad enough that the end of a school would mean the end of an inquiry and that the potential scientists were isolated. What is worse is that science had to conform to the philosophy of that school, since it was secondary to the study of the philosophy. The consensus on a philosophic system then forced an apparent consensus on the science as well. Coupled with this was the secrecy of the Pythagoreans, a secretiveness which struck at the very heart of science as a consensus discipline and made failure inevitable.

The fact that science was pursued by people who were basically philosophers virtually ensured that extensive experimentation would be impossible. The Greeks were prepared to gather data by observing nature, but artificial experiments, with tortured approximations, were on the whole rejected. Consequently the study of astronomy was a favorite, since it involved ideal point sources of light, no friction, and data which repeated naturally. As far as the Aristotelian school was concerned, whatever nature wanted to be known she made visible; the only duty of scientists was then to interpret the data, data which everyone else had equally available. There was not opportunity to take the third step in the scientific method; that is, no imaginative predictions could be made.

Finally, the Greeks were aristocrats who believed in moderation. They had made their social choices; their priorities were not large-scale possessions:

> One should realize that human life is weak and brief and mixed with many cares and difficulties, in order that one may care only for moderate possessions, and that hardship may be measured by the standard of one's needs. (Democritus, *Fragment*, as quoted in Ref. 6.1, p. 260.)

The Greeks asked what technology can do for man; and they concluded: not much. Perhaps because they had slaves, and certainly
because of their moderation, they had no significant technology; they
seemingly despised it. The Greek temples were aesthetic, but they
were technically inferior to the Egyptian accomplishments. There
seemed to be no reason to improve the technological achievements
already available; the only people who might want life to be improved
were the slaves, and these were to be kept ignorant of the possibilities
of improvement through science and technology. A few quotations
from Aristotle's *Metaphysics* illustrate the Greek contempt for technology:

> Hence we think also that the master-workers in each craft are
> more honourable and know in a truer sense and are wiser than the
> manual workers, because they know the causes of the things that
> are done (we think the manual workers are like certain lifeless
> things which act indeed, but act without knowing what they do,
> as fire burns—but while the lifeless things perform each of their
> functions by a natural tendency, the labourers perform them
> through habit.) ... But as more arts were invented, and some
> were directed to the necessities of life, others to recreation, the
> inventors of the latter were naturally always regarded as wiser
> than the inventors of the former, because their branches of knowl-
> edge did not aim at utility.... Hence when all such inventions
> were already established, the sciences which do not aim at giving
> pleasure or at the necessities of life were discovered, and first in
> the places where men first began to have leisure. This is why the
> mathematical arts were founded in Egypt: for there the priestly
> caste was allowed to be at leisure.... Therefore since they philos-
> ophized in order to escape from ignorance, evidently they were
> pursuing science in order to know, and not for any utilitarian
> end. And this is confirmed by the facts; for it was when almost all
> the necessities of life and the things that make for comfort and
> recreation had been secured, that such knowledge began to be
> sought.... (As quoted in Ref. 6.1, pp. 258–259.)

It appears from the Greek experience that pure science cannot
stand by itself. It is possible to set the social priorities in such a way as
to exclude technology, but then science also is not viable. It seems almost as if in order to obtain a satisfactory enthusiasm about and

an understanding of science we must ultimately bring the knowledge out into the open through technological exposure.

REFERENCES

Prime reference

6.1 S. Sambursky, *The Physical World of the Greeks*, New York: Collier Books, 1962; particularly Chapter 10, "Limits of Greek Science."

Interesting reading

6.2 B. Farrington, *Science and Politics in the Ancient World*, New York: Barnes and Noble, 1966; agrees with the explanation of the Greek failure as presented in Ref. 6.1.

6.3 S. L. Jaki, *The Relevance of Physics*, Chicago: University of Chicago Press, 1966; Chapter 1, "The World as an Organism," pp. 1−51; the introductory quotation is on p. 3.

6.4 G. Gamow, *Biography of Physics*, New York: Harper Torchbook TB567, 1961; Chapter 1, "The Dawn of Physics," pp. 1−24.

6.5 M. K. Munitz, Ed., *Theories of the Universe*, (Ref. 5.9).

6.6 A. Pannekoek, *A History of Astronomy*, (Ref. 5.1).

6.7 J. L. E. Dryer, *A History of Astronomy*, (Ref. 5.2).

6.8 W. C. Dampier and M. Dampier, *Readings in the Literature of Science*, (Ref. 5.14); excerpts from works of Aristotle, Archimedes, etc.

6.9 G. Sarton, *A History of Science*, (Ref. 5.12); Volumes 1 and 2 contain a very enthusiastic and impressive account of the Greek accomplishments in the sciences.

6.10 M. Clagett, *Greek Science in Antiquity*, New York: Collier Books, 1963.

QUESTIONS FOR DISCUSSION

1. What might Aristotle and Archimedes have said if they had watched the first moon-walk on TV?

2. If being prepared for new things is a measure of knowledge, which one of these two men might be more knowledgeable?

3. How might the ownership of slaves prevent the rise of science?

4. In what ways is the organismic concept of nature related to the humanistic culture, and numbers to the scientific culture?

5. If the Greeks had been plagued with a rising birthrate leading to overpopulation, might they then have developed technology? Could they ever have had overpopulation?

6. Could we take ancient Greece as *the* model of a successful society which deliberately rejected technology?

7 | GALILEO AND THE SCIENTIFIC REVOLUTION

I am inclined to believe that it is the function of the authority of the Holy Scriptures to convince men of those truths which are necessary for the salvation of their souls and which—since they exceed all human understanding—cannot acquire credibility by any science other than that of the revelation of the Holy Ghost.

Galileo Galilei

The influence of Christianity on the rise of science after the Middle Ages is discussed. Galileo is then taken as the model of the new scientist. His conflict with the church points up the changes that were taking place during the Renaissance. The gradual modifications which took place in Bertold Brecht's view of Galileo over a period of 15 years illustrate the development of the modern concept of the social responsibility of science.

INTRODUCTION

In 1928 there took place in Berlin the first performance of the musical, *The Three-Penny Opera*, with the score by Kurt Weill written to the libretto by Bertold Brecht. This opera was a quite bitter commentary on the social problems of the poor at that time. Then, a few years later in 1938, Brecht began writing a play, *The Life of Galilei*, which continued to occupy him off and on for the rest of his life, as different versions of it were written paralleling his own social experience. In this play, Brecht's social concerns are presented by focusing on the late-Renaissance physicist, Galileo Galilei, as the symbol of all of modern science.

This use of Galileo as a symbol to relate the rise of modern science to social and political conditions is not unique with Brecht. Galileo's life illustrates several aspects of the new science-society interaction induced by the Renaissance. Galileo was, after all, the last of the "victims" of the conflict between science and religion, when in 1633 he was forced by the Inquisition of the Holy Catholic Church to recant his view that the earth moves around the sun. Furthermore, the way in which he pursued his research and published his results relates directly to the consensus definition of science and shows what the "new" scientist might be like.

In this chapter, using Galileo as an illustration, we shall examine the origins of modern science in Christianity. Then we will consider the conflicts which took place between science and religion before science finally established its independence. The basic question will be whether Christianity ultimately did more to help or to hinder the development of science.

But beyond this, the Galileo-Church confrontation is also obviously the stuff of which a dramatist can make a great deal. Galileo may not be a Hamlet struggling against a very basic and emotional wrong; however, as the founder of science as we now know it, he was involved in an enormously significant conflict. This conflict, and its reflection in modern affairs, was Brecht's central interest. Therefore we will conclude by looking at Brecht's play to see how Galileo's conflict relates to contemporary thoughts on science.

SCIENCE FROM THE GREEKS TO THE RENAISSANCE

Let me first indicate what happened to the development of science after the Greeks and how its revival was related to the Renaissance. Greek attempts toward science went astray after Aristotle and terminated with Ptolemy about 150 A.D. Of course, the Greek scientific influence by then had spread through a large portion of the world; but this influence waned as the Roman Empire declined; in 389 A.D. the great library at Alexandria was burned down (for the last time) by an irate Christian mob. This was a symbolic death knell.

By then the leaders of the Christian church demanded a literal interpretation of the cosmology described in the Bible; so astronomy was the discipline which regressed the furthest, due to its close connection with the Book of Genesis. The pictures of the world inherited from the Greeks were, for example, inconsistent with the supercelestial waters mentioned in Genesis—waters which some Christians felt would be very helpful in putting out the fires of the sun, moon, and stars on Judgment Day. Early in the 4th century A.D., Lactantius remarked on the absurdity of a round earth, since that implied the existence of places where people would have their feet above their heads, and where rain and hail and snow would fall upward. And Kosmas wondered how a spherical world, floating in space, could have emerged from the waters on the third day of creation, or how it could have been flooded in the days of Noah. He preferred to see the world as a tabernacle, with the earth the footstool of the Lord.

During the Dark Ages in Europe, the Greek scientific writings were not totally lost, but rather were dispersed, sometimes as far as India. After 600 A.D., the Arabic nations were united by Mohammed under the banner of Islam and took over the intellectual leadership of the Western world. We still use Arabic numerals because the mathematics (and astronomy) of the Arabs was very good. The *Rubaiyat* of Omar Khayyam shows his background as astronomer:

Quatrain LXVIII
We are no other than a moving row
Of Magic Shadow-Shapes that come and go
  Round with the Sun-Illuminated Lantern held
In Midnight by the Master of the Show.
        (Ref. 7.12, p. 98)

The difficulty with Arabic science was that a man was respected for being learned rather than for being a creator. In addition, there was too much of a concept of fate, of the will of Allah. So the biggest contribution of the Arabs to science was the collection and preservation of Greek knowledge. And slowly this knowledge drifted from the Arab nations into Europe. Foremost in this drift were the writings of Aristotle, whose ideas initially forced a tremendous improvement in thought and understanding. Through Albertus Magnus (1193–1280 A.D.) and his pupil Thomas Aquinas (1227–1274 A.D.), Aristotle's view of the world was reconciled with the Christian faith. It then came to be adopted as church doctrine, until it finally became a congealed religious commitment which was to last through the 17th century to plague Galileo. (See, e.g., Ref. 7.5 on the Thomistic synthesis.)

COPERNICUS AND KEPLER

There were slow encroachments on the Aristotelian views of science in the 13th and 14th centuries, through such people as Buridan, Oresme, Bradwardine, and Grosseteste. These led, for example, to the work of Nicolaus Copernicus (1497–1529), who thoroughly developed the concept that the earth was moving around the sun and rotating as well. Actually these new developments were frequently inspired by a rediscovery of diverging Greek views. Copernicus appealed to ancient authorities (such as Plutarch) to buttress his arguments:

> ... but Philolaus the Pythagorean says that she (the earth) moves around the (central) fire on an oblique circle like the Sun and Moon. Heraclides of Pontus and Ecphantus the Pythagorean also make the earth to move, not indeed through space but by rotating round her own centre as a wheel axle from West to East. (Preface to *De Revolutionibus* as quoted, for example, in Ref. 7.6.)

Copernicus still believed that the orbits of the planets must be circles, because circular motion is perfect.

Johannes Kepler, in the period 1600–1619, then worked out his three laws of planetary motion. Astrology as a doctrine of world unity dominated his mind—not astrology as a fearful spying upon the stars to discover human destinies but as a way to penetrate into the secrets of this unity. So Kepler finally was able to leave the Aristotelian circles and go to ellipses for the planetary motions, but only after trying some 70 other conceivable orbits. He found quantitative relationships between various aspects of planetary motion, but primarily through application of the concept of a harmony of the spheres. In some ways Kepler was a mixture of mystic and modern scientist; underneath the religious mysticism something new was appearing—something which perhaps tells us a little about what we have become since then.

CHRISTIANITY AND SCIENCE

A most decisive question, which must be asked sooner or later, is why the West has become since the Renaissance the dominant power on the earth. Why did the scientific and industrial revolutions take place only in the last 400 years and then first in Europe and North America? Alfred North Whitehead gave an interesting answer to this question in his book *Science and the Modern World* (Ref. 7.1). He suggested that this breakthrough was due to the Christian idea of a rational Creator. What has happened since the Renaissance is not so much the discovery of scientific facts as the emergence of a new intellectual climate. The growth of science has recolored our whole mentality: we now work with realistic fact as well as with general principles; we now believe that these two are reconcilable. This mentality is due to a belief, an instinctive conviction, in an *order of nature*. There is nothing rational about this belief itself. There is only blind and stubborn faith that we can study nature and make sense out of it. The Middle Ages may be characterized as the Age of Faith based upon reason (Aristotelian scholastic reason), while the scientific 18th century may be called the Age of Reason based upon faith.

The Christian faith in the rationality of God and nature had not always been there. Aquinas had accepted the Aristotelian concepts that there could be only one world at the center of the universe and that rectilinear motion was impossible. Therefore, some scholars date the origin of modern science to the year 1277, the year that the Bishop of Paris condemned these propositions of Aristotle (about possible motions) as placing limitations on the capabilities of God. The monotheistic belief in a rational Creator since then has led to the firm expectation that every occurrence can be related to earlier events in a very definite way through general principles. It is as though God after the flood had set the rainbow up as a sign that no undue number of miracles was to be imposed on nature in the future and that God and the physical universe were henceforth to be more or-less decoupled.

It is this faith in rationality which had not existed before. The Greeks believed instead in a dramatic fate in which every individual event is pregnant with meaning. With the world being an organism, there was then love and hate, with a mover for every motion. The Chinese also had enough time to produce science, yet developed very little. For them there was no conviction that mere mortals could ever understand the inscrutable divine code of laws which rule nature. The Egyptians and Persians in turn believed in an astrology, in the constant interference of the star-gods in events on earth. Since astrology has interpretation, it does not lend itself to the establishment of a faith in rationality. And to the Mohammedans the inevitable fate was too intimately good-willed to be understood by mere humans.

The world as the work of a rational, though infinitely superior, Creator had to appear to man's intellect as anything but simple. Time and again it was pointed out that the subtlety of nature is far beyond sense or understanding; and none of the 17th-century physicists failed to refer to the infinite richness of possibilities implicit for the Creator. But some sense could be made of it all. In a way the Renaissance represents the first real thoughts about the possibility of a consensus in science. Once the universe became something rational, it became possible for all people to agree on its meaning—because there was a definite meaning built in by God. Nothing was totally hidden; there were only things obscured. Now science could develop as a proper consensus discipline, and with this development came the meteoric rise of scientific knowledge.

THE LIFE AND WORK OF GALILEO

Galileo Galilei reaped the benefits of this atmosphere of rationality in natural philosophy and therefore could become the first of the modern scientists. He was born in 1564 in Pisa, Italy, 47 years after the beginning of the Reformation and three days before the death of Michelangelo. His father was a Florentine aristocrat of modest means, whose beliefs in scholarly investigation must have influenced Galileo considerably:

> It is my opinion that the censure of unreason is deserved by those who strive to prove the validity of a statement by relying exclus- ively on the weight of authorities without making use of any other argument. I for one desire that controversial questions be posed freely and be debated freely as behooves any man honestly quest- ing after the truth. (As quoted in Ref. 7.3, p. 66.)

This is the consensus view of science. A brief sketch of Galileo's life might go as follows. In 1592 he became Professor of Mathematics at the University of Padua, where he taught until 1610, and where he made most of his major discoveries. In 1597 he wrote to Kepler that he believed the Copernican theory that the earth moves, three years before Giordano Bruno was burnt at the stake for suggesting that there might be other inhabited planets. In 1610 Galileo went to teach in Florence. In 1612 the bloody 30-year religious war started in Europe; four years later Galileo was told by the Church to stop

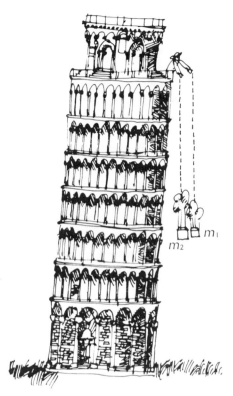

m_1

m_2

Fig. 7.1 The leaning tower of Pisa.

advocating the Copernican theory. In 1633 he was forced by the Inquisition to recant his belief in this theory, and lived under house arrest until his death at age 79 in 1642.

While working at Padua under the protection of the Republic of Venice, Galileo carried out a variety of studies which gave results contradicting the Aristotelian physics. In mechanics he came very close to the concept of inertia—to the concept that a moving body would continue to move even with no external mover acting on it. Aristotle had taught that only perfect bodies going in a circle (like the planets) would keep going perpetually. In gravitational studies, Galileo concluded that in the absence of friction all objects would fall in an identical manner. Scientific legend (most likely false) has it that he dropped two objects with very different weights from the leaning tower of Pisa and found them to strike the ground at about the same time (Fig. 7.1). The very concept of such an experiment contradicted Aristotle's statement that the time of falling of an object should be inversely proportional to the weight.

Finally, Galileo's astronomical studies supported in his mind the anti-Aristotelian aspects of the Copernican world picture. In 1609 he heard about the discovery in Holland of telescopes, and by thorough studies he was able to come up with a superior design which allowed as much as nine-fold magnification. These telescopes he offered to the Venetian Republic for military use:

> The advantages are inestimable that can acrue to all ventures on land and on the sea from the possibility provided by this instrument of seeing objects closer by. On the sea we shall be able to discover the vessels and the sails of the enemy two hours before we ourselves are within the enemy's sight. As in this fashion we can distinguish the numbers and types of the enemy's ships we can evaluate his strength and reach a decision as to whether we should take up the chase, accept battle, or withdraw. In the same way we are able on land to have the enemy's camp or his fortifications inside his strongholds observed from high places and can also see in the open field to our own advantage his movements and preparations and distinguish them in great detail. (As quoted in Ref. 7.3, p. 70.)

According to Ref. 7.3, the next day his salary was raised and he was given tenure. With these telescopes he observed four moons of Jupiter, which acted like a miniature Copernican planetary system; this made a moving earth appear much more reasonable. The telescopes also showed that neither the moon nor the sun were perfect spheres; instead the moon clearly had mountains, and the sun had spots and rotated once every 15 days. This contradicted the Aristotelian idea of the perfectness of the heavenly bodies. All these anti-Aristotelian ideas were incorporated into his book, *Dialogue Concerning the Two Chief World Systems*, published in 1632.

THE CONFRONTATION OF GALILEO AND THE CATHOLIC CHURCH

The confrontation of Galileo and the Church was closely connected with his advocacy of these anti-Aristotelian views. With the threat of the Protestant Reformation, the Church could not afford unlimited challenges to its authority. But the situation was somewhat more complicated than that, because Galileo to some extent actually forced this confrontation. Initially he was hesitant to enter into any public debate on the topic. His 1597 letter to Kepler said:

> ... for years I have been an adherent to the Copernican view which explains to me the causes of many natural phenomena that remain utterly inexplicable within the limits of the commonly accepted hypothesis. To disprove this latter I have compiled numerous arguments but I dare not bring them to the light of public attention for fear lest my fate become that of our master Copernicus who, although in the esteem of some his fame has come to be immortal, stands in the opinion of infinitely many (for such are the numbers of fools) as an object of ridicule and derision. (As quoted in Ref. 7.3, p. 68.)

Besides the fear of laughter there was also the fear of burning, as Bruno burned in 1600. (Note that 1620 was the year of the landing of the pilgrims at Plymouth rock to escape religious persecution.) There was, however, a difference between Galileo and Bruno. Bruno drew conclusions from the Copernican world picture which contradicted the Biblical world picture. Galileo, on the other hand, was never prepared to interpret the Copernican teachings in an anti-Christian way. For all of his life he was convinced that the concept of a stationary sun and moving earth was completely consistent with the Bible, if only the Bible was read properly. There is no evidence that Galileo ever had any struggles with his religious conscience; it appears that he not only started the modern age of science but also was the first representative of that group of scientists who had no difficulty reconciling science with possible supernatural intervention. Of course, even the Church did not initially object to the Copernican teachings; Copernicus, in fact, dedicated his *De Revolutionibus Orbium Caelestium* to Pope Paul III, confident that it would be well received. And when Galileo showed his telescope and the moons of Jupiter in Rome in 1611, the Jesuits publicly supported him and Pope Paul V received him and indicated support. Underneath, however, there was less unanimity.

Part of the difficulty was that Galileo felt encouraged to push the Catholic Church into declaring belief in Copernicus, i.e., to go beyond just presenting the Copernican view as a possible alternative to be debated, and considered, and gradually adopted. There was simply too much resistance from academic Aristotelian believers who had committed themselves to that view and who could not accept being proved wrong. Galileo's experiments with sunspots, for example, brought him into conflict with the Jesuit Christoph Schreiner, who not only disagreed with the Copernican interpretation of the spots but furthermore claimed priority in the discovery of the sunspot motion. In 1613 Galileo wrote in a letter:

> It seems to me, therefore, that no work of nature that is taught us by our eyes' experience or that is otherwise demonstrable by proof should be cast into doubt by reason of passages in Holy Scripture ... for no statement in Holy Scripture is subject to laws as rigid as those governing every work of nature. . . . Since it is patently impossible for two truths to be at odds, it is the task of the wise exegetes of Holy Scripture to endeavor to find the true meaning of the statements to establish their accord with those necessary inferences which must be made by reason of definite evidence or certain proof. (As quoted in Ref. 7.3, p. 80.)

Galileo believed that the Holy Scriptures are intended to convince man of those truths which science cannot examine; that since God gave us our senses, we certainly must be allowed to use them to study what we can. Galileo's letter was circulated with his approval and fell into hand of his enemies. It was passed on to the Roman Inquisition:

> ... those responsible for the document aim to interpret Holy Scripture in their own way and against the accepted interpretation of the Holy Fathers, upholding an opinion entirely and evidently contrary to Holy Scripture, and since I have been told that these men speak with little respect of the Holy Fathers of old and of Saint Thomas, trampling under foot the entire philosophy of Aristotle of which scholastic theology makes so much use... (As quoted in Ref. 7.3, pp. 81–82.)

Galileo's letter to the Grand Duchess of Tuscany is a more detailed statement of what he wants to have accepted:

> Some years ago ... I discovered many things in the heavens that had remained unseen until our own era ... these discoveries

conflicted with certain propositions concerning nature which were commonly accepted by the philosophical schools. Hence no small number of professors became stirred up against me— almost as though I, with my own hand, had placed these things in heaven in order to disturb and obscure nature and the sciences. But who could with all certainty insist that the Scripture has chosen rigorously to confine itself to the strict and literal meaning of words when it speaks incidentally of the Earth, water, the Sun, and other creatures?

From this it would seem that natural effects, either those which sensory experience sets before our eyes or those which are established by logical demonstration, ought never on any account to be called into question, much less condemned, on the basis of Scriptural passages whose words may appear to support a conflicting opinion. For not every Scriptural dictum is connected to conditions as severe as those which hold with respect to effects of Nature; nor does God reveal Himself less excellently to us in the effects of Nature than He does in the sacred utterances of Scripture.

It is obvious, then, how necessary it was (for Scripture) to attribute motion to the Sun and stability to the Earth. It was necessary in order not to confuse the limited understanding of the vulgar, and in order not to render them obstinate and antagonistic, and in order that they should have faith in the principal doctrines which have altogether to do with Faith. (As quoted in Ref. 7.10, pp. 724–727.)

Galileo was so anxious to get these views accepted by the Church that in 1615 he stayed in Rome for half a year, participating in public discussions. And finally the Inquisition could no longer concentrate on the Copernican teachings themselves but had to do something about Galileo as well. Early in 1616 the Pope ordered the theologians of the Holy Office to decide whether or not (a) the sun is the center of the world and hence immovable and (b) the earth is not the center of the world and is not immovable, but rather moves with respect to itself in daily motion (i.e., rotates). The decision came that both were wrong and that the first definitely contradicted the scriptures. Two days later Galileo was told by the Inquisition to stop advocating his erroneous Copernican belief, while Copernicus' book was banned until it could be appropriately revised.

And now Galileo's decision of 1610, to leave Padua to go to Florence, showed itself clearly to have been a mistake; he had traded the anti-Jesuit Venetian Republic for the Florentine Jesuit stronghold. For seven years Galileo did not publish anything. Then in 1623 his friend and supposed supporter of science, Cardinal Barberini, became Pope Urban VIII. Urban could not retract the anti-Copernican decision, but he did not forbid discussion of the theory as a speculative hypothesis. So in 1632 Galileo published his *Dialogues*, which held to this limitation in appearance but in fact quite strongly supported the Copernican theory. In the *Dialogues*, Salviati, the representative of the Copernican school, ultimately convinces the layman, Sagredo, while the Aristotelian, Simplicio (who sounded like a poor version of Pope Urban VIII), comes off very much second best, as when he says:

> Even though the Copernican system may seem to be more correct than the system of [Aristotle], the conclusion that the Copernican system is true must still be deferred, for such a conclusion is tantamount to placing God under duress. (As quoted in Ref. 7.3, p. 96.)

After initial approval by the censors, the book was taken out of circulation. The Church at that moment simply could not ignore such a strong challenge. After all, in 1630 King Gustavus Adolphus of Sweden had turned the scales against the Catholic forces in the North so that the Catholic religion hung in the balance. In addition, the Aristotelians at the Roman court were overwhelming and were only waiting for a chance to get even with Galileo. And the Pope's support of Galileo was more in the nature of a bid for a reputation as a supporter of the arts and sciences than a reflection of a real interest in science as such.

At the end of 1632, the Holy Office asked Galileo to come to Rome to face the Inquisition. In the hearings the accusation and decision were based on records which indicated that the interview of 1616 had led to a papal order to stop all discussion of the Copernican theory. Galileo denied ever having received such an order and said he had since 1616 only discussed the theory as a hypothesis: "I do not consider the opinion of Copernicus to be true; and have disbelieved it, ever since I have been ordered to give it up." On June 22, 1633, the

Dialogues were publicly banned; Galileo was sentenced to jail and had to kneel and recant his belief in the theory that the earth moves. (See Ref. 7.9 for a detailed discussion of this case.) Within a few months he was back in Florence and stayed under house arrest at his villa. Four weeks after the judgment, he sent the banned *Dialogues* to Strassburg and asked that a Latin translation of it be prepared and published. While he held to the external appearance of the restrictions imposed on him, he certainly did not follow the sense behind them. And clearly the Church was only interested in the appearance; it was quite willing to ignore Galileo's contacts with the outside world. To his dying days Galileo could say:

> ... I find at all times strength and consolation from two sources. The one is the knowledge that on examining all my works no one will be able to find even the trace of a shadow of anything deviating from the spirit of love and veneration for the Holy Church. The other is my own conscience which is fully known here on earth only to myself and in heaven to God. He knows that ... no one ... would have been able to proceed and to speak with greater piety and greater zeal for the Holy Church or with greater purity of intent. (As quoted in Ref. 7.3, p. 108.)

BRECHT'S LIFE OF GALILEI

In a sense, Galileo is the first hero of modern science. He rebelled against a religious imposition on the content of science and tried to foster a spirit of public discussion of the issues. But in his role as the first of the modern scientists, Galileo has suffered much criticism for selling his services to Venice and for surrendering to the Inquisition. One of the more interesting of these criticisms was written by Brecht in the form of the play *The Life of Galilei*. (See also Ref. 7.4 for another anti-Galilean viewpoint.)

Brecht was an active playwright in Berlin between the two world wars; besides *The Three-Penny Opera*, his *Mother Courage and Her Children* has been well received in New York as a commentary on the social condition of man. In 1933 he moved to Denmark, in 1940 he fled further to Finland, and in 1941 he settled in the United States. In 1948 he finally returned to East Berlin, where he was placed in charge of his own theater group until his death. His play, *The Life of*

Galilei, is of particular interest because its various versions mirror the change in attitude of Brecht (and others) as science began to play a bigger part in world developments during and after World War II.

The first version was written in 1938/39 in Denmark. Brecht had already been a leftist for a long time, but the Russian purges in 1937/38 and the 1939 nonagression pact of Stalin with Hitler had confused all antifascist friends of communism and the U.S.S.R. So this initial version is more or less apolitical, antireligious, and true to the actual life of Galileo. In the United States, Brecht rewrote the play for and with Charles Laughton; under Laughton's influence, he changed Galileo to an Epicurian, to a vain and opportunistic coward. There occurs, for example, a very cynical scene in which Galileo collaborates with the political powers and dictates a letter discussing how the Bible can be used to suppress peasant workers. Part-way through the writing of this version, the first atomic bomb was used in war, and Brecht's Galileo now began to represent all *those* scientists. As Brecht put it:

> The atomic age made its debut in the middle of our work. Overnight the biography of the founder of the new system of physics read differently. (As quoted in Ref. 7.2, p. 16.)

In the third version, Galileo's changeover from fighter for progress to villain was completed. This version was written by Brecht for use in his own theater in East Berlin. In this final version, Galileo represents the modern nuclear physicist who is very competent but does not feel like being a martyr and prefers to save his life and work by adjusting and submitting. This third Galileo is not only not a hero, he is in fact a social criminal. And Brecht considers his capitulation before the Catholic Church the original sin of science.

CONCLUSIONS

Who is right? Was Galileo a hero or a criminal coward? Actually he was generally a man of his time, with both faults and virtues. He did indeed sell his applied science to the highest bidder, but that was the way of life in the period when an independent science did not exist. He did indeed capitulate to the Inquisition, but was there any choice? The issue there was clear-cut, the conflict obvious. To allow progress in the sciences, the old authorities had to be challengable; this was the spirit of the time. In turn, the Church could not at that moment afford such a challenge. So Galileo was squelched. But not really; the "persecution" was mainly *pro forma*, and the truth spread. So now Galileo is considered the first modern scientist, and the Inquisition is the goat. Religion held up science, but only for a moment; science, in turn, made a small contribution toward reform of the organized church.

It is equally interesting to look at the way Galileo viewed the discipline of science. He very much tried to achieve public discussions of scientific questions, and tried to separate consensus science from religion. In that sense he was indeed the premier scientist. But he may have overdone it. He perhaps pushed his views harder than his data warranted. Much of his evidence was either wrong or inconclusive. For example, he totally ignored Kepler's theory of elliptical planetary orbits, and therefore his interpretation was simply not convincing enough to overcome all the existing Aristotelian prejudice. It is possible that, if Galileo had attached the proper weight to the data supporting his viewpoint, the Catholic Church might not have been forced to react quite so strongly, and the public consensus might have been better served.

REFERENCES

Prime references

7.1 A. N. Whitehead, *Science and the Modern World*, Mentor Books 1948, Chapter I, pp. 1–20.

7.2 Eric Bentley, *Galileo (English Version by Charles Laughton)*, New York: Grove Press BC–128, 1966; particularly the Introduction.

Interesting reading

7.3 G. Szczesny, *The Case Against Bertold Brecht: With Arguments Drawn from His Life of Galileo*, (translated by Alexander Gode), New York: Frederick Ungar Publishing Co., 1969; introductory quotation is on pp. 80–81.

7.4 A. Koestler, *The Sleepwalkers*, New York: MacMillan Co., 1959.

7.5 E. J. Dijksterhuis, *The Mechanization of the World Picture*, London: Oxford University Press, 1961.

7.6 M. K. Munitz, ed., *Theories of the Universe* (Ref. 5.9); Quotations from Copernicus and Kepler.

7.7 A. Pannekoek, *History of Astronomy* (Ref. 5.1); Chapters 15–18 and 23, pp. 164–198 and 253–260.

7.8 J. L. E. Dreyer, *History of Astronomy from Thales to Kepler*, (Ref. 5.2); Chapter 10, "Oriental Astronomy," pp. 207–239.

7.9 G. deSantillana, *The Crime of Galileo*, Chicago: University of Chicago Press, 1955.

7.10 *Introduction to Contemporary Civilization in the West*, a syllabus, Vol. I, 2nd Ed., New York: Columbia University Press 1957; pp. 724–729.

7.11 S. L. Jaki, *The Relevance of Physics*, (Ref. 6.3); Chapter 10, "Physics and Theology," pp. 412–457.

7.12 E. Fitzgerald, *The Rubaiyat of Omar Khayyam*, Garden City, N.Y.: Doubleday and Co., Dolphin Book.

QUESTIONS FOR DISCUSSION

1. Does the humanistic culture believe in a rational Creator? Is an organic universe consistent with such a Creator?

2. Why was this rational Creator not incorporated into Christianity from the beginning?

3. Can we export science to India with its sacred cows if science requires an instinctive faith in a rational Creator?

4. What happens to science if we give up our belief in God?

5. What do we give up when we adopt a blind faith in a rational God? Some Venetians refused to look through Galileo's telescopes; since there could be no moons around Jupiter, they could only be optical illusions, so why bother looking? Is this so unreasonable?

6. Was it proper for Galileo to try to force the Church to change its stand?

7. Is there a limit to the public consensus which can be attained at any given moment?

8. Is it wrong to twist the past to your purpose as Brecht twisted the life of Galileo?

8 | THE WORLD AS A CLOCKWORK MECHANISM

My aim in this is to show that the celestial machine is to be likened not to a divine organism but rather to clockwork.

Johannes Kepler

Look around the world: contemplate the whole and every part of it: You will find it to be nothing but one great machine, subdivided into an infinite number of lesser machines. . . .

David Hume

The contribution of Newtonian physics to the view of the world as a clockwork mechanism is presented. The impact of this world view on philosophy, theology, and politics is examined.

INTRODUCTION

"All men are created equal." This statement in the Declaration of Independence is so basic to the political development of the United States that it is vitally important to know its historical antecedents. This attitude comes from the 18th-century Age of Enlightenment, from that age when the whole universe was viewed as one vast machine. This mechanistic outlook strongly contrasts with the Aristotelian organismic outlook; it characterizes the scientific culture in the same sense as the animistic view characterizes the humanistic culture. In fact, the mechanistic laws of nature authorized the American Revolution, and decreed that all men were born with equally unconditioned minds. The U.S. Constitution itself is mechanistic in the sense

Fig. 8.1 Prophetic in 1490, Leonardo da Vinci suggested this flying machine. (Photo courtesy The Bettmann Archive, Inc.)

that it has incorporated into it checks and balances, just as a precision clockwork has in it checks and balances to keep accurate time. (See, e.g., Ref. 8.2.)

This chapter will review the origins of the clockwork concept, indicating why it developed when it did. It was Newton who put the capstone on the development of the non-Aristotelian mechanics with his three laws of motion and his law of gravitation. And the resulting Age of Enlightenment had a tremendous impact in such areas as philosophy, theology, and politics.

THE CLOCKWORK MODEL

The details of the process by which the model of the universe as a clock developed are rather interesting. Renaissance man was fascinated not only by clockworks but by all mechanical devices. To enhance the status of the owner, gadgets had to be not only useful but beautiful as well. One of the most famous examples of such an interest in gadgets, is, of course, Leonardo da Vinci (Fig. 8.1). His application for a post with the Duke of Milan is nothing more than a catalog of Renaissance devices and mechanisms:

> 1. I have a process for the construction of very light bridges, capable of easy transport, by means of which the enemy may be pursued and put to flight. . . .

2. In case of the investment of a place, I know how to drain moats and construct scaling ladders and other such apparatus. . . .

5. By means of narrow and tortuous subterranean tunnels, dug without noise, I am able to create a passage to inaccessible places, even under rivers. . . .

7. I can make cannon, mortars, and engines of fire, etc., of form useful and beautiful, and different from those at present in use. . . .

10. In times of peace, I believe I can compete with anyone in architecture, and in the construction of both public and private monuments and in the building of canals; I am able to excecute statues in marble, bronze and clay; in painting I can do as well as anyone else. . . . (*Codex Atlantico*, as quoted in Ref. 8.5, pp. 167–168.)

And gradually these ornaments, toys, and devices, became technological masterpieces, precise enough to be useful in scientific research. It is quite possible that the availability of experimental apparatus during the Renaissance led indirectly to the rise of consensus science.

About 100 years before Leonardo, Oresme already felt that the whole configuration and motion of the heavens reminded him of "a man making a clock and letting it go and be moved by itself." All the pieces of the clock contributed to the working of the whole; no part was nobler than another. The Aristotelian world model implied that the heavens were noble while the earth was base, but the newer clockwork model inevitably challenged the old views. Similarly, this newer model of the universe was used by Rheticus to support the Copernican system. Surely, he argued, God's skills could not be second to that exhibited by the clockmakers whose products contained no superfluous wheels. And what else is the system of Copernicus if not the most economical description of the heavenly clockwork? Not only does the clockwork model indicate rapid advances in the design of technical gadgets; the very thought of drawing an analogy between the world and a mechanical device was new.

Actually the use of this analogy and the development of technical devices, at this point in time, is not merely a result of the Renaissance. Rather it is a consequence of the sudden importation of very complicated astronomical devices from China, where they had been improving for some time. (Some evidence even suggests that their history started as far back as Archimedes.) Without any apparent prior development, huge clocks appeared in Europe in the 14th century; even Chaucer in 1391 wrote a treatise on the astrolabe. And, in fact, clocks for some time actually declined in complexity to simple time-telling machines. So in the Renaissance, clocks were startlingly new and beautiful.

NEWTON'S PHYSICS

Isaac Newton capped the development of this mechanistic picture by laying down the unifying laws which allow the calculation of the configuration of the universe at any moment from the previous configuration. Born in 1642, the year of Galileo's death, he returned home from Cambridge University at the age of 23 to escape the plague. There he formulated the basic concepts of his three laws of motion and of the universal law of gravitation. The three laws of motion deal with the interaction of masses with external forces and with each other. As important as the laws themselves is the way in which they demand quantifiable formulations of such terms as distance, speed, acceleration, mass, and force. These three laws permit the complete prediction of all future motions of an object if only its starting point and its initial speed are known, together with the forces which act on it.

One of the more critical steps in the use of these laws is the insertion of the relevant forces. And it is here that Newton inspired an age by relating the way in which apples fall here on earth to the forces which keep the solar system in operation. By means of his universal law of gravitation he was able to calculate the 28-day period of revolution for the moon (in fact, he predicted the rotation period of an artificial earth satellite); and he was able to explain the elliptical orbits of the planets as well as the orbits of other astronomical objects such as comets. With his four laws, all of astronomy could seemingly be explained; they once and for all took the mysterious organismic concepts out of the sky. It appeared that once the universe was set into motion and the laws were fixed, it would simply go its predetermined way, just as a clock, once wound, will run on and on. As Alexander Pope expressed it:

> Nature and Nature's laws lay hid in night.
> God said, Let Newton be! and all was Light.

In 1687 Newton's *Mathematical Principles of Natural Philosophy* (the *Principia*) was published. Immediately, leading members of the Royal Society embraced his system enthusiastically. The impact on physics of this successful mechanistic approach has been tremendous. The making of mechanical models for natural phenomena then began and has persisted well into the 20th century. The great physicist Lord Kelvin still said late in the 19th century:

> I never satisfy myself until I make a mechanical model of a thing. If I can make a mechanical model I can understand it. As long as I cannot make a mechanical model all the way through I cannot understand.... (*Baltimore Lectures*, as quoted in Ref. 8.1, p. 75.)

The contrast with the nonmechanistic approach toward relativity and quantum mechanics, as described in Chapter 13, will be obvious.

Mechanism soon became an article of faith in all the physical sciences. Leibnitz, for example, argued that to abandon mechanism would either reintroduce perpetual miracles or else would impute contradictions to God and thereby make him unintelligible. Chemistry was called by James C. Maxwell:

> ... [a study] to determine, from the observed external actions of an unseen piece of machinery, its internal composition. (As quoted in Ref. 8.1, p. 71.)

And the French physicist E. V. Jamin could say:

> Physics will one day form a chapter of general mechanics. (As quoted in Ref. 8.1, p. 72.)

THE IMPACT OF NEWTONIAN MECHANICS

The impact of Newtonian mechanics went far beyond just changing scientific attitudes. Within five years of its appearance, Newton's work was publicly referred to from an English pulpit as "incontestably sound." And it was the godparent to the whole Age of Enlightenment. The new thinking was reflected in a change in vocabulary. In the 13th century the important words, words whose meanings were taken for granted, included God, sin, grace, salvation, and heaven; in the 18th century these were replaced by nature, natural law, reason, humanity, and perfectibility. This new vocabulary allowed the change from the pessimistic Christian doctrine of man's depraved nature, burdened from birth with original sin, to the optimistic view that all men are born with their minds a clean slate on which either good or evil can be written by society.

With the word "nature" there came the impact of the mechanistic doctrine of "natural" law. Newton's science inspired Thomas Jefferson to say that under the laws of nature a broken contract authorized the Americans to rebel against King George III. Jean Jacques Rousseau felt that the "state of nature" of the "noble savage" was a state of virtue. Jeremy Bentham was inspired to identify utility or the "greatest happiness" principle as the social law of gravity in legislation. Adam Smith talked about economics in a Newtonian way: in a supply-and-demand market the actual prices tend to "gravitate" toward the natural price. In politics the rationalists tried to use the "contrary-to-nature" argument to replace the old institutions of Europe with an enlightened "natural" humanitarianism; and the authority of Newton's system lent power to their attempts. Rationalism reigned supreme; Hume was willing to believe in a miracle only if the falsehood of the testimony for the miracle was even harder to accept than the miracle itself.

NEWTONIANISM AND THEOLOGY

Two of the results of this Newtonianism are particularly interesting, namely its impact on theology and ethics. In theology the effect was primarily to remove God from the running of the universe and to reserve for Him instead the act of creation. A limit was placed on the miraculous. As Newton put it:

> For miracles are so-called not because they are the works of God, but because they happen seldom and for that reason create wonder. (As quoted in Ref. 8.11, p. 645.)

This, of course, runs totally counter to the belief in Divine Intervention. Yet the theology derived from Newton's mechanics had a very strong belief in God the Creator. We may remember Newton for his scientific accomplishments, but he himself felt his science had intrinsic worth only insofar as it demonstrated the power of God to produce a perfect creation. God's truth was now to be found in nature as well as in the Bible. Voltaire proclaimed that Newton's philosophy

> ... leads necessarily to the knowledge of a superior being who has created everything, arranging everything freely ... [there is]

no Newtonian who was not a theist in the strictest sense. (*Elements of Newtonian Philosophy*, as quoted in Ref. 8.1, p. 432.)

The Newtonian physics was constantly called upon to give witness to God's existence. In 1697 Chaplain Richard Bentley gave several lectures in which he dealt with proofs of God's existence based on conclusions about the solar system as presented in Newton's *Principia*. Newton supported this presentation, and gave the following arguments (see Ref. 8.6).

1. The sun gives heat and light to help man survive. As Newton put it, "I know no reason, but because the author of the system thought it convenient."

2. The planets all move in the same plane around the sun, as opposed to the random paths of comets.

3. God must have specifically selected the masses, velocities, and distances of planets to let man survive.

4. God must have inclined the earth with respect to its orbit in order to produce the seasons, and given it rotation to separate day from night.

5. Only a supernatural power could have made the solar system out of a lump of mass.

Such "gap proofs" for God's existence, based on gaps in scientific knowledge, were abundant. Huygens in 1665 discovered the satellite Titan. This brought the known number of planets and satellites to 12, a number which "can be considered as predetermined by the counsel of the Supreme Artifex." W. Derham in 1713 published a book called *Physico-Theology* in which he proved God's existence from various aspects of nature such as the atmosphere, the winds, clouds, and rain. There were published books with titles like *The Theology of Stones* and *The Theology of Insects*. The skeptic Voltaire finally exposed the ludicrousness of this approach when in *Candide* he had Dr. Pangloss (a professor of metaphysico-theologico-cosmolonigology) prove to simpleminded Candide that:

'Tis demonstrated that things cannot be otherwise; for since everything is made for an end, everything is necessarily for the best end. Observe that noses were made to wear spectacles;

and so we have spectacles. Legs were visibly instituted to be breeched, and we have breeches. (As quoted in Ref. 8.2, p. 145.)

NEWTONIANISM AND FREE WILL

Another invocation of the Newtonian system and approach was in the discussion of ethics, particularly of free will. Once the universe is wound up, then it must run its course, and all that a person does is predetermined at the beginning by the clockmaker. There can then be no real free will, and no one is responsible for what he does. From the configuration of the universe right now, Newton's laws allow a complete prediction of the future. God is certainly capable of such predictions. And even though we may not have the capacity to duplicate this prediction, we certainly cannot hope ever to change the future. So there is no good, no evil, and man has no soul. (See Bishop Berkeley's writings for a contrary view.)

As a consequence of mechanism, the philosophers Hobbes and Spinoza were forced to deny free will. This led them to consider that the motions of the mind, such as the appetites and volition, must be amenable to explanations based on the Newtonian philosophy, and that as such they can be studied and predicted. Voltaire certainly wondered about the concept of free will; it seemed to him strange

... that all nature, all the planets, should obey eternal laws, and that there should be a little animal, five feet high, who in contempt of these laws, could act as he pleased, solely according to his caprice. He would act at random, but we know randomness means nothing. We have merely invented the word to denote the known effect of all unknown causes. (As quoted in Ref. 8.1, p. 375.)

The next step in the development of Newtonianism was pure materialism, which left absolutely no room for God, nor for a soul. As De la Mettrie put it, the only difference between a dog and a man is then one of degree of complexity:

A few more wheels, a few more springs then in the most perfect animal, the brain proportionately nearer the heart and for this reason receiving more blood—any of a number of unknown causes might always produce this delicate conscience so easily wounded, this remorse which is no more foreign to matter than to thought, and in a word all the differences that are supposed to exist there. (*Man, a Machine*, as quoted in Ref. 8.1, p. 376.)

Ethics become pure mechanism and man was reduced to a machine. d'Holbach said that the physical man

... is a man acting under the impulse of causes which our senses make known to us, [while the moral individual] is a man acting under the influence of causes which our prejudices prevent to recognize. (*System of Nature*, as quoted in Ref. 8.1, p. 377.)

SUMMARY

Newton solved the puzzle of nature so well that the world never was the same after him. His mechanics led to the clockwork model of the universe; the concepts coming out of this model included: a natural religion, a natural government, and a natural economy. Even the American Revolution was based on these natural concepts, on the inalienable rights of man; the United States is a result of this Newtonianism, of this rationalism. In fact, for a whole century all of intellectual society was dominated by ideas derived from the Newtonian mechanics. For a whole century the scientific culture reigned supreme.

There were attempts to place other disciplines, like philosophy and politics, on a similar basis of quantitative law, to put them into a scientific form aiming toward universal agreement. These attempts at a scientific consensus outside science were magnificent, but inevitable failures. And their excesses provoked the revolution of the resurgent humanistic culture in Romanticism.

REFERENCES

Prime references

8.1 S. L. Jaki, *The Relevance of Physics*, (Ref. 6.3); Chapter 2, "The World as a Mechanism," pp. 52–94.

8.2 Everett W. Hall, *Modern Science and Human Values*, New York: Van Nostrand, 1956; Chapter 3, "The Scientific Revolution and the Age of Reason," pp. 90–184.

Interesting reading

8.3 Ref. 8.1; Chapter 9, "Physics and Ethics," and Chapter 10, "Physics and Theology," pp. 371–457.

8.4 C. C. Gillespie, *The Edge of Objectivity*, Princeton: Princeton University Press, 1960; Chapter 5, "Science and the Enlightenment," and Chapter 4, "Newton with his Prism and Silent Face," pp. 117–201.

8.5 J. D. Bernal, *The Social Function of Science*, Cambridge, Mass.: The M.I.T. Press, 1967, pp. 19–23.

8.6 M. K. Munitz, Ed., *Theories of the Universe*, (Ref. 5.9); "Four Letters to Richard Bentley," pp. 211–219.

8.7 G. Gamow, *Biography of Physics*, (Ref. 6.4); Chapter 3, "God Said, Let Newton Be!" pp. 51–88.

8.8 C. L. Becker, *The Heavenly City of the Eighteenth Century Philosophers*, New Haven, Conn.: Yale University Press, 1932.

8.9 R. A. Baker, Ed., *Stress Analysis of a Strapless Evening Gown*, Englewood Cliffs, N.J.: Prentice Hall, 1963; J. E. Miller, "How Newton Discovered the Law of Gravitation," pp. 128–139, a tongue-in-cheek tale.

8.10 D. J. de Solla Price, *Science Since Babylon*, (Ref. 3.3); Chapter 2, "Celestial Clockwork in Greece and China," pp. 23–44.

8.11 L. T. More, *Isaac Newton*, New York: Dover Publication Co., 1962.

8.12 M. Nicholson, *Science and Imagination*, Ithaca, New York: Cornell University Press, 1956; tells of the impact of the Newtonian philosophy on literature.

8.13 A. D. White, *The Warfare of Science and Theology*, any one of several editions after 1897.

8.14 R. H. Hurlbutt, IIIrd, *Hume, Newton and the Design Argument*, Lincoln, Nebraska: University of Nebraska Press, 1965.

QUESTIONS FOR DISCUSSION

1. What might the Age of Enlightenment have said about Limbo? About Divine Grace?

2. How could the Age of Enlightenment resolve the discrepancy between slavery and the fact that everyone is supposedly created equal? Is slavery natural?

3. Many scientists see God in natural phenomena. My wife sees him in a baby. Is this a significant contrast?

4. Plants grow toward the sun. Did God design them to do this?

5. We have an appendix which seems worse than useless. Is the God who designed it therefore imperfect?

6. God apparently designed the universe so that an atomic bomb was feasible. Does that mean he wanted us to build and use one?

9 | ROMANTICISM, PHYSICS, AND GOETHE

. . . Do not all charms fly
At the mere touch of cold philosophy?
There was an awful rainbow once in heaven:
We know her woof, her texture; she is given
In the dull catalogue of common things.
Philosophy will clip an Angel's wings,
Conquer all mysteries by rule and line,
Empty the haunted air, and gnomed mine. . . .

John Keats

The Romantic revolt against the mechanistic world view resembled Aristotle's organismic approach toward nature; as such it illustrates the gap between the two cultures. Goethe is cited as an example of a man who tried to unite these two cultures and failed.

INTRODUCTION

From the publication in 1687 of the *Principia*, the Newtonian rationalism ruled the Western world, in the humanities as well as in the sciences. There was then no recognized gap between the two cultures, because the scientific world view was so overwhelming. Excesses were inevitable. One of the worst offenders was d'Holbach, who wrote in 1770 the following.

'O thou,' cries this Nature to Man, 'who, following the impulse I have given you, during your whole existence, incessantly tend toward happiness, do not strive to resist my sovereign law. . . . Dare then to affranchise yourself from the trammels of superstition, my self-conceited, pragmatic rival, who mistakes my rights; denounce those empty theories, which are usurpers of my priviledges; return under the dominion of my laws, which, however severe, are mild in comparison with those of bigotry. It is in my empire alone that true liberty reigns. . . . Enjoy thyself, and cause others also to enjoy those comforts, which I have placed with a liberal hand for all the children of the earth, who all equally emanate from my bosom. . . . These pleasures are freely permitted thee, if thou indulgest them with moderation, with that discretion which I myself have fixed. Be happy then, O man!' O Nature, sovereign of all beings! and ye, her adorable daughters Virtue, Reason and Truth! remain forever our revered protectors! it is to you that belong the praises of the human race . . . cause knowledge to extend its salubrious reign; goodness to occupy our souls; serenity to occupy our bosoms. (*Système de la Nature*, as quoted in Ref. 9.8, pp. 278–279.)

Equally inevitable was the reaction which then arose against these excesses of mechanistic philosophizing, against this objective realm of facts and procedures.

The rebellion was most immediately noticeable in such humanistic fields as poetry and music. But it also manifested itself in the Luddite protests against the Industrial Revolution and in the political return to imperialistic nationalism. There was even an impact of this revolt on the sciences through *Naturphilosophie*, an approach in which nature was looked upon as a living whole. In this chapter we will examine this romantic revolt against the Newtonian world view, a revolt which used the Aristotelian image of an organic nature. To further illustrate the "gap" between the two cultures, we shall consider the poet Goethe as a man who tried to unite the two cultures—and failed.

ROMANTICISM AND ENGLISH POETRY

When one speaks of Romanticism, one is generally referring to the end of the 18th and the beginning of the 19th centuries, when there was a general rebellion against the intellectual dominance of the mechanistic world view. This was a rebellion against the rule of nature, against the laws of physics, the laws of music, and the laws of literature; and it argued for a return to the picture of nature as an organic, animistic being, to the heroic classicism of the Greeks, and to nationalism away from world empire and cosmopolitanism. Ultimately it was a revulsion against the cruelties and confusions of the rising machine age.

The political setting for Romanticism was the fevered French Revolution of 1789, with its excesses in the name of rational liberalism. This revolution was derived from the concept of natural liberty and equality of all men, which in turn had come from the Enlightenment's view of perfect nature being perverted by imperfect human laws—laws which the French Revolution tried to change. Even Napoleon did not really represent a change from rationalism. The romantic revolt was represented in a political context by the decision at the Congress of Vienna in 1815 to return to the old national arrangements, with their censorship and tight control; this was a return to the old order, the old nonrational order. There was a parallel reaction to the economic situation at that time; the agricultural revolution had already driven the farmer off the land, and the Industrial Revolution was well begun. Between 1811 and 1816 there occurred the Luddite rebellions in England, in which weavers who had been displaced from their jobs by mechanization tried to destroy the machines. Instead of solving all the economic problems, the mechanistic approach was creating new ones.

The intellectual rebellion against the Enlightenment is clearly apparent in religion. In the revivalism of John and Charles Wesley, salvation through individual ecstatic conversion became once again very personal. But this intellectual rebellion shows up most clearly in the poetry of the time. As William Blake put it, "Art is the Tree of Life. . . . Science is the Tree of Death"; to him reason was the very Devil, and the goal of life was unity and spirituality. In his poem "The Tiger," he expresses his anathema toward everything mechanistic, replacing it with wonder on a grand scale. Blake very prophetically foresaw all the evils of industrialization when he asked about the vision of the Lamb of God:

And did those feet in ancient time
Walk upon England's mountains green?

And was the holy Lamb of God
  On England's pleasant pastures seen?
And did the Countenance Divine
  Shine forth upon our clouded hills?
And was Jerusalem builded here
  Among these dark Satanic Mills?
(From "Milton," as quoted in Ref. 9.5, pp. 84–85.)

and when he drew the following pessimistic picture of mechanical progress:

... intricate wheels invented, wheel without wheel,
To perplex youth in their outgoings & to bind to labours in Albion
Of day & night the myriads of eternity; that they may grind
And polish brass & iron hour after hour, laborious task,
Kept ignorant of its use: that they might spend the days of wisdom
In sorrowful drudgery to obtain a scanty pittance of bread ...
(As quoted in Ref. 9.5, p. 85.)

In a similar way Wordsworth portrayed man's feeling of self-alienation in an industrialized and moneyed society;

For a multitude of causes, unknown to former times, are now acting with a combined force to blunt the discriminating powers of the mind, and, unfitting it for all voluntary exertion, to reduce it to a state of almost savage torpor. The most effective of these causes are the great national events which are daily taking place, and the increasing accumulation of men in cities, where the uniformity of their occupations produces a craving for extraordinary incident, which the rapid communication of intelligence hourly gratifies. To this tendency of life and manners the literature and theatrical exhibitions of the country have conformed themselves. (As quoted in Ref. 9.5, p. 95.)

His view of nature matches this feeling:

The world is too much with us; late and soon,
Getting and spending, we lay waste our powers:
Little we see in Nature that is ours;
We have given our hearts away, a sordid boon!
The Sea that bares her bosom to the moon;

The winds that will be howling at all hours,
And are up-gathered now like sleeping flowers;
For this, for everything, we are out of tune;
It moves us not.—Great God! I'd rather be
A Pagan, suckled in a creed outworn,
So might I, standing on this pleasant lea,
Have glimpses that would make me less forlorn;
Have sight of Proteus rising from the sea;
Or hear old Triton blow his wreathed horn.
                    ("Nature," as quoted in Ref. 9.5, p. 95.)

Lord Byron, who was to be the spokesman for the working class against the Industrial Revolution, said:

... knowledge is not happiness, and science
But an exchange of ignorance for that
Which is another kind of ignorance.
                    (As quoted in Ref. 9.5, p. 100.)

And, finally, Tennyson wanted to crush the cold and impersonal natural philosophy.

And all the phantom Nature, stands—
    With all the music in her tone,
    A hollow echo of my own—
A hollow form with empty hands.
And shall I take a thing so blind,
    Embrace her as my natural good,
    Or crush her, like a vice of blood,
Upon the threshhold of the mind?
(From "In Memoriam," as quoted in Ref. 9.3, p. 189.)

In all this poetry it is the individual whom the Romanticists emphasized. It is no coincidence that the countryside was preferred to the squalid factory towns; as Cowper put it: "The town has tinged the country; and the stain appears a blot upon the vestal's robe, the worse for what it soils," and "God made the country and man made the town." The individual soul was seemingly threatened by masses and mass production.

GERMAN ROMANTICISM

In Germany Romanticism took a perhaps even firmer grip. There this approach was largely initiated by Johann G. Herder, who was a theologian turned historian. In his *Ideas to a Philosophy of the History of Mankind* (1774–75) he presented history as a realization of the spirit of God. He believed that it was both "anatomically and physiologically true that the analogy of an organism dominates through all the living realm of our earth;" to Herder, history "lived." It is interesting that only after him did historical studies develop as a separate discipline.

The compositions of German composers of that time reflect many of the features of the Romantic movement. There was a revolt against the laws of music, as the art song broke away from the stanza form; Schubert wrote his two-movement *Unfinished Symphony*; and rhapsodies became favorite compositions. Nationalism reflected itself in Mendelssohn's *Italian* and *Scottish* symphonies and in Beethoven's opera *Fidelio* and his *Egmont Overture*. Fantasy was prevalent in Schubert's art song about the supernatural "Erlkönig" and in Mendelssohn's *Overture to a Midsummernight's Dream*. And the emphasis was on the individual, as shown by the importance of the concerto form with its soloist of demonic ability, such as Paganini and Liszt. Later derivatives of this period, like the fairy tales of the brothers Grimm, the romantic interest in the medieval period, and the music of Wagner, were simply a deepening of the revolt.

We can trace these romantic influences down to the present century, where they have done more than merely keep alive the cultural gap. They have ultimately had a significant impact even on contemporary history. It is no coincidence that the nationalistic fascist movement of the 1920s and 1930s was overlaid with the overtones of Wagnerian music and of mystical heroes like Siegfried and Brünnhilde.

GOETHE AND ROMANTICISM

The German poet Goethe is an excellent example of the attitudes of the Romantics and of their relationship with the sciences against which they rebelled. Johann Wolfgang von Goethe is important because he is the German equivalent of Shakespeare, with the added fact that his thoughts have been much more influential not only in literary developments but in all spheres of German thought. And he is interesting here not only because he characterizes some aspects of Romanticism, but also because he made an attempt to unite in one person the two cultures. It was unfortunately an attempt which failed and which may ultimately have split the two cultures even further apart.

Goethe was born in Frankfurt/Main in 1749. By the age of 18 he had written a lot of "Rococo" or "Enlightened" poetry, with witty phrases and stylized "sheperd and maiden" situations. Then he came in contact with the medieval literature of Paracelsius and other magical and mystical animistic writings, became acquainted with several pietists, and finally met Herder. These experiences were immediately reflected in his writings. In 1774 he achieved instantaneous world-wide fame when he published *The Sorrows of Young Werther*. This very autobiographical novel deals with a young man who desperately wants to become one with nature, to dissolve in nature. The style of the writing makes everything totally subjective and nonrational; the novel consists of letters written in the very personal "I" form. The letters are never answered in the book; the external world never replies, so the reader sees the whole universe mirrored in one soul. In fact, the whole novel describes an attempt to take all the world into one individual, to dissolve subject and object. And there is something very erotic in this; it is a love affair with organismic nature. It is in a sense a protest against the Establishment by a young soul which refuses to be restricted; the failure to erase the boundary between subject and object leads to death. There is a trancelike love affair, which starts in spring. Nature's seasons then parallel the development of the relationship. Werther finally and inevitably loses out to a rival who is a stable and productive individual. And at 11 p.m. on December 23, when nature is closest to death, Werther shoots himself.

The Romanticism of this book struck a very responsive chord in the youth of Europe. It became the most widely read book of the 18th century; in 20 years there appeared 20 English and 20 French translations of it, and it was, in fact, the first European book ever translated into Chinese. Furthermore, as a result of this book there spread throughout Europe a deadly illness—the so-called *Wertherfever*; young men went into the woods dressed in blue pants and a yellow vest, and with a copy of a certain play nearby, shot themselves just as Werther had committed suicide. It became so bad that Goethe, in the foreword to a later edition, asked the reader not to take Werther's example too seriously: "Be a man and don't follow me."

FAUST

In Goethe's work and thought and in the influence he had there was a very clear contrast between an Aristotelian-humanistic view of the world as something organic as opposed to the world-machine view of the Newtonian tradition. The desire of Werther to be an integral part of nature was a reflection of a belief in something greater than any individual and an opposition to dry scientific knowledge. This anti-mechanistic attitude permeates the most famous and most puzzling of Goethe's works, namely, his play *Faust*.

Faust is an ancient figure dating from the Middle Ages. Christopher Marlowe, almost 200 years before Goethe, also wrote a play, *Doctor Faustus*, on the same theme; this is the play in which there occurred the famous lines concerning Helen of Troy: "Was this the face that launched a thousand ships, and burnt the topless towers of Ilium?" Marlowe in the very beginning of that play expresses the Aristotelian origins of the Faustian view of science when he has him say:

> Settle the studies, Faustus and begin
> To sound the depth of that thou wilt profess.
> Having commenced, be a divine in show,
> Yet level at the end of every art
> And live and die in Aristotle's works:
> Sweet analytics, 'tis thou hast ravished me!
> (Ref. 9.6, p. 3)

This attitude toward nature as something more than cold rationalism, as something Aristotelian, carries over to Goethe's version. The Goethe play presents Faust as a seeker after the meaning of life. As the play begins, Faust has been searching for years for this meaning in study and in the sciences, and he finally realizes that it may all be meaningless, that after all this time he is no wiser than he was before. In a final effort to find this meaning, he signs a contract with Mephistopheles, a contract according to which he is to be shown all the attractions the world has to offer. The collection of Faust's soul is to take place if he ever says: "this moment I like; I wish it would last forever." Most of the play then deals with the attractions which Mephistopheles invokes in order to tempt Faust. Throughout the play there are reflec-

Fig. 9.1   Conversation in the study between Faust and Mephistopheles. After a lithograph of Eugene Delacroix.

tions (both subtle and blunt) of Goethe on science as a soul-deadening
activity:

> Unless you feel it, you will never achieve it.
> If it doesn't flow from your soul
> With natural easy power,
> Your listeners will not believe it. . . .
> How can anyone cling to such trash
> Keep any hope in his head?
> With greedy hands he digs for treasure,
> And is happy when he finds earthworms instead. . . .
> Gray and ashen, my friend, is every science,
> And only the golden tree of life is green.
>
> (Ref. 9.4, p. 29–33)

Goethe made it clear in many ways that he considered the sciences to
be a cultural wasteland. As then practiced, the Newtonian sciences
seemed to him to run completely contrary to man's relationship to
nature. The whole of *Faust* is in a sense an exploration of cultural
alternatives to musty science.

GOETHE AS A SCIENTIST

As a man who fancied himself a universal man, as a man who was a
statesman and administrator as well as a poet, Goethe also attempted
to make a contribution to the sciences. He expected, of course, that
this contribution would substantiate the scientific correctness of his
view of the world as an organic and purposive whole. He did actually
gain some success with this view in his biological studies, studies
which were then still almost purely descriptive. He found, for example, on intuitive grounds, similarities between certain bones of
animals and of man; in fact, he predicted a previously unknown bone
in man (the *os intermaximare*). In the field of biology, his attentiveness,
good memory, and fertile imagination could couple successfully with
his organically teleological approach.

But then in 1786 Goethe traveled to Italy and was enormously
impressed, like so many before him, by the colors of the many paintings and of the countryside. He then felt the need to develop a theory
of color. Newton himself had already proposed a theory of color, but
to Goethe that theory was clearly unsatisfactory. After all, Newton's

theory was based on many complicated experiments which were designed to take human subjectivity out of the data. One of Newton's conclusions was that white light contained all the colors in it and that a prism could be used to separate these color components. This idea disturbed Goethe greatly. He was committed to an Aristotelian-like preference of opposites, in this case of light versus dark rather than of a whole range of colors. The breakthrough came for him when he inserted the "I" of the observer back into the experiment by looking at a white object through a prism. Instead of seeing this object in all the colors, as he interpreted Newton's theory to predict, he saw color only on the edges. "I immediately exclaimed that Newton's theory is false," he wrote. Goethe's interpretation was that the eye creates the colors out of the various admixtures of the two opposites of light and dark. This makes man the center of the observation process. Goethe felt that "Man himself, if he uses his common sense, is the best and the most exact physical apparatus possible." The problem with the Newtonian physics was that it wanted to recognize nature only when "restricted in artificial apparatus."

Goethe spent much time on his optical studies. This resulted in the book, *The Theory of Colors*, of which he was so proud that at the end of a life rich in superlative literary accomplishments, he said:

> As for what I have done as a poet, I take no pride in it whatever.... Excellent poets have lived at the same time with me, poets more excellent lived before me, and others will come after me. But that in my century I am the only person who knows the truth in the difficult science of colors—of that, I say, I am not a little proud, and here I have a consciousness of superiority to many. (*Conversations with Eckerman*, quoted, for example, in Ref. 9.2, p. 39.)

This is a little like Newton saying "my laws of motion are nothing; but my chronology of the Bible, that will make me immortal."

The Theory of Colors included a historical part about previous color theories, with the emphasis on Greek and medieval sources and no clear analysis or understanding of Newton's contribution. Goethe's comment is self-explanatory. "I would rather be wrong with Plato than be right with his enemies." The third part described Goethe's experiments and his analyses of them; many interesting visual effects are described there. But from our distant perspective, the most interesting part is the middle section, the polemical part; it is entertaining just because of its language. In it Goethe charged Newton with obdurate resistance to the light of evidence, labeled him a bandleader of Cossacks, called him a mere twaddle, and described Newton's version of the scientific method as follows:

> First he finds his theory plausible, then he convinces himself with excessive haste, even before he realizes how contrived a sleight-of-hand he will need to apply his hypothetical insight to the real order of things. But once he has openly expressed it, he does not fail to make use of all his mind's devices to see his thesis through. In this he asserts with unbelievable sangfroid before the whole world, the whole absurdity as the obvious truth. (*The Theory of Colors: Historical Part*, quoted, for example, in Ref. 9.2, p. 44.)

Physicists were spoken of as Newton's herd. And Goethe decried their eagerness to

> ... cement, patch-up, and glue together, as witchdoctors do, the Newtonian doctrine, so that it could, as an embalmed corpse, preside in the style of ancient Egyptians, at the drinking bouts of physicists. (Quoted for example in Ref. 9.1, p. 198.)

This may have been an entertaining commentary, but it was not a very responsible attack on a substantial theory by a most reputable scientist.

Goethe's theory of colors was, of course, rejected by all physicists —in its scientific sense. His frantic fear that mathematics destroyed the beauty and immediacy of personal observation was an echo of the attacks by Aristotle on the Pythagoreans. Here, however, the challenge was against the complete and successful Newtonian system. His demand that light be left alone as an indivisible phenomenon, and his feeling that the various aspects of optics are subjective, were cries that went unheeded by the mainstream of physics. Later generations of physicists have, nevertheless, tried to be tolerant and to see some good in Goethe's struggle against the coldness inherent in the unfeeling mechanics. For example, Max Born, Nobel prize winner in physics, asked that we "learn from them [Goethe and his followers] not to forget the meaning of the whole amidst the fascination of details." Goethe is simply too imposing a figure to be ignored, even when totally wrong.

CONCLUSION

We have here in Goethe a man who failed to unite the two cultures. He represents the revulsion of the Romantic revolution against all the mechanistic philosophies and sciences and machinery. He went back to the Aristotelian view of the world as an organism, and desperately tried to reimpose it on the sciences. To be frank, Goethe's physics would probably be rejected as the babbling of a crackpot by most physicists—except that it is hard to reject something which occupied such a significant fraction of the life of a truly great poet. Goethe failed in his attempts to unite the two cultures because he did not try to take the then existing consensus in physics as a starting point. Instead, he totally rebelled, and in the process, alienated the scientific culture.

We see here in the Romanticists in general, and in Goethe in particular, the deep split in society which is still with us. We can now see that C. P. Snow recognized only the visible part of the "culture gap"; that underneath the modern conflict between the humanities and technology lies this ancient conflict between the organic and the mechanistic views of nature. This gap may be much harder to bridge than the simplistic one between the humanists and the technologists.

REFERENCES

Prime references

9.1 S. L. Jaki, "Goethe and the Physicists," *American Journal of Physics* **37**, 195–203 (1969); see also a subsequent letter exchange, **38**, 544–546 (1970).

Interesting reading

9.2 S. L. Jaki, *The Relevance of Physics*, (Ref. 6.3); Chapter I, "The World as an Organism," pp. 3–51.

9.3 E. W. Hall, *Modern Science and Human Values*, (Ref. 8.2); Chapter 4, "Romanticism and Science," pp. 185–236.

9.4 J. W. von Goethe, *Faust*, (translated by Carlyle F. MacIntyre), Norfolk, Conn.: New Directions Publishing Corp., 1949; quotation by permission.

9.5 D. Bush, *Science and English Poetry*, New York: Oxford University Press, 1950; Chapter 4, "The Romantic Revolt Against Rationalism," pp. 79–108, has introductory quotation from Keats' "Lamia" on p. 102.

9.6 C. Marlowe, *Doctor Faustus*, (edited by L. B. Wright and V. A. LaMar), New York: Washington Square Press, 1959.

9.7 J. W. von Goethe, *The Sorrows of Young Werther*; any one of many editions.

9.8 J. H. Randall, *The Making of the Modern Mind*, Boston: Houghton Mifflin Co., 1940; Chapter 16, "The Romantic Protest Against the Age of Reason," pp. 389–426.

9.9 A. Thorlby, *The Romantic Movement*, London: Longmans, Green and Co., 1966; a collection of excerpts from writings on Romanticism.

QUESTIONS FOR DISCUSSION

1. Romanticism has certainly produced great music and literature. Do we perhaps need a cultural conflict for stimulation?

2. Is magic, as in *Faust*, unscientific or antiscientific?

3. If looking at nature as an organism leads to new discoveries, is this then not a very appropriate approach?

4. In what ways is Mary Shelley's *Frankenstein* a literary work representative of Romanticism?

10 | SCIENCE AND THE INDUSTRIAL REVOLUTION

To say that the economic life of society in general, and processes of manufacture in particular, were unaffected by science until the beginning of the last century is hardly an exaggeration.

A. R. Hall

One century ago not one person in five hundred wore [stockings]; now not one person in a thousand is without them.

C. Knight, *The Results of Machinery*, 1831

When asked by Prime Minister Gladstone what was the use of electricity the physicist Faraday replied, "Some day you will tax it."

The relationship between science and the Industrial Revolution is examined. The steam engine is cited as an example where the industrial development preceded the scientific understanding, while the electrical industry is an example where the scientific knowledge preceded the industrial applications.

INTRODUCTION

We have seen that the Newtonian synthesis inspired a whole age to adopt a mechanistic view of the universe—a view which in turn induced a romantic reaction. Yet only the educated man responded to this controversy, for the traces of science were visible primarily to the cultured society. It was the Industrial Revolution which finally brought the "common man" into contact with technology and science. And when one considers that the communist ideology of Marx and Engels was, in fact, basically a protest against some of the negative consequences of this upheaval for the common man, and that the Industrial Revolution is constantly being repeated in the newly emerging nations, then it becomes clear that industrialism is one of the major aspects of the science-society interaction.

Therefore in this chapter we will briefly review the origin and nature of the advance in technology, particularly in Great Britain. By considering the steam engine and the electric power industry as examples, we shall then try to show that the coupling between science and technology was not very close during much of the 19th century.

THE INDUSTRIAL REVOLUTION

Before analyzing the interplay between science and the Industrial Revolution, we must first get a picture of this so-called revolution. The word "so-called" is used here because there isn't even universal agreement on whether there actually was anything that could be called a "revolution," or whether there was instead simply a gradual change in the character of British economic enterprise over an extended period. Nor is there agreement concerning the effect of this revolution on British society—whether it was a triumph or a disaster (Ref. 10.2). It should not be surprising that the scientific antecedents of this revolution are equally hard to determine.

The Industrial Revolution, as depicted by most historians, is considered to have occurred first in Great Britain between about 1750 and 1850. During this interval, the doubling period of the human population increased from a low of 234 years to about 50 years; i.e., from a very slow rate of increase to essentially the contemporary rate. During this time, the nature of agriculture changed from one of many very small farms to one of fewer but larger ones. As a result of this change, and due to the population increase, many people lost their farm-based livelihood and became an inexpensive source of labor for industry. Intermingled with the economic changes were the effects of the Napoleonic wars, which lasted until 1815. There was child labor, the growth of towns, technological mass production, and riots by workers against the competition of machines.

THE LUNATICS

As a beginning one needs to ask how much science had to do with the early development of this revolution. The first quotation at the beginning of this chapter points out how little contact the science of the Enlightenment made with utilitarian technology. There were, however, dilettante scientists among the early movers in the Industrial Revolution in the 1770s in England, including one rather interesting group called the Lunar Society of Birmingham (inevitably nicknamed the "Lunatics"). This group met once a month on the night of the full moon when they had widesweeping discussions on any and all topics, such as medicine, poetry, pottery, philosophy, knife edges, nature, and human experience. The group included such diverse individuals as Josiah Wedgwood—the prince of potters, Joseph Priestley—the discoverer of oxygen and friend of Benjamin Franklin, Matthew Boulton—an ornament maker, William Small—who imbued Thomas Jefferson with Newtonianism, James Watt—the inventor of the condensing steam engine, Erasmus Darwin—the grandfather of Charles Darwin and a speculator about creative evolution, and Wilkinson—the cannon-maker (of sword-edge razor blade fame).

It was through interactions inside this society that Watt's engine developed; Wilkinson, for example, lathed the barrels for the engine. A member of the society by the name of Withering discovered that digitalis was good for the treatment of heart disease and dropsy. Members developed synthetic alkalis, sulphuric acid, and bleaching by chlorine. Their cooperation led to the production of the famous blue of Wedgwood Jasperware by the addition of barium carbonate and sulphate to the coating. But when the society supported the French Revolution, it suffered persecution, and the turn of the century saw it die out. By that time scientific specialization had already begun.

THE STEAM ENGINE AND THERMODYNAMICS

In a more detailed consideration of the interaction of science and the Industrial Revolution, there are two outstanding examples that can be examined. The first of these is the development of the steam engine as related to the science of thermodynamics. The industrial aspects of the steam engine are clear; it was developed to provide large-scale power for water pumps, railroads, and machinery. The problem was how to convert the heat contained in steam into work. This turned out to be basically a technological question rather than a scientific one. The original designs were made by dilettantes such as Watt, who were tinkerers at heart. The primary interest was in the technological efficiency and economic utility rather than in the scientific aspects; i.e., there was more concern with labor saving than with the exact energy content of steam and the theoretically possible efficiency. For example, Watt defined the horsepower in order to set royalty payments for his machines. The question was how many horses his engines replaced in the work of pumping water out of the mines in Cornwall. The horsepower is therefore basically an economic unit of energy flow.

After the engines for pumping water out of mines, the next large-scale development of the steam engine came in using it to power railroads for hauling coal from the mines to boats. From 1780 to 1880 coal production in England increased by a factor of 15 (the demand for iron went up 115 fold in the same time); this provided a tremendous market for powerful devices. The use of the railroads to carry passengers developed considerably later. And here again the developers were largely self-taught men, who were concerned with building engines which had a lot of power rather than efficiency close to the theoretical limit.

The relevant science here was the concept of conservation of energy. To make a contribution to the theory of engines and heat flow, it was first necessary to understand that heat and work are simply different forms of energy. The number needed was that one calorie of heat could theoretically be used to lift one pound by about three feet. This idea was not generally accepted until after 1841. The discoverers of this principle included a very diverse group of individuals, among them J. R. Mayer, a German medical doctor who approached it from the viewpoint of energy conversion in animals; Hermann von Helmholtz, a German physicist with a great interest in the physiology of sound and vision; and James P. Joule, the independently wealthy son of an English brewer, who had as his background the desire and curiosity to improve manufacturing by improving mechanical power. (The resulting priority squabble about the discovery, as told in Ref. 10.11, pp. 65–66, is both fascinating and amusing, with the Victorian equivalent of a challenge being issued in a scientific journal by one of the physicists.)

There were several reasons why the science of thermodynamics lagged so far behind the technology. To begin with, the whole business appeared too repulsively utilitarian for the academicians. Such a repulsion was an attitude which persisted through all of the 19th century. As Professor Rowland of Johns Hopkins University expressed it in 1879:

> He who makes two blades of grass grow where one grew before is the benefactor of mankind; but he who obscurely works to find the laws of such growth is the intellectual superior as well as the greater benefactor of the two. (As quoted in Ref. 10.5, p. 8.)

The physicist James C. Maxwell made the same point in his remark about the inventor of the telephone, Alexander G. Bell:

> ... a speaker, who to gain his private ends, has become an electrician. (As quoted in Ref. 10.5, p. 8.)

The second difficulty with the energy concept was that many of the phenomena involving such energy interconversion processes were simply too crude to allow accurate measurements and theoretical predictions. As indicated earlier, the relevant technology was simply not advanced enough. The final difficulty had to do with the very concept of energy conservation. There was something faintly Aristotelian-organismic about energy as an all-pervasive fluid. One might, in fact, characterize the First Law of Thermodynamics, which says that energy can be neither created nor destroyed, by the statement, "you can't win." This law contradicts all perpetual-motion machines, so that the U.S. patent office now refuses to even consider such devices. The Second Law of Thermodynamics (to be discussed in Chapter 11) goes even further and says, "you can't even break even," because in all real energy exchange processes there are always nonrecoverable losses in usable energy. And when one thinks of these laws in terms of winning and losing, one does get the organismic feeling of fighting nature.

ELECTROMAGNETIC THEORY AND THE ELECTRICAL INDUSTRY

The second major interaction between physics and industry took place in the later stages of the Industrial Revolution, when the scientific knowledge of the field of electricity and magnetism inspired the electrical communications and power industry. In this case the situation was completely reversed from that of the steam engine; here the science led the industry.

The knowledge required for these developments involved an understanding of:

1. Electric charges and their motion in materials, which was thoroughly investigated immediately after the discovery of batteries in 1800;

2. the interaction between moving charges and magnetic fields, which was reasonably well understood by 1832; and

3. a consistent theory of the nature of electromagnetic radiation such as light, which was described in the equations of Maxwell in 1864.

The timetable for the applications of this knowledge ran consistently more than 30 years late. Morse did not develop the battery-powered telegraph until 1832, 32 years after the battery became available. The electrical power industry did not develop until after 1860, 28 years after the knowledge about the behavior of currents in motors and generators was substantially complete. The industry began with such applications as electroplating and arc lamps for lighthouses (about 1860) and street lamps (in the 1870s). But before the electrical industry could really expand, there had to be developed completely new applications in the household market, like the tungsten light bulb. That, in turn, became possible only when good vacuum pumps were built, in part to evacuate the scientific toys called spectral analysis tubes (which later led to the discovery of x-rays). And it took a man of Thomas Edison's stature to get investors to contribute the large sums of money required to simultaneously build power stations, lay out the wiring for a square mile of New York, and sell the inhabitants on the usefulness of electricity. The amount of development work involved in this power production and consumption was actually quite small; it has been estimated that no more than 5000 man-years was invested from 1831 to 1881; i.e., less than 100 people worked on it each year. The science was there—it was a matter of developing a market. The final step in this sequence was the application of Maxwell's equations. Heinrich Hertz in 1887 discovered the predicted electromagnetic radiations, now called radio waves, a discovery which then led directly to the radio of Guglielmo Marconi and thence to our modern communications industry.

CONCLUSIONS

The Industrial Revolution was certainly strongly involved in technology; but this was primarily a technology which was only very loosely coupled to contemporary science. The demand on industry was more for enlarged production, for more machinery and automation (particularly in the labor-short United States), rather than for improvements in products through better understanding of their scientific basis. The period in general experienced such an expansion in economic activity that new products were not really necessary; the demand was always for more of the same at less cost.

The fact that the connection between science and technology was not very strong at this time is clearly evident in the two examples cited. The steam engine reached a high level of development before its scientific basis was ever seriously analyzed. In the example of the electrical industry, the exact opposite happened; the knowledge in the scientific field of electricity and magnetism predated applications by typically 30 years. There was, of course, some direct contact; the electrical technology in turn provided employment and precision equipment for further scientific studies. But this was on the whole a limited contact.

During this time, however, the character of science began to change from an elegant ornament of society, practiced by virtuosi as in the Lunar Society, to an essential factor in the everyday production of goods and services. The age of the basement inventor was changing to the age of the research worker of Edison's Menlo Park; even the universities were becoming research minded. This was a time when through technology the sciences for the first time penetrated into the general public consciousness; the question of "Newton or Aristotle" was no longer restricted to a very small elite segment of the population; the "culture gap" began to concern everyone, as some of the consequences of the new technologies seemed very threatening to the existing way of life. Even the American Civil War had overtones of struggle between an agricultural society (the South) and an industrial society (the North). But primarily the losses in the way of life were then measured in the same economic terms as were the industrial gains; it is only very recently that other factors in the quality of life have become generally recognized.

REFERENCES

Prime reference

10.1 J. D. Bernal, *Science and Industries in the 19th Century*, London: Routledge and Kegan Paul, Ltd., 1953; has the third introductory story on p. 44.

Interesting reading

10.2 P. A. M. Taylor, *The Industrial Revolution in Britain: Triumph or Disaster?*, Boston: D. C. Heath and Co., 1958.

10.3 A. R. Hall, *Ballistics in the 17th Century*, Cambridge, England: Cambridge University Press, 1952; has the introductory quotation on p. 1.

10.4 R. Calder, *Science in Our Lives*, New York: New American Library, 1954; Chapter 1, "The Lunatics," pp. 7–16.

10.5 J. B. Conant, *Modern Science and Modern Man*: New York: Columbia University Press, 1952.

10.6 H. W. and S. Rapport, Eds., *Great Adventures in Science*, New York: Harper and Brothers, 1956; C. B. Wall "Incandescent Genius," pp. 209–226, on Edison.

10.7 N. Reingold, *Science in 19th Century America*, New York: Hill and Wang, 1964.

10.8 Books by Dickens like *David Copperfield* paint a rather grim picture of some of the effects of the Industrial Revolution.

QUESTIONS FOR DISCUSSION

1. How does Mark Twain's book *A Connecticut Yankee at King Arthur's Court* fit into the Industrial Revolution? If you were this Yankee, what books would you take with you?

2. How can we export the Industrial Revolution to underdeveloped countries?

3. The first applications for steam engines were for water fountains in gentlemen's gardens. Comment?

4. It has been suggested that the discovery of the cotton gin led to a resurgence of cotton production, and hence of slavery. Is science and technology hence to blame for the Civil War?

5. The Industrial Revolution involved child labor. Was that a loss of quality of life?

11 | MAXWELL'S DEMON, THE HEAT DEATH, AND EVOLUTION

Once or twice I have been provoked and have asked the company how many of them could describe the Second Law of Thermodynamics. The response was cold: it was also negative. Yet I was asking something which is about the scientific equivalent of "Have you read a work of Shakespeare's?"

C. P. Snow in *The Two Cultures*

There is no scientific equivalent of that question . . .; equations between orders so disparate are meaningless.

F. R. Leavis in *Two Cultures? The Significance of C. P. Snow*

This chapter traces the impact of the concepts of thermodynamics on geology, on the theory of evolution, and on religion and philosophy.

INTRODUCTION

In Dayton, Tennessee, in 1925 there took place perhaps the most amazing trial in America's history. The Scopes antievolution case involved not only two of the most outstanding personalities of the day in William Jennings Bryan and Clarence Darrow but also the almost unbelievable question: whether the teaching of biology and zoology could be forced to conform with the Bible. Before the trial there were strong antievolution laws in many of the states; there was even talk of an antievolution constitutional amendment. At the end of the trial, the biology teacher, John T. Scopes, had been convicted of teaching evolution in his classes, but the fundamentalist demand that the Bible be accepted as "gospel" had been discredited.

In a sense this trial was the peak in the reaction against the theory of evolution, a theory which was one of the most significant developments of the 19th century. Interestingly enough, even physics was involved in this antievolution sentiment; for some time physics actually weakened the case supporting the theory of evolution. The last chapter considered the relationship between steam-engine technology and the science of thermodynamics. And it is the Second Law of Thermodynamics which had such a significant effect not only on the theory of evolution, but more generally on the whole intellectual climate of the 19th century. This chapter will try to justify Snow's belief in the intellectual equivalence between this law and Shakespeare's works.

19th-CENTURY CYCLES IN THE HUMANITIES AND IN PHYSICS

Let us first examine the overall coupling between physics and the intellectual climate of the 19th century. There was during that century a constant ebb and flow in ideas, with the two cultures alternately opposing and reinforcing each other. Very direct contacts between them are difficult to establish, but there are certainly many parallels in the developments within the cultures. The 19th century had three major movements in philosophy and the arts, and each of these had a parallel in the sciences. There was the Romantic period, which lasted until about 1835 and was followed by Realism (or Enlightenment tempered by Romanticism), with its maximum influence about 1870. Finally there was a reaction back to neo-Romanticism near the turn of the century.

As indicated in Chapter 9, the Romantic movement produced such writers as Goethe, Coleridge, or Wordsworth, Blake, Shelley, Byron, Keats, and Tennyson, such painters as the pre-Raphaelites and Delacroix, such composers as Spohr, Weber, Mendelsohn, Schumann, and Berlioz, and the whole Gothic revival in architecture as exemplified by the most recent portion of the British Parliament building. The scientific aspect of Romanticism was *Naturphilosophie*, the belief that nature was infused by a living spirit (Vitalism), that everything in nature had a unifying concept behind it, a basic principle such as that of contrasts. In medicine, for example, some doctors then attributed all diseases to a single cause. One reaction to the French Revolution was a lack of interest in social planning and public health and welfare during the Romantic period. This lack may have been responsible for the rise in the death rate in England after 1810. In fact, the cholera epidemic of 1832, which killed Hegel (one of the chief exponents of Romanticism), exposed the inadequacy of medicine at the time and thereby may have accelerated the termination of this movement. Interestingly, the theory of Vitalism is reflected in the idea of energy conservation of the First Law of Thermodynamics —a fact which is somewhat surprising when viewed in the light of the mechanistic trappings which this law acquired after its mathematical formulation. Of course any romantic thoughts on this subject were nebulous and qualitative, and as suggested in the last chapter, the association in tone may have delayed the acceptance of the law by contemporary physicists.

The subsequent intellectual countermovement of Realism or Naturalism was exemplified by writers who tried to show life in all its sordid details: Flaubert (*Madame Bovary*), Balzac, Zola, Dostoevsky, Tolstoi, Hardy, (*Far from the Madding Crowd*), Dickens, etc. There were realist painters like Goya, Daumier, and Courbet, functional architecture, and operas like Mascagni's *Cavalleria Rusticana* and Leoncavallo's *I Pagliacci*. Realist philosophers included Comté, H. Spencer, J. S. Mill, and Feuerbach, and religious trends included toleration of such groups as the Unitarians and the agnostics. During this period of Realism, great developments took place in the social and biological sciences as they were released from the animistic strictures of Romanticism. There was the theory of evolution of Wallace and Darwin, the materialistic theory of history of Marx and Engels, the theory of population statistics of Galton, the biological cell theory of Brown, Schwann, and Schleiden, and the medical germ theory of Koch and Pasteur. During this period, the steam engine had reached a stage of development advanced enough to warrant theoretical analysis, so that the whole field of thermodynamics was thoroughly explored. This study included the Second Law of Thermodynamics, a thoroughly quantitative statement about the direction of energy flow. Paradoxically enough, this rather mechanistic statement led to the seemingly antimechanistic conclusion that the universe is not a constant clockwork but is rather running down toward a predictable end.

In turn, this running down of the universe became a part of the rather pessimistic intellectual climate of the neo-Romantic movement. In fact, one aspect of thermodynamics helped directly to bring on this new period. In the kinetic theory of heat, all heat phenomena were interpreted as mechanical motion of the atoms in the gas or solid. This further mechanization of man's view of nature helped to trigger the neo-Romantic reaction, as T. H. Huxley pointed out in 1868 in his remarks about materialism:

> The consciousness of this great truth weighs like a nightmare, I believe, upon many of the best minds of these days. They watch what they conceive to be the progress of materialism, in such fear and powerless anger as a savage feels, when, during an eclipse, the great shadow creeps over the face of the sun. The advancing tide of matter threatens to drown their souls; the tightening grasp of law impedes their freedom; they are alarmed lest man's moral nature be debased by the increase of his wisdom. (*Collected Essays*, as quoted in Ref. 10.1, p. 526.)

One characteristic of the neo-Romanticism was the proclaimed independence of such sciences as sociology and psychology from the mechanism of physics. Conservatism grew very strong, with nationalism leading to imperialism, the "divine right of expansion," and "a manifest destiny." Mysticism and spiritualism grew with Christian Science, Yogi, and Theosophy. And the musical aspects of the pessimism may be found in the works of Mahler and Bruckner.

THERMODYNAMICS

To us the relevant parts of thermodynamics are the first two laws and the kinetic theory. The first law concerning the conservation of energy has already been discussed in Chapter 10. The second law came out of studies of the theoretical efficiencies of engines. Discovered by both Sadi Carnot and Rudolf Clausius, it was publicized about 1852 by (the later) Lord Kelvin. In its final form, this law states that in an isolated system the amount of entropy is always increasing. Entropy is a quantitative measure of the disorder of a system, of the amount of energy which is no longer available to do work (like the heat in the oceans); in information theory it would be noise or the lack of information. If, for example, there is a system made up of two bodies, one very cold and one very hot, then this system has very little disorder; i.e., the entropy is very small. When these two bodies are brought into contact and reach the same final temperature, then the system has the maximum possible disorder (or the minimum organization) and hence the maximum possible entropy. The Second Law of Thermodynamics then states that, as time progresses, the entropy of an isolated system can only increase.

The other influential physical concept of thermodynamics is the kinetic theory of heat. Heat in a gas or a solid is considered to be in the form of kinetic energy; i.e., the temperature of a material is a measure of how rapidly the atoms in it are moving; the hotter it is, the faster they are traveling. To analyze a specific system, like a given gas or crystal, quantitatively is of course not necessarily easy; there are involved, for example, extensive statistical calculations. But at least theoretically such systems can be analyzed in a mechanistic way.

MAXWELL'S DEMON

Many attempts have been made to override these laws. The first law, for example, has inspired countless perpetual-motion machines. And the game to beat the second law has led to the invention of one very interesting player, namely "Maxwell's Demon." This demon, who is very small and very quick, stands at a frictionless gate separating two parts of an enclosure filled with a gas. As the gas molecules travel toward the gate, he opens it in such a way that they can pass in only one direction. Gradually one side of the enclosure comes to have in it all of the gas molecules. Then the organization of the gas has increased; i.e., the entropy has decreased, and the second law is violated. If one wants an air conditioner, all one has to do is catch such a demon, place him in the window, and tell him to let into the room slow molecules (cold air) and let out fast molecules (hot air). Since demons eat very little, this seemingly makes for very cheap air conditioning.

There are, of course, objections to this scheme, in addition to the problem of catching such a demon. To perform efficiently, the demon must be small and fast enough to rapidly open the gate (which must be very light). But the demon and the gate are struck by the atoms of the gas, and being so light, they are then knocked about sufficiently to negate the violation of the second law. The demon is nevertheless an interesting concept since human beings are essentially Maxwellian demons. Entropy is decreased every time music is made, a painting is painted, or a book is written, since then something is more highly organized than it was before. But in each case the human demon converts the energy from food very inefficiently into sound waves or muscular motion or thought, so that the total entropy of the world is still necessarily increased, in spite of the local decrease. This concept of entropy is particularly useful in information theory. Information can be considered a lack of entropy, and any breakdown in communication (and hence loss in information) can then be quantitatively evaluated as an increase in entropy.

PHYSICS AND EVOLUTION

The greatest cultural impact of thermodynamics has probably come about through the second law. Its effects were perhaps most noticeable in geological and biological evolutionary theory, and through inducing the pessimism which led to the philosophy of ultimate human degradation. Through these attitudes, it influenced the mental concepts of every 19th-century intellectual, from Henry Adams through Friedrich Nietzsche to John Dewey. Unfortunately, the impact, as on evolution, was frequently a negative one, as thermodynamics was aligned on the side of the antievolutionists.

As Romanticism gave way to Realism, in geology the catastrophic view of the earth's creation was replaced by the uniformitarian view of evolution. Under the leadership of Sir Charles Lyell, physical causes such as erosion were assumed to have led to the earth's present configuration. However, this uniformitarian view of the earth's geology required that there should have existed for long times relatively constant temperatures and circumstances on the earth's surface, so that processes like erosion could have operated. Unfortunately, Lord Kelvin refused to grant the geologists this much time. He drew a seemingly obvious conclusion from the Second Law of Thermodynamics; namely, that all of the earth must be slowly cooling toward the same temperature, and that

> ... within a finite period of time past the earth must have been, and within a finite period of time to come the earth must again be, unfit for the habitation of man as at present constituted, unless

operations have been, or are to be performed, which are impossible under the laws to which the known operations going on at present in the material world are subject. (*Philosophical Magazine* 4, 304 (1852), as quoted in Ref. 11.1, p. 494.)

From that time the universe would be in a state of eternal rest. This is the "heat death" of the universe, when everything is at the same temperature. (It could more appropriately be called the "cold death".) Under such a condition of equilibrium there could then no longer be any heat flow, since heat only flows to a colder body. And since without heat flow nothing happens, everything is then dead (see Fig. 11.1).

From detailed calculations involving the rate of heat conduction in the earth and the rate of arrival of solar energy, Kelvin set an absolute upper limit of 200 million years to the age of the solid earth. The uniformitarian geologists required billions of years for the natural evolution of the earth's present features. And the reputation of Lord Kelvin was so high (after all, he was responsible for the success of the transatlantic cable, besides being probably the best-known British physicist of the time) that he could not be ignored. Finally the geologists tried to accommodate their time schedules to the limits set by Lord Kelvin, but ultimately no one was satisfied.

This attack was coupled with one on biological evolution. Lord Kelvin did not object to evolution per se, but he did not like the aspect of randomness and lack of conscious direction implied by the theory of natural selection. In 1871 he said that Darwin's proposed mechanism for evolution was unsatisfactory insofar as

... it did not sufficiently take into account a continually guiding and controlling intelligence. ... The argument of design has been greatly too much lost sight of in recent zoological speculations. ... But over-powering strong proofs of intelligent and benevolent design lie all round us ... teaching us that all living beings depend on one ever-acting Creator and Ruler. (As quoted in Ref. 11.1, p. 502.)

And Darwin was quite concerned about this attack. In 1871 he wrote to Wallace, "I should rely much on pre-Silurian times; but then comes Sir W. Thomson [Kelvin] like an odious spectre." There have been speculations that Darwin may have lost some faith in his theory of evolution, as evidenced by the fact that he eliminated some supporting

Fig. 11.1 The Heat Death. (From Camille Flammarion's *La Fin du Monde*,
Paris, 1894; p. 115).

arguments in later versions of his work. This loss of confidence was directly related to Lord Kelvin and his theory of the heat death. Some biologists and geologists even felt compelled to try to reinsert, to a limited extent, the theory of the inheritance of acquired characteristics back into the theory of evolution.

Of course, once radioactive radium was discovered, the source of the continual heat which kept the earth warm over the evolutionary time period was recognized to be nuclear energy. By 1905 an estimate of 2.4 billion years was proposed for the age of the earth on the basis of the uranium dating technique. Lord Kelvin saw this reversal of opinion and was deeply disturbed, since he had actually considered his work on the age of the earth as the most important of all his contributions to science. The physicist Ernest Rutherford tells of a lecture he gave in 1904 in which he discussed the changes in estimates of the age of the earth due to the discovery of heating by radioactive substances:

> I came into the room, which was half dark, and presently spotted Lord Kelvin in the audience and realized that I was in for trouble at the last part of my speech dealing with the age of the earth, where my views conflicted with him. To my relief, Kelvin fell asleep, but as I came to the important point, I saw the old bird sit up, open an eye and cock a baleful glance at me! Then a sudden inspiration came, and I said Lord Kelvin had limited the age of the earth, *provided no new source was discovered*. That prophetic utterance refers to what we are now considering tonight, radium! Behold! The old boy beamed upon me. (As quoted in Ref. 11.1, p. 504.)

DEGENERATION

The dissipation idea derived from the Second Law of Thermodynamics was also applied in the field of biology in framing the theory of the degeneration of man. As Alfred Lord Tennyson said in 1886 (in the poem "Locksley Hall Sixty Years After"):

> Evolution ever climbing after some ideal good
> And Reversion ever dragging Evolution in the mud.
> (As quoted in Ref. 11.1, p. 505.)

The degeneration principle affected intellectual life near the end of the 19th century in areas far beyond the subject of biology. All the evils of society were blamed on individuals showing symptoms of degeneration: a degeneration which dissipated all those good qualities back out of man that evolution had tried to concentrate into man. Baudelaire wrote poetry on this theme, and Emile Zola concerned himself with this problem in the Rongon-Marquart novels. After France was defeated in 1870 by Germany, some intellectuals proclaimed that the Latin races had reached the final stages of decadence and were to be succeeded in power by the Nordic races. Oscar Wilde's *The Picture of Dorian Gray* is a portrayal of decay in a specific individual. There were traces of dissipation of available energy in the philosophy of Herbert Spencer and in the historical writings of Henry Adams (who felt that he was a final decayed product in the fourth generation of a family which had started fresh with President Adams). There are many other hints of this kind in the intellectual repertoire of the period, but the ones we have mentioned here suffice to give the flavor.

SUMMARY

In this chapter we have tried to establish an interconnection between the science of thermodynamics and the intellectual climate of the 19th century. It may not always have been a helpful interaction between the two cultures, but at least there was no mutual indifference. The poets were inspired by the science, even if sometimes in a negative sense; and the developments in thermodynamics in turn were at least parallel to the intellectual climate, even if it may be difficult to show any one-to-one correspondences. There is indeed some truth in Snow's thought that the Second Law of Thermodynamics has a large intellectual content.

There was also an impact of thermodynamics on other sciences such as geology and biology, an impact which was partially negative. It was an example of the physicists feeling in some sense superior to the representatives of these seemingly less quantitative disciplines; their feeling was that a concept, like evolution, could never evoke the same concensus that physics could compel. This type of intolerance has survived to this day.

REFERENCES

Prime reference

11.1 S. G. Brush, "Thermodynamics and History," *The Graduate Journal* **7** (2), 477–565 (Spring, 1967).

Interesting reading

11.2 G. Gamow, *Biography of Physics*, (Ref. 6.4), pp. 105–115.

11.3 W. Ehrenburg, "Maxwell's Demon," *Scientific American* **217** (5), 103–110 (Nov. 1967).

11.4 J. Dewey, *The Influence of Darwin on Philosophy*, Bloomington, Ind.: Indiana University Press, 1965.

11.5 T. M. Brown, "Resource Letter EEC–1 on the Evolution of Energy Concepts from Galileo to Helmholtz," *American Journal of Physics* **33**, 759–765 (1965).

11.6 H. G. Wells, *The Time Machine*, any one of many editions.

11.7 O. Wilde, *The Picture of Dorian Gray*, any one of many editions.

11.8 O. Spengler, *The Decline of the West*, any one of many editions.

QUESTIONS FOR DISCUSSION

1. In the modern steady-state theory of the universe, neutral hydrogen atoms are thought to be created in space at the rate of about one per 100 years in a volume the size of an office building. This creation counteracts the expansion of the universe in the sense of keeping the average density of matter constant. Does this violate the First and Second Laws of Thermodynamics?

2. How does man increase or decrease the entropy of the universe when he plays music?

3. How can we answer the following objection to the theory of evolution: God created the world yesterday, and in creating it incorporated the evidence which we now interpret as proving evolution?

4. Shouldn't Lord Kelvin have said that, since the evolutionists establish such a long age for the earth, hence there must be something wrong with thermodynamics?

5. It is interesting how the same refrain runs through the old age of so many brilliant people: "What I did in my field of specialty is nothing compared to what I did in other fields" (Newton: physics and Biblical chronology; Goethe: poetry and optics; Lord Kelvin: thermodynamics and geology). Is this significant?

6. Who was right about the value of the Second Law of Thermodynamics, Snow or Leavis?

12 | X-RAYS AND ART

Lines on an X-ray Portrait of a Lady
She is so tall, so slender, and her bones—
Those frail phosphates, those carbonates of lime—
Are well produced by cathode rays sublime,
By oscillations, amperes and by ohms.
Her dorsal vertebrae are not concealed
By epidermis, but are well revealed.

Around her ribs, those beauteous twenty-four,
Her flesh a halo makes, misty in line,
Her noseless, eyeless face looks into mine,
And I but whisper, "Sweetheart, Je t'adore."
Her white and gleaming teeth at me do laugh.
Ah! Lovely, cruel, sweet cathodograph!

L. K. Russell, *Life* magazine of 3/12/1896

Within one year of their discovery, virtually all the potentially useful applications of x-rays were known. As an example of an interaction between the two cultures, uses of x-rays in art criticism are discussed.

INTRODUCTION

In the spring of 1945, after the end of the European part of the Second World War, the Dutch members of an Allied art commission were intrigued to find a hitherto unknown painting thought to be by Vermeer, entitled the *Adultress*, in the collection of the Nazi second-in-command Herman Goering. From records of Goering's purchase (for one-half million dollars), the painting was finally traced to a Dutch dealer, Han Van Meegeren. When asked about the origins of the painting, he refused to reveal the name of his supposed Italian supplier. He was then promptly arrested for collaboration with the German enemy. Under intense questioning, and in the face of this very serious charge, Van Meegeren finally blurted out that he could not be guilty of selling a Dutch art treasure to the Germans since he had painted the picture himself. He claimed, in fact, to have faked seven other paintings as well, with a total sales price of $2\frac{1}{4}$ million.

The shock of this revelation reverberated throughout the art world. Not only was this a great deal of money, but furthermore some of the most reputable art critics, art dealers, and art collectors were involved. Could they all have been fooled? If so, how many other "original" paintings in collections were actually fakes? Van Meegeren had successfully duplicated not only the style and physical attributes of 300 year-old paintings by Vermeer, but had infused enough genius into them so that to this day some art critics are still convinced of the the authenticity of one of them. To finally persuade the doubters about his ability as a forger, Van Meegeren painted yet another "Vermeer" before police witnesses. He was convincted of forgery, but died before serving his one-year sentence, a hero to many people who are suspicious about the abilities of art critics and who felt that he had been a hero in tricking Goering.

To us the relevant aspect of this story is the fact that most of these forgeries could have been so easily detected by the use of a technique taken from the modern scientific revolution: namely, analysis by x-rays.

As will be explained in the next chapter, at the end of the 19th century a great upheaval in the very concepts of science took place, as the atomic and nuclear revolutions occurred. In this chapter there will be presented one breakthrough in physics, which is not only characteristic of this modern scientific revolution, but which also had some immediate technological and even humanistic applications. This is the discovery in 1895 of x-rays. By looking at this example, one may perhaps learn what makes possible a swift technological application of a scientific discovery, and whether any thoughts should be given in advance to possible social implications of such a discovery. Finally, this example will raise the question: under what circumstances may applications of scientific techniques to the arts be humanizing?

ROENTGEN'S DISCOVERY OF X-RAYS

One of the more interesting unexplained phenomena which was being widely studied in the 1890s was the flow of electrical charges through a vacuum. By taking an evacuated tube (e.g., a Crookes tube) and putting a large voltage between two plates in it, it is possible to get a flow of charged particles through the vacuum. (This is now known to be a current of electrons.) The electrons could be deflected by nearby electric charges and by magnets, and could induce a glow in various materials. It was this phenomenon which Wilhelm Conrad Roentgen was beginning to investigate in Würzburg in Bavaria when he discovered x-rays. Being a very thorough man, he had just begun to repeat the previously published work of others. To improve the experiments, he covered his Crookes tube with black paper; and to test the blackness of the paper, he even covered the main fluorescent screen. At that point he was surprised to observe some flashes of light in some crystals of barium platinocyanide on a nearby table. Something was penetrating the black paper, something which obviously was not ordinary visible light.

This first observation of x-rays took place on November 8, 1895. Roentgen then proceeded to investigate the causes of the flashes, and on December 28, only 50 days later, he submitted a "preliminary communication" of it to the President of the Physical Medical Society of Würzburg. When the electrons strike the screen, after being accelerated to high speeds by the applied voltage, some of their energy is converted into very penetrating rays which Roentgen called x-rays. X-rays are now known to be very energetic "light rays," bits of pure energy which travel at the same speed as visible light, but which contain as much as 10,000 times the energy contained in visible light. (Incidentally, in Germany they are known as Roentgen rays. A few years ago in talking, in German, to a German Roentgenographer, I used the word x-rays, and he very strongly corrected me. Of course, once he discovered I was actually American, he forgave me as simply not knowing better.)

During those 50 days, Roentgen investigated many aspects of these x-rays, particularly their penetration properties. He discovered

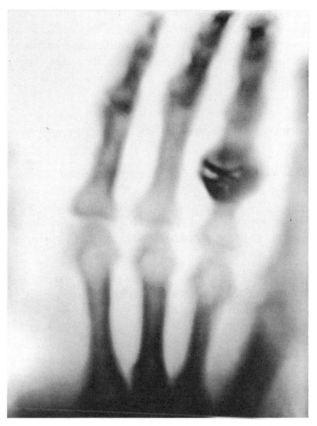

Fig. 12.1   X-ray of his wife's hand taken by Roentgen in December of 1895. (Photo courtesy Deutsches Museum München.)

that they could penetrate not only paper and glass, but light metals such as aluminium and zinc, while being absorbed very well by lead. If he had stopped with these experiments, then all the relevant physical facts from his experiments about the absorption of x-rays would have been known, and physicists could have gradually developed the theory of x-rays. But Roentgen had a slightly different approach from that of the average physicist, and as part of his first experiments he not only included absorption coefficients, but he also illustrated these absorption properties in a very striking manner by a series of pictures. These included x-rays of his wife's hand (Fig. 12.1), of metal weights in a wooden box, of the uneven density in a metal foil, and of absorption by lead paint on a door. In all these, the heavier elements cast the shadows: the calcium of the bones, the metal of the weights, or the lead in lead paint. It is these pictures which stimulated the rapid practical applications of x-rays.

THE SPREADING OF THE NEWS ABOUT THE DISCOVERY OF X–RAYS

The news about this discovery spread with almost unbelievable rapidity. On the 4th of January of 1896, there was an exhibition of some of these photographs at a meeting of the Berlin Physical Society, only six days after submission of Roentgen's first article. On January 5, the first press reports appeared in Germany. On January 6, London received the news via cable:

> The noise of war's alarm (the Boer war) should not distract attention from the marvellous triumph of Science which is reported from Vienna. It is announced that Prof. Routgen [sic] of Würzburg has discovered a light which, for the purposes of photography, will penetrate wood, flesh and most other organic substances. The professor has succeeded in photographing metal weights which were in a closed wooden case, also a man's hand, which shows only the bones, the flesh being 'invisible.' (Quoted for example in Ref. 12.1, p. 199.)

From there the news went to all the newspapers of the world:

> The *Presse* (of Vienna) assures its readers that there is no joke or humbug in the matter. It is a serious discovery by a serious German Professor. (*London Standard* of January 7, 1896, quoted for example in Ref. 12.1, p. 200.)

Le Matin of Paris reported on x-rays for the first time on January 13; *The New York Times* on January 16. German reprints of Roentgen's communication were printed in the first days of January; French and English translations appeared on February 8 and 14, respectively. Roentgen gave a demonstration of these phenomena for Emperor Wilhelm II in Berlin early in January; his first public talk was not until January 23, but in the course of it he made an x-ray of a living hand, which convinced any possible remaining skeptics. In 1901 Roentgen received the first Nobel prize in physics; and he died in 1923 (not of leukemia).

Public interest in x-rays was enormous. Edison's laboratory in the United States was literally besieged by curiosity seekers:

> Edison himself has been having a severe attack of Röntgenmania. The newspapers having reporters in attendance at his laboratory did not suffer for copy, as the yards of sensational matter emanating from this source attest, and we learn that last week Mr. Edison and his staff worked through seventy hours without intermission, a hand organ being employed during the latter hours to assist in keeping the force awake. (*Electrical World* of February 1896, quoted for example in Ref. 12.1, p. 204.)

Edison had a special exhibition in New York in May of 1896 at the Electrical Exhibit, where everyone could see the shadows of hands of visitors on a fluorescent screen. (Incidentally, one of Edison's assistants in his x-ray experiments, Mr. Dally, died in 1904 of x-ray burns; Edison never again worked with x-rays.)

There were some interesting views on the usefulness of the x-rays. Miss Frances E. Willard, for example, stated:

> I believe the X-rays are going to do much for the temperance cause. By this means drunkards and cigarette smokers can be shown the steady deterioration in their systems, which follows the practice, and seeing is believing. (The *Electrical Review* of June, 1896, quoted for example in Ref. 12.1, p. 206.)

And there was published a certain amount of nonsense about x-rays:

> ... roentgen rays were used to reflect anatomic diagrams directly into the brains of the students, making a much more enduring impression than the ordinary methods of learning anatomic details. (*Science* [of New York] of March 3, 1896, quoted for example in Ref. 12.1, pp. 204–205.)

Supposedly x-rays could even turn ordinary metals into gold! And inevitably some spiritualists and somnambulists took advantage of the x-rays.

The humor of the time reflected the interest in x-rays. Some sample jokes: (1) Dealer (pointing toward a thin horse): "There, sir!

That's what I call a picture!" Prospective buyer: "M'm, yes, he does rather suggest one of those Roentgen photographs!" (2) Guest (to waiter who has brought him chops with a large bone and little meat): "Waiter, is this a chop *à la* Roentgen?" (3) "Shah Kal-Y-Jula had all of his court officials photographed with Roentgen's Rays. In spite of one hour's exposure no backbone could be detected in any of them." (As quoted in Ref. 12.1, pp. 364–366.) And, of course, there were the cartoons in *Life* and *La Nature*, and even advertisements for ladies' x-ray-proof underwear.

THE APPLICATIONS OF X-RAYS

Scientists and technologists, inspired by Roentgen's pictures, quickly followed up the various implied applications. Medical diagnosis came immediately (by January 15). For example, on January 28, 1896, the following was published:

> A few years ago the hand of one of the assistants of the Urania (a school) was injured in the explosion of a glass flask. He complained continuously of pain in the scar and it seemed possible that a piece of glass remained in the hand. Now this piece of glass has been detected by the new photographic method. (*Münchener Medizinische Wochenschrift* **43**, 86 [1986], quoted for example in Ref. 12.1, p. 246.)

On February 2 there appeared reports of dental x-rays and of x-rays of Egyptian mummies. In March opaque materials were used in medical visualization of cavities in the body. Ref. 12.1 has many pretty pictures taken in 1896 of skeletons, gall stones, kidney stones, fractures of legs, and outlines of veins. Queen Amelia of Portugal had x-ray pictures made of several of her court ladies in order to illustrate the evils of tight lacing. Even in war, x-rays found immediate acceptance, as they were used to hunt for bullets embedded in flesh, for example. In May of 1896 the British Nile expedition carried with it two portable x-ray units. By the end of 1896, movies of moving bones were obtained. And x-rays were already used as evidence in court to show that a Miss Ffolliot (a burlesque dancer) had injured her foot while on the job. So within a year the whole spectrum of uses of x-rays in medical diagnosis had been explored. Now in the United States each year there are in excess of 100 million x-ray visits, more than 50 million dental x-rays are taken, and there are over 200 thousand x-ray units in operation.

The therapeutic uses of x-rays also came very quickly. In late January of 1896, E. Grubbe of Chicago noticed that after exposure to x-rays his hands itched and turned red and swollen and that the hair on them fell out. So, on January 29, he gave the first x-ray treatment for cancer of the breast. And he actually achieved remission; however, there was no cure, since the cancer had already spread. Unfortunately, these potentially bad consequences of the uses of x-rays were more or less ignored; instead, the hair-removal effect of x-rays was taken as a possible beneficial effect:

> If the time that elapses before positive baldness was effected could be reduced, what an incalculable benefit would Rontgen's discovery confer on shavers. Thus to remove the beard would only require the placing of a Crookes tube for a few minutes over the chin before retiring to rest, when next morning the ordinary application of soap and water would complete the operation. Under these circumstances, the "new barber" may not impossibly be one of the new outcomes of the "new photography." (The *Lancet* of May 9, 1896, quoted for example in Ref. 12.1, p. 297.)

So instead of proper precautions being taken concerning x-rays, there were intentional hair removals for beauty treatments.

Nonmedical uses of x-rays, of course, also developed quickly. Roentgen himself took pictures of a defective shotgun and saw the internal flaws. Edison suggested the use of x-rays to temper aluminum. X-rays were used to examine infernal machines. Plant structures were studied with x-rays. The list could be endless.

X-RAYS IN ART CRITICISM

Some of these developments in technological and scientific applications of x-rays we will touch upon later (e.g., in Chapter 19). But now we will briefly explore one application which has a bearing on the humanities: namely the uses of x-rays in art criticism. This use consists of taking x-rays of a painting in an attempt to obtain information about the painting which might lie below the surface features. The method hinges on the following facts. (1) The old masters used leaded white paint to shape and delineate the underlying structure of their paintings; since lead absorbs x-rays very well, this underlying shaping can therefore be explored with x-rays. (2) Modern paints differ in chemical content from older paints, leading to differences in x-ray absorption. (3) Overpainting still leaves the old paint underneath, so that original pictures or sketches may appear in the x-rays along with the surface features.

As with all applications of x-rays, the study of paintings was developed long ago. There are essentially two different applications of x-rays to art criticism. The first is in the technical use to either distinguish original paintings from outright forgeries, or else to detect belated changes in, or repairs to, the original conception. The second use is in studying the style of a painter by examining brush technique and conceptual development as the painting progressed from rough draft to final form.

FORGERIES, FAKES, AND MODIFICATIONS

A few examples will suffice to show what kinds of modifications can be detected in paintings (e.g., Ref. 12.3, pp. 114–121). In the *Crucifixion* by the 16th century painter Cornelius Engelbrechtsen, there was a woman in the right foreground. When x-rayed, the painting of a priest of far better quality was seen underneath. It appears that the donor of the painting decided to have herself immortalized, and had her portrait added as an afterthought. In the *Madonna* by Geertgen van St. Jeans (about 1500) the arms seemed very stiff and unnatural. X-rays showed the hidden baby which had been in her arms, making the pose much more natural. The art critic Martin de Wild once noticed in a painting by Frans Hals that the main figure in it had a wine glass of inferior craftsmanship in his right hand and wore a red cap which looked painted on top of his hair. Later, an etching was found of a similar pose with a ram's horn in the hand, and no hat. X-rays revealed that, indeed, the wine glass had been painted over a ram's horn and that the hat was a later addition.

The fake and forgery market in paintings is a flourishing one; Van Meegeren is not a solitary example of a successful forger. (In fact, a real success would be one that we would never know about because it would never be found out.) However, the modern forger does face certain difficulties in carrying on his craft, in part because of the increasing use of x-rays to examine paintings.

To begin with, the forger must use the right chemicals; for example, zinc-oxide white was not used before 1870, and titanium-oxide white not until this century, so these had better not appear in a painting which is supposedly 300 years old. Van Meegeren was quite careful with this. Also, the painting must appear properly aged, with the right kind of cracks and surface characteristics. Van Meegeren excelled at this. (Infrared radiation is also quite useful testing for the age of surfaces.) A canvas of the right age must be used. That means removing a poor painting from an old canvas; this has to be done very thoroughly, otherwise traces of the old picture can be seen in the x-rays. Here Van Meegeren could have been caught, because he became more and more careless about this as he become more and more successful. Alternatively, if an old wooden background is used, one can sometimes detect with x-rays the wormholes that had to be filled with paints. And, finally, even the strokes with which the underlying base of paint is laid on must be controlled to conform with the style of the imitated artist. Usually done with lead paint, the strokes are very prominent in the x-ray pictures; frequently forgers are far too precise in their background outline. Figures 12.2 and 12.3 illustrate some of these possibilities of x-rays.

STYLES OF PAINTING

More subtle effects of style have been discovered with x-rays. Let me cite just one example of what can be done in this respect. The painter Veronese had long been considered a very facile artist, an artist who used broad easy strokes with an apparent absence of thoughtful effect. But then his painting *Mars and Venus* was studied by means of x-rays:

> Although the richly colored picture, lavish in form, has a tapestry-like effect and a highly decorative, easy quality which is consistent with the artist's mature work, the X-ray films record a struggle for design which reveals the critical effort put into the achievement of this apparently graceful composition. As the several parts of the picture were X-rayed and the shadowgraphs pieced together, the general aspect of Veronese's first conception of the

Fig. 12.2 St. Agnes by Ambrogio Lorenzetti (on the left) together with a studio-exercise copy by A. Everett Austin (on the right). (Photos courtesy of the Fogg Art Museum, Harvard University.)

Fig. 12.3 Radiograph of Ambrogio Lorenzetti, St. Agnes (left) and of Austin's copy (right). Note the difference between Lorenzetti's delicate and precise touch and Austin's struggle to imitate the surface appearance of the original painting. (Photos courtesy of the Fogg Art Museum, Harvard University.)

scene, hidden beneath the surface, appeared in conjunction with the forms visible on the surface. The revisions in the composition reveal the complexity of Veronese's creative process.

The detail of Venus' head contains a large revision of pose. . . . Venus' left hand also was different in the underpainting. . . . Instead of the rather elegant gesture of the finished painting, one finds a heavy pose. . . .

Summing up these changes, we see that, if Veronese "had no knowledge at all of the agony of conceiving and thinking in his work," at least he went through the process of struggling with pose and composition, which usually accompanies the agony of conceiving. . . .

One hesitates to say that the evidence of control proves Veronese to have had intellectual profundity, for he might have made these alternations merely through a desire to experiment with his figures, or at the suggestion of a patron. What is apparent, however, is that Veronese must have been supremely sensitive to niceties of design, and that he must have exercised a vigorous degree of intelligence in changing Venus so simply and concisely from a half-draped human being into a nude Renaissance goddess. Altogether the shadowgraphs suggest an unsuspected conscientiousness and analytical power which the easy manipulation of the painted surface tends to hide. (Ref. 12.2, pp. 93–96, by permission of Greenwood Press, Inc.)

To a good art critic it is this additional information about the development of styles which is of interest. With x-rays, each picture becomes several pictures; the subsurface sketches reveal the development of the painter's thoughts and his changes in attitude. His personality often comes out more clearly in the sketchlike undercoating; the progressively more compact overcoating gives hints at the thoughts behind the changes. It is as though the art student or critic could watch the painter at work.

SUMMARY

This chapter has tried to indicate how and why the applications of x-rays came so soon after their discovery. In part, the explanation may lie in the mind of the discoverer. Roentgen went beyond a dry, scientific discussion of x-rays and pointed out some of their fascinating possibilities. His x-ray of a living hand particularly appealed to the general public, stimulating the curiosity toward further experiments. Through considering possible applications, Roentgen may have accepted some social responsibility for the consequences, although he did not foresee the ultimate bad radiation-damage effects. Was he mixing science and technology?

In considering the impact of x-rays on art, one can ask whether they had an ultimately humanizing effect. Has art, as a creative experience, improved or progressed due to the technique of x-ray analysis? Or is this simply a case of allowing some scientists to pretend to be intellectuals and some art critics to pretend to be scientific? This is a question closely related to thoughts about changes in the quality of life due to technology.

REFERENCES

Prime references

12.1 O. Glasser, *Wilhelm Conrad Roentgen and the Early History of the Roentgen Rays*, Springfield, Ill.: Charles C. Thomas, 1934; quotes introductory poem on page 42.

12.2 A. Burroughs, *Art Criticism from a Laboratory*, Westport, Conn.: Greenwood Press, 1965.

Interesting reading

12.3 A. R. Bleich, *The Story of X Rays*, New York: Dover Publishing Co., 1960.

12.4 G. W. C. Kaye, *The Practical Applications of X Rays*, New York: E. P. Dutton and Co., 1923.

12.5 F. Mendax, *Art Fakes and Forgeries*, New York: Philosophical Library, 1956.

12.6 P. Brown, *American Martyrs to Science Through the Roentgen Rays*, Springfield, Ill.: Charles C. Thomas, 1936.

QUESTIONS FOR DISCUSSION

1. Are there any modern scientific discoveries which have found particularly rapid applications? What about nuclear fission, transistors, lasers? Are there any parallels with x-rays in these cases?

2. Did the quacks hinder or harm the development of x-rays?

3. Should the possible deleterious consequences of x-rays have been thought about in 1896? Does anyone bear a responsibility for these bad consequences?

4. Has the discovery of x-rays improved art (and hence the quality of life)?

13 | THE MODERN SCIENTIFIC REVOLUTION: RELATIVITY AND QUANTUM MECHANICS

There once was a fellow named Fisk,
Whose fencing was exceedingly brisk.
* So fast was his action*
* The relativistic contraction*
Reduced his rapier to a disk.

Relativistic limerick

I simply cannot believe in a God who plays dice.

Comment by Einstein about the Copenhagen
statistical interpretation of quantum mechanics

The modern age of physics was ushered in by the theory of relativity, which overthrew the Newtonian absolute of space and time. The quantum theory then led to a dualism and uncertainty in experimental science, which stood in sharp contrast to the earlier absolutism. Both these aspects of the modern scientific revolution reintroduced the observer into experiments—relativity by making his position and local time the central facts of the universe, and quantum mechanics by once again linking the very act of observation with the resultant value for the observed parameter.

INTRODUCTION

In 1900 Lord Kelvin felt he could say that there were only two minor 19th-century "clouds" which dimmed the otherwise brilliant sky of the new scientific century (e.g., Ref. 13.3, p. 14). These two clouds were the controversy over the nature of the ether and the nonexistence of the ultraviolet catasrophe in light emission. As a matter of fact, these two minor clouds were not so minor after all; the first led to the theory of relativity and the second to quantum mechanics. And it is precisely these two theoretical developments which make up the different character of contemporary physics, which provide such a contrast with the preceding views of the physical universe, and which have led to the suspicion that we can never really know all the complexities of the universe—that there are limits to our observational abilities.

Both these theories are derivatives of the controversy over the nature of light; both became entangled in the impossibility of describing light uniquely as either waves or particles. The difficulty of deciding whether there exists an ether to propagate light waves was ultimately resolved by Einstein's theory of relativity. (See Ref. 13.5 for a detailed discussion of the relationship between that problem and that theory.) In this theory he points out that there is no such thing as an absolute motion, that all motions can be discussed only relative to some specific observer. The most powerful conclusion from this theory is, of course, the equation $E = mc^2$, an equation which states that an energy E can be converted into a mass m, and vice versa, in a quantitatively specifiable way, with the proportionality constant being the square of the speed of light, c^2.

We are all already familiar with the concept of quantization from our everyday life; for example, there is such a thing as a quantum of financial value: the cent. Money always changes hands in amounts which are multiples of cents; when one pays no tax on a 10¢-candy bar but a 1¢ tax on a 20¢-Coke, then quantization is very evident; however, in the federal budget of $200 billion such quantization is hardly noticeable. Quantization of energy in physics is similar; when an experiment involves big things like automobiles, or people, the effect of quantization is not noticeable, but when an experiment deals with small things like atoms, then the quantization plays a major role. Quantum mechanics arose out of the fact that light always occurs in nature as very specific quanta of energy. Its importance is not only that it has improved our understanding of atomic and nuclear phenomena. More importantly, quantization appears to set another limit on the certainty with which man can know anything, just as the relativistic limits restrict man's capability to fix an absolute of space and time. One of the results of quantum mechanics is the Heisenberg Uncertainty Principle, which suggests that we cannot simultaneously know everything about all the particles in the universe, no matter how hard we try to measure things precisely. In fact, this principle puts a quantitative limit on our accuracy, on our imperfectness.

There are two particularly fascinating aspects to this 20th-century revolution. One has to do with the development of the theories, a development which displayed an extensively metaphysical character. The founders of relativity and quantum mechanics frequently seemed more like philosophers than scientists in their speculations. Yet in all cases the ultimate test was comparison with reality. The second fascination lies in the interaction of these physical theories with philosophy and political ideology (as described in Chapters 16 and 21). Modern scientists were involved in World War II not only through their science but also through the contact of their theories with political thought.

THE NATURE OF LIGHT

The background of the 20th-century revolution in physics lies in the history of the scientific studies of light. The interpretation of the nature of light has been a varied one. Newton, for example, was the chief proponent of one of the two opposing views of light; he believed that light consists of moving particles. He believed this on the basis of the fact that light appears to travel in straight lines and make sharp shadows, and that light can be separated into various colors, suggesting that it is made up of distinct constituent entities. Then in the 18th century, interference phenomena were observed for light—interference similar to that observed in the crossing of the ripples from two stones thrown simultaneously into a pond. One consequent article of faith was then that these waves of light must be transmitted by a medium, just as water waves travel in the water medium and sound waves are transmitted by air. This medium was called the ether, a word used earlier by Aristotle to describe nonearthly material.

If the ether exists, then it should be possible to measure the motion of the earth in this ether, just as one can measure the position of a boat relative to the water in which it floats. In the period 1882–1887, A. A. Michelson and E. W. Morley performed such an experiment in Cleveland at the Case School of Applied Science. With a $10,000 grant, they built an extremely precise device, now known as the Michelson-Morley interferometer, with many mirrors, lights, and lenses mounted on a huge slab floating in a pool of mercury on top of cement poured onto bedrock. In this device, light was sent along two different paths; one path was parallel and the other path was perpendicular to the suspected motion of the earth through the ether. Just as it is harder to swim against a current in a river than at a right angle to it, so the light in the parallel path should be slowed down by the ether flow. Interference effects were then used to try to detect this slowing down. The beautiful thing about the experiment was that *no* motion relative to the ether could be detected. The simplest conclusion which agreed with the Michelson-Morley experiment was that the ether did not exist. (See Ref. 13.4 for the detailed history of this experiment, and of other attempts to explain this null result.) Something was clearly wrong with the attempt to explain the behavior of light by classical wave theory.

The other difficulty about the nature of light had to do with its origins. In particular there was the puzzle known as the "ultraviolet catastrophy." This catastrophe has to do with the color distribution of the light emitted by hot bodies such as the tungsten filament in light bulbs. This color distribution can be calculated using classical theory, but the prediction is wrong. Classically, hot bodies should radiate primarily very high-energy photons of light (i.e., ultraviolet), so that if one opened the door of an oven at home one should get bombarded by high-energy x-rays. Since x-rays are rather deadly, it is lucky for us that an actual oven emits mostly red light; the ultraviolet catastrophe is notable for not occurring.

EINSTEIN'S THEORY OF RELATIVITY

The lack of an ether was not the only unexplained problem in 1905. For example, by 1901 it was already known that an electron moving at high speeds behaved anomalously. Albert Einstein provided the answer to these problems with his special theory of relativity.

Einstein was born in 1879 in Ulm, Germany (a small town distinguished primarily by having in its center a church with the highest steeple in the world). After obtaining his Ph.D. in Switzerland with difficulty (because he studied what he, rather than the professors, felt to be important), he worked as a patent examiner. This job left him enough leisure to work in his real avocation, and in 1905 he published three papers, any of which was worthy of the Nobel prize. One of these papers explained Brownian motion (such as dust particles dancing in the air); one showed that in the photoelectric effect, light does at times act like a particle when knocking electrons out of a metal (this won Einstein a Nobel prize); and the third proposed the special theory of relativity.

Let me first illustrate the nature of Einstein's starting assumptions in explaining the relativistic phenomena.

1. He assumed that the speed of light is measured to be the same by all observers who are moving at a constant speed. This assumption goes utterly against common sense. If a ball is thrown at 60 mph due East, parallel to a car going 54 mph due East, the driver of the car will see the ball slowly passing him at 6 mph. If an astronaut passes us in his spaceship at 167,400 mph (90% the speed of light), and we shine light after him (traveling 100% the speed of light), we would by analogy expect the astronaut to measure the speed of the light to be 18,600 mph (10% the speed of light). This, however, is not true; the astronaut would also measure the speed of that light to be exactly 186,000 mph. It seems to make no difference who measures the speed of light; it always comes out to be the same. This explains the Michelson-Morley experiment: there is no ether to slow down the light; it travels at the same speed c in both arms of the interferometer.

2. The second Einsteinian assumption was that all laws of nature hold equally well in all nonaccelerating systems; this simply brought out again the fact that no one reference frame is preferred over another.

Einstein's special theory of relativity predicts many puzzling and anti-common-sense phenomena. For example, it shows that, since energy and mass are equivalent, a body has more mass when moving rapidly than when it is at rest, since its kinetic energy appears as an increase in the mass. This explains why no material object can ever reach the speed of light; as it goes faster and faster, and hence becomes heavier and heavier, the same force (as in a rocket motor) will produce

Fig. 13.1   Einstein at the blackboard. (Cartoon courtesy of Sidney Harris.)

less and less acceleration. Since the mass of the body approaches in-finity as its speed approaches the speed of light, an infinite force would be required to break the light barrier. (This is relevant to the discus-sion on interstellar space travel in Chapter 24.) There also is the rel-ativistic "twin paradox." The theory of relativity says that time passes more slowly in a moving system than in a stationary one. This can be illustrated by means of identical twins. One of these we send off as an astronaut at a high velocity into space, while the other stays behind. When the twins are finally reunited upon the return of the astronaut, the traveler turns out to be younger than the stay-at-home. (The paradox lies in the fact that it is the initial acceleration which defines which is the moving twin.) A final puzzle is that of the relativistic contraction of objects at high speed. Note that all these phenomena become noticeable only at speeds close to that of light, i.e., at speeds not on the order of miles per hour but rather of thousands of miles per second. But if you wanted to play basketball with 7'-1" Wilt Chamberlain on more even terms, perhaps this might be the way: if Wilt would go up for a rebound at 90% the speed of light, he would appear only 4'-3" tall, a much more manageable opponent. Of course, it may be somewhat difficult to play any kind of game with an opponent who is moving that fast, but that is a minor detail. (Another minor detail is the fact that at the same time the basket would seem to Wilt to be only six feet high, so that he seemingly wouldn't even have to jump.)

QUANTUM MECHANICS

The other 19th-century cloud was finally resolved by Max Planck at the end of 1900, when he suggested that light is emitted in a quantized way. As finally made clear by Einstein, the energy carried by each quantum of light (called a photon) is then proportional to its frequency, the constant of proportionality being Planck's constant h. For example, if a 100-watt light bulb is burnt all day, it will emit about 20 million-billion-billion light quanta; i.e., the energy carried per quantum is quite small by human standards. Note that this relationship between the energy and the frequency incorporates the particle-wave duality in the sense that the energy implies a quantum or particle, while the frequency implies a wave characteristic. This assumption nicely explains away the ultraviolet catastrophe, and ultimately led to all of the developments of quantum mechanics.

One of the more beautiful quantum effects occurs when gases have an ionizing current passed through them; light is then emitted which has certain very distinct frequencies (colors) which are characteristic of the particular gas. This phenomenon is not explainable on any prequantum basis. The Danish physicist Niels Bohr took the first step toward a satisfactory solution of this problem in 1913 when he suggested that the electrons travel around the atomic nucleus in certain very definite orbits, and that light quanta are emitted when the electrons jump from one orbit to another. This theory predicted frequencies for the light from hydrogen which agreed very well with already existing experimental data, and it put quantum mechanics into a very heady period of development. Much of the subsequent work was inspired by, and performed at, the Institute for Theoretical Physics in Copenhagen, an institute directed by Niels Bohr until his son Aage took it over, and funded by the Carlsberg Brewery (an example of the impact of beer on physics?).

The full-fledged quantum theory extended this particle-wave duality of light to all matter. In this formulation all particulate matter is a wave—or has a wave associated with it—whose wavelength is inversely proportional to the particle's mass. This explains why we do not see wave phenomena in our day-to-day living; a car, for example, is simply so massive that its wavelength is vanishingly small. But an electron has such a small mass that the wavelength associated with it can be fairly large, that the electron can actually behave *noticeably* like a wave on an atomic scale. When water waves pass through two openings, interference phenomena occur where the parts of the wave from the two openings overlap. In this case, it makes sense to say that the wave went through both holes. In a similar way, it is possible to make a discrete electron pass simultaneously through several holes on the atomic scale of a crystal lattice—or rather it is possible to set up an experiment in which it is impossible to determine through which of several holes an electron actually passed. (See Ref. 13.9, Chapters 37 and 38, for a nice discussion of this point.) In general, quantum mechanics is a method of looking at all matter as waves and then asking the probabilities of certain events, probabilities which one can then proceed to check by repeated experiments. One does not know how to predict exactly what will happen in a given case; only probabilities are predictable. However, for large-scale (nonatomic) phenomena, the uncertainties in the predictions are ordinarily quite small in this wave-distribution sense.

THE HEISENBERG UNCERTAINTY PRINCIPLE

All the implications of the wave-particle duality, and of this statistical uncertainty, are contained in the Heisenberg Uncertainty Principle.

It states that it is impossible to do any experiment in which all the variables can be measured with unlimited accuracy. If one wants to measure the position of a particle with extreme precision, then one gives up the ability to measure simultaneously the speed of the particle with a similar unlimited precision. In fact, the Uncertainty Principle sets a quantitative lower limit on the product of the precision of these two simultaneous measurements.

THE IMPLICATIONS OF RELATIVITY
AND QUANTUM MECHANICS

The physical implications of the theory of relativity run frequently counter to common sense. One might be tempted to say that, since the effects we have described become significant only at high speeds, they do not make the theory very revolutionary. And it is true that the classical Newtonian laws still hold except for objects moving at nearly the speed of light. But in a sense, Newton's laws, or at least some of their implications, have been totally overthrown.

The theory of relativity says that we can no longer give preference to one central coordinate system in space (a central system originally associated with the ether) or to a specific time system. We cannot say how fast we are moving in space; we can only say how fast we are traveling relative to some other object. An element of indefiniteness is introduced. With relativity, the observer once again becomes the center of the universe. Where the whole Galilean astronomy labored to destroy the idea of the uniqueness of the earth, and hence of man, now the Einsteinian mechanics indicated that it is important to talk about phenomena only in terms of observation by a real observer. Only by observation can sense be made of the measures of space and time.

Quantum mechanics raises similar fundamental questions. In classical Newtonian mechanics, man was limited in what he could know, and hence predict, because it required effort to measure with sufficient accuracy the position and speed of many particles. Now quantum mechanics says man does not need to bother to try for a better precision, since it is unattainable in any case due to the Heisenberg Uncertainty Principle. And no one has been able to discover a way to defeat this principle. It seems to be just as the romantics have been claiming for so long: the observer cannot be separated from the experiment. When measurements are carried out on microscopic phenomena, then the observer adds enough disturbance to the system to affect the observed data. In quantum mechanics there are rigorous limits on our capability to know, as opposed to the classical limit on our capacity to know. We are limited in our ability to know all about nature; there are certain questions which we cannot ask because they are unanswerable. This is, in a sense, a very pessimistic new view about the universe and about our role in it; there is no longer a Creator who opens the universe like a book for us to read. If all of science is statistical probabilities, how can we even talk about ultimate consensus on anything?

But there is an even deeper question involved in quantum mechanics, a question which is answered very differently by the two primary schools of quantum-mechanical thought. One school is represented by the older generation of physicists like Einstein, who are reluctant to believe in a dice-playing God, feel that there is a basic reality to all phenomena, and believe that only the observational interference makes the universe appear nonclockwork. On the other hand, the Copenhagen school, as represented by Bohr and Heisenberg, believes that there is no basic underlying reality except that which we can physically measure; only contact with measurable reality is ultimately significant. In this approach there is no point in discussing something which can never be seen or measured, which is simply not real. Reference 13.12 describes the many debates between Einstein and Bohr, in which Einstein tried very hard to invent thought experiments which might circumvent the Uncertainty Principle.

It is such debates, so necessary to the development of both relativity and quantum mechanics, which make the modern physics seem at times very metaphysical (see Refs. 13.2 and 13.11). The equations, numbers, and usefulness of the various points of view are not so much under discussion. But considering the influence of the Newtonian mechanical viewpoint of the universe, it is not surprising that these metaphysical problems have wide-ranging implications. Modern physics has added elements of uncertainty and indefiniteness; it has in a sense recombined the quantitative aspects of physics with the organismic reintroduction of the observer into the phenomenon.

REFERENCES

Prime references

13.1 G. Gamow, *Thirty Years That Shook Physics*, Garden City, New York: Doubleday and Co., 1966: a history of quantum mechanics.

13.2 W. Heisenberg, *Encounters and Conversations* (translated by A. J. Pomerans), New York: Harper and Row, 1970; gives a feeling for the thought processes involved in the development of quantum mechanics.

Interesting reading

13.3 M. Jammer, *The Conceptual Development of Quantum Mechanics*, New York: McGraw-Hill, 1966; a very detailed but technical history of quantum mechanics.

13.4 R. S. Shankland, "The Michelson-Morley Experiment," *The American Journal of Physics* **32**, 16–35 (1964); and B. Jaffe, *Michelson and the Speed of Light*, New York: Doubleday Anchor Science Study Series S13, 1960.

13.5 G. Holton, "Einstein, Michelson and the 'Crucial Experiment'," Isis **60** (#2), 133–197 (1969).

13.6 H. Bondi, *Relativity and Common Sense*, New York: Doubleday Anchor Science Study Series S36, 1964.

13.7 G. Gamow, *Mr. Thompkins in Wonderland*, Cambridge: Cambridge University Press, 1939; has nice discussions of the puzzles of relativity.

13.8 A. Baker, *Modern Physics and Antiphysics*, Reading, Mass.: Addison-Wesley Publishing Co., 1970; quite readable material on relativity and quantum mechanics.

13.9 R. P. Feynman, R. B. Leighton, and M. Sands, *The Feynman Lectures on Physics*, Vol I, Reading, Mass.: Addison-Wesley Publishing Co., 1964; see Chapters 37 and 38 for discussion of interference phenomena for particles.

13.10 G. Gamow, *Biography of Physics*, (Ref. 6.4); pp. 209–271 on quantum mechanics.

13.11 W. Heisenberg, *Physics and Philosophy*, New York: Harper and Brothers, 1958; Chapters 2, 3, and 8 on quantum mechanics and philosophy.

13.12 J. Bernstein, *A Comprehensible World*, New York: Random House, 1967; on the Einstein-Bohr debates, pp. 110–134.

13.13 A. M. Bork and A. B. Arons, "Collateral Reading for Physics Courses," *The American Journal of Physics* **35**, 71 (1967); a bibliography which gives, for example, references on the impact of relativity on art.

QUESTIONS FOR DISCUSSION

1. Alexander Graham Bell supported the early Michelson experiments on the speed of light. Why?

2. Research cost money even in the 1880s; Michelson, for example, received $70,000 to do his ether experiment. Einstein, however, was content to be a patent examiner and work on physics in his leisure time. Which is the better way to do science?

3. Michelson worked with high precision. Was this a characteristic of American science, or of physics in general, at the turn of the century?

4. Does quantum mechanics at all contradict Newtonian mechanics?

5. Could the atom be a miniature solar system?

6. Are there any modern attitudes which have grown out of the "new" nonabsolute outlook in physics (morals? existentialism?)?

7. Why have the theory of relativity and quantum mechanics been so much used as inspiration for philosophy?

8. The Uncertainty Principle has in the past been linked with the problem of free will. How?

9. Is there currently any area of science which interests the non-scientist as much as the theory of relativity and quantum mechanics did the nonscientist of the 1920s?

14 | THE DATING GAME

How can one tell apart two samples of pure alcohol where one is extracted from corn, and the other from petroleum products?
Question on chemistry Ph.D. examination

Nature is particulate. This allows the use of both stable and radioactive isotopes in determining the age of materials. Examples are taken from geology, anthropology, archeology, and bootlegging.

INTRODUCTION

Picture the following: a report is published that the wreck of a Spanish galleon, with a large cargo of well-preserved wine, has been found off the eastern coast of Florida. There follows then a big influx of tourists to view the collection of old bottles, professional wine tasters declare the contents to be delicious, and the local chamber of com merce is ecstatic. Then some skeptics begin to wonder whether this find of wine might not be a fake. It turns out that nuclear physics can check on the veracity of the finders of this treasure. At the cost of about a case of the liquid, it is possible to tell whether the wine is contemporary or quite old, simply by measuring its radioactivity. If the wine contains a significant amount of tritium (a radioactive isotope of hydrogen), then it is not old and the whole affair is a hoax.

In preparation for some of the future chapters, and as a further illustration of modern science, some of the physics related to radioactivity will be briefly presented here. Then we will see how the method of dating objects by radioactive and stable isotopes has been used in other disciplines such as geology and archeology. The connection of these examples with both the scientific merit of nuclear physics and the two-culture controversy will be clear.

THE PARTICULATENESS OF MATTER

Beyond relativity and quantum mechanics, the 20th-century physics is also characterized by the reintroduction of the concept of the particulateness of nature. While the ancient Greeks had speculated that matter consisted of particles, and while the periodic table of 19th-century chemistry supported this idea, it was only as part of the modern scientific revolution that the quantization of matter was quantitatively established.

One of the first demonstrations that matter was particulate came out of the same experiment which led to Roentgen's discovery of x-rays. J. J. Thomson, of the Cavendish laboratory at Cambridge, England, was able to show in 1897 that current flowing through the gas in a Crookes tube consisted of particles (electrons) with a specific ratio of charge to mass. Later the American physicist Robert A. Millikan was able to determine the quantity of charge carried by each electron, a quantity which has since been considered the basic unit of charge. Interestingly enough, now some evidence exists that there are particles, called quarks, which carry a charge which is either one-third or two-thirds that of the electron.

NATURAL RADIOACTIVITY

In 1896 the French physicist Henri Becquerel discovered natural radioactivity, a process involving the emission of discrete particles. This discovery is a case of true serendipity. Becquerel was studying fluorescence, which is the ability of certain crystals to glow in the dark after exposure to light. In one of the drawers of his desk, Becquerel kept a collection of various minerals that he used in his studies, together with some photographic plates. When Becquerel tried to use these plates after a month's break in his work, they all turned out to be fogged, even though they had been thoroughly wrapped up in black paper. The serendipity occurred when, instead of blaming the plate manufacturer, he investigated the possibility that his minerals were responsible for the fogging. And, indeed, the culprit turned out to be a piece of uranium ore (pitchblende) from Bohemia, which continuously emitted radiations energetic enough to penetrate the paper wrapper. By 1898 Madame Marie S. Curie and her husband Pierre Curie were able to separate 200 milligrams (or 1/140 of an ounce) of the radioactive element radium from a ton of pitchblende. (Note that Marie Curie died of leukemia in 1934.) The emission from these radioactive sources were found to consist of three types of discrete radiations, namely α-, β-, and γ-rays. The γ-rays are similar to x-rays; they too can penetrate through thick layers of paper and glass, and are actually high-energy photons, or quanta of energy traveling at the speed of light. The β-radiations are simply energetic electrons. The α-radiations consist of the nuclei of helium atoms.

THE PARTICULATE MODEL OF THE NUCLEUS

By 1911 a discrete model of the atom was proposed by Lord Ernest Rutherford. In this model each atom contains a central particulate core of positive charge called the nucleus. Around this nucleus there are electrons moving in orbits. The Danish physicist Niels Bohr used this particular model to explain long-known data on the color spectra emitted by excited atoms. Thomson soon found that chemical elements, as they occur in nature, are made up of isotopes with the same chemical character, but with differing masses per atom. The discovery of the neutron by Chadwick in 1932 then allowed an explanation of the nature of these isotopes by a subdivision of the nucleus into further discrete components; namely, each nucleus consists of some number of heavy neutral particles (neutrons) and some other number of heavy positively charged particles (protons). The chemical properties of an atom are controlled by the number of electrons and hence by the number of protons in the nucleus, while the mass depends on both the numbers of protons and neutrons. Therefore, isotopes of the same element have the same number of protons in the nucleus, but differing numbers of neutrons. In this model, radioactive decay is then a change in the nucleus, accompanied by the emission of one or more of these α-, β- or γ-rays, a change which may involve a transmutation from one chemical element to another.

Since that time many more elementary particles have been discovered. There is the positron (a positively charged electron), a negatively charged proton, and about 100 others. One of the more interesting elementary particles is the neutrino, whose existence was predicted in 1930. However, it has little interaction with matter, so that it was not observed until 25 years later. John Updike wrote a poem about the neutrino which not only gives the reaction of one humanist to elementary-particle physics, but also nicely characterizes its most apparent property.

> Cosmic Gall
> Neutrinos, they are very small.
> They have no charge and have no mass
> And do not interact at all.
> The earth is just a silly ball
> To them, through which they simply pass,
> Like dustmaids down a drafty hall
> Or photons through a sheet of glass.
> They snub the most exquisite gas,
> Ignore the most substantial wall,
> Cold-shoulder steel and sounding brass,
> Insult the stallion in his stall,
> And scorning barriers of class,
> Infiltrate you and me! Like tall
> And painless guillotines, they fall
> Down through our heads into the grass.
> At night, they enter at Nepal
> And pierce the lover and his lass
> From underneath the bed—you call
> It wonderful; I call it crass.

(As quoted in Ref. 8.9, p. 30. Originally published in the *New Yorker* magazine, and used by permission of Random House, Inc.)

TRANSMUTATION OF ELEMENTS

Once Rutherford became convinced that radioactivity was due to instabilities of nuclei, he tried to induce such instabilities by bombarding nuclei with heavy charged particles. And in 1919 he succeeded in changing nitrogen into oxygen by bombardment with alpha particles from the decay of uranium. The alchemists' old dream had come true; transmutation of the elements had become reality. Of course, the dream was not quite fulfilled; such methods of transmutation are far too expensive to mass-produce gold.

Soon this cumbersome method of transmutation was replaced by expensive devices which accelerate protons, alpha particles, etc., to very high velocities in order to break up target nuclei in a more controlled manner. Both the Van De Graaff accelerator and Ernest O. Lawrence's cyclotron could give bombarding particles enough energy to transmute many of the elements. In none of these devices is much money to be made by transmutation; gold may go into them in the form of cash, but certainly very little gold comes out. (In fact, in the Second World War, silver was used to make some low-resistance wires for such devices.) In 1934 the transmutation to artificially radioactive substances was observed with such accelerators, making possible the production of many new isotopes.

These are the major threads which weave through the fields of atomic and nuclear physics. By 1928 the major constituent components of the atom had been found and its construction clarified. The stage was then set for the uses of this knowledge in the Second World War. Before leaving this topic of particulateness, we might use it to show what it means for a scientific discipline to have scientific merit. As pointed out in Chapter 3, this merit hinges on the contact of a discipline with neighboring disciplines. And studies into the structure of the atom had such merit from the very beginning, because the acquired knowledge was immediately relevant to studies in other fields such as geology, biology (evolution), and archeology. To illustrate this, we will now look at several applications of both stable and radioactive isotopes in studies which might be called "studies of time" or "The Dating Game."

THE AGE OF THE EARTH

As pointed out in Chapter 11, when the theory of evolution was first proposed there was dissent from Lord Kelvin on the grounds that so much heat was being radiated by the earth that it was cooling off at too rapid a rate to have allowed sufficient time for the evolutionary processes. This objection was, of course, invalidated by the discovery of substances like uranium, which are found everywhere in the earth's crust and emit heat in the process of radioactive decay. Beyond just rescuing the concept of evolution, radioactivity allows more reliable quantitative estimates of the geologic times involved in the evolutionary processes.

Prior to the discovery of radioactivity, the geological dating process was very difficult and uncertain (Ref. 14.3). Estimates were made of the earth's age (some of them surprisingly good) based both on the evolution time of species and on the erosion and sedimentation rates of geologic stratas. Halley (after whom the comet was named) even tried to fix the age of earth from the salt content of the ocean. Assuming that the oceans originally consisted of salt-free precipitation, and taking into account how salt is washed out of the earth into the ocean, this method led to estimates of 700 million to 2.4 billion years. But some independent substantiation was needed for such projections.

In 1913 Joly and Rutherford proposed a more definitive way of determining the age of geological materials. The radioactive decay process of uranium is quite complicated, with many sequential steps, but ultimately the U^{238} isotope decays into Pb^{206}, with a halflife of 4.5 billion years. This means that out of a million U^{238} atoms, only $\frac{1}{2}$ million will be left after 4.5 billion years (the other $\frac{1}{2}$ million having turned into Pb^{206}); after 9 billion years, only $\frac{1}{4}$ million U^{238} atoms will be left (the other $\frac{3}{4}$ million will have become Pb^{206}); after 13.5 billion years, only 125,000 U^{238} atoms will be left; etc. Such decay processes are described by the law of exponential decay and are characterized by a halflife. The age of geological deposits which contain uranium can therefore be measured by determining how much Pb^{206} has been produced in them; i.e., if we measure the lead-to-uranium ratio in such deposits, we can extract the date on which the rock crystallized. Actually the measuring process is not quite so simple, because various other uranium isotopes also decay into lead isotopes. But all these complications can be accounted for. This technique gives a maximum age for the earth's crust of about 2 billion years.

More reliable ways of dating geologic times are through the use of either the decay of Rb^{87} (rubidium) into Sr^{87} (strontium) with a halflife of 60 billion years, or of A^{40} (argon) into K^{40} (potassium) with a halflife of 1.3 billion years. With these techniques the oldest earth rocks are determined to be about 2.8 billion years old.

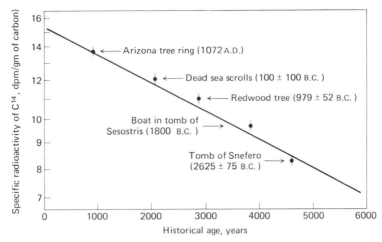

Fig. 14.1   Predicted versus observed radioactivity of carbon samples of known age. (Data from Ref. 14.2.)

Of course, the existence of the earth predates these crystallized rocks by a large period. Stony meteorites, which might be expected to represent some cataclysmic event on the earth, seem to have a maximum age of about 4.5 billion years. At that time, the earth's core and mantle probably separated, and then about 1.7 billion years later, the crust hardened. One of the most interesting series of experiments being performed on the Apollo lunar rock samples consists of such dating measurements. The question is how the age of the moon compares with that of the earth. Such information will hopefully, in turn, reveal more about the history of the earth.

CARBON-14 DATING

Perhaps, the most exciting contribution of the dating technique is to archeology through the radio-carbon or carbon-14 technique. This technique consists of measuring the relative fraction of radioactive C^{14} in the total carbon content of the sample which is to be dated. It hinges on our knowledge of the origin of this C^{14}. C^{14} has a halflife of about 5600 years, and is constantly being produced in the atmosphere by cosmic rays producing secondary neutrons, which in turn react with nitrogen. From there it circulates until it is homogeneously mixed with the stable carbon(C^{12}), so that in the long run the air has a constant fraction of C^{14}—enough so that in one gram ($\frac{1}{28}$th of an ounce) of carbon in the air there are about 15 C^{14} atoms decaying each minute. Since air is involved in photosynthesis, the carbon in living plants will then also contain this ratio of C^{14} atoms (the C^{14} is chemically identical to stable carbon). However, when a plant is cut, it will stop recirculating its carbon, and gradually the C^{14} in it will decay. Carbon dating thus consists of extracting all the carbon from a sample of the material of interest and measuring the radioactivity (and hence the number of C^{14} atoms) left in it.

Figure 14.1 shows the usefulness and accuracy of this method for various samples whose ages are known from other information. To give an example: when Pharaoh Sneferu died in 3000 B.C., he had some supporting beams incorporated into his grave. When analyzed for C^{14}, they were found to have only 55% the number of C^{14} atoms of a similar contemporary carbon sample. The estimated archeological age of 5000 years agrees with this fraction. This carbon-dating technique has a wide range of usefulness. Hammurabi's reign can be fixed to within 100 years; the period of the cliff dwellers in New Mexico can be determined quite well; from the remains of the trees pushed over by the furthest reaches of the glaciers in Wisconsin, the last glacial age has been found to be much more recent (about 11,000 years ago) than thought earlier; it is now known from C^{14} studies that man had entered the New World by 9000 B.C., and had penetrated to extreme South America within 1000 to 2000 years. And if ever a bootlegger should claim that his "corn juice" is just alcohol bought from a petroleum distillery, it would be very easy to disprove this. The presence of C^{14} in the juice would mean that it cannot be from petroleum; petroleum which has been out of contact with the air's carbon pool for millions of years would have no C^{14} atoms left in it.

OTHER DATING TECHNIQUES

There are many other dating procedures. As indicated at the beginning of this chapter, one of these provides the answer to the question: how old is a given wine? The test involves the measurement of the tritium content of the wine, where tritium is the radioactive hydrogen isotope H^3. Just like C^{14}, tritium is also produced by cosmic rays and mixes with the ordinary hydrogen in all water. Once wine is bottled, the tritium decays with a halflife of 12.5 years. Wine from a Spanish galleon should not be at all radioactive.

Even stable isotopes can provide valuable information. It is known, for example, that there have been many ice advances and recessions in the recent past; these might be expected to be closely related to man's emergence to a position of dominance. Geologists are fairly well agreed now that there have been four ice ages in the last 300,000 years. In fixing the times of these ages quantitatively, the question is essentially a matter of determining the average temperature for the last 300,000 years. One of the ways of fixing the dates of the ice ages involves the ratio of the stable isotopes O^{18} to O^{16} in *foraminifera*, a single-celled water organism (e.g., Ref. 14.4). Harold C. Urey found that in processes such as evaporation or biological secretion, there tends to be a slight difference in the movement of various isotopes of the same element simply because of their different nuclear mass. In the foraminifera, this ratio of O^{18} to O^{16} depends on the temperature of the surrounding water; one degree centigrade ($1.8°F$) makes a difference of about $\frac{2}{100}$ of one percent in this ratio in the carbonate of these organisms. And from such isotopic temperature analyses in deep-core samples of the ocean floor, it is actually possible to determine the dates of the four ice ages.

SUMMARY

Although the particulateness of nature was proposed as long ago as ancient Greece, it was only during the 20th century that the unraveling into constituent particles could be done quantitatively, in a consensus way. Various fascinating phenomena, such as natural and artificial radioactivity and nuclear transmutation, were discovered in the process. And from the very beginning, nuclear physics, particularly studies of radioactivity, found immediate applications in other disciplines, as illustrated by the isotopic dating techniques used in the "hard" science of geology and in the "soft" sciences of archeology and anthropology. Early nuclear physics was very high in scientific merit. And to the extent that the origin of man is a humanistic concern, these applications even span the "two-culture" gap.

REFERENCES

Prime reference

14.1 P. M. Hurley, *How Old Is the Earth?*, New York: Doubleday Anchor Book 55, 1959.

Interesting reading

14.2 W. F. Libby, *Radiocarbon Dating*, Chicago: University of Chicago Press, 1955, 2nd Edition.

14.3 F. E. Zeuner, *Dating the Past*, London: Methuen & Co., 1959, 4th Edition.

14.4 G. E. Hutchinson, *The Itinerant Ivory Tower*, New Haven: Yale University Press, 1955; "Time, Temperature and the Birth of Aphrodite," pp. 6–18.

14.5 G. Gamow, *Biography of Physics*, (Ref. 6.4); pp. 272–294 on the science of this chapter.

14.6 M. Renault, *The King Must Die* and *The Bull from the Sea*; any one of several editions; literature based on myth and archeology.

QUESTIONS FOR DISCUSSION

1. In 1937 the Carlsbad caverns were uranium-dated as 3 million years old. Now the guides say the caverns are 3 million and 35 years old. Is this a proper statement?

2. So we now know when Hammurabi lived, when man developed, and how old the earth is. Who cares?

3. Both the Industrial Revolution and the nuclear-bomb tests have affected the future of the C^{14} dating method. How?

15 | SCIENCE AND MODERN ART

Blue is the masculine principle, robust and spiritual. Yellow is the feminine principle, gentle, serene, sensual. Red is matter, brutal and heavy.

Franz Marc

The suffering of a man is of the same interest to us as the suffering of an electric lamp, which, with spasmodic starts shrieks out the most heartrending expression of color.

Umberto Boccioni

Yellow light has a wavelength of 0.000052 centimeters.

Textbook on optics

This chapter contains an examination of the response of painters and allied artists to science and technology in the early 20th century. The German Expressionists exemplify a retreat to an organic nature, while the Italian Futurists represent an exploration of the feelings induced by modern technology. The Bauhaus is presented as an example of a successful fusion of art and technology.

INTRODUCTION

This chapter will explore the impact of science and technology on painters and architects during the first third of this century. Needless to say, it is not very easy to establish any direct connection between these very different human activities. In addition, the approach and interpretation will necessarily be quite personal and subjective. Since there is then the possibility that I may be try-

ing too hard to make the facts fit a preconceived conclusion, this whole discussion must not be taken too seriously. The overall objective will be to try to outline possible artistic responses to science and technology and, in the process, to convey the atmosphere in which the modern scientific revolution was taking place.

TECHNOLOGY AND ART: 1900–1933

The paintings I like best date from the period 1900-1933. My two favorite paintings were painted in 1914; *Three Riders*, by Wassily Kandinsky, and *Tyrol*, by Franz Marc. I have at times wondered why my preference should lie there. One guess is that this is so because this period contains many varied responses to the ever-increasing pervasiveness of science and technology.

Science has always had some interaction with painting; Goethe with his *Theory of Colors* is a prime example of this. There was, of course, a great change in painting in the later part of the 19th century due in part to the introduction of photography, which eliminated the need for painting as a faithful record of the visible (see, e.g., Ref. 15.4). Painting then became more and more a subjective and ultimately nonrepresentational picture of what the artist felt rather than a picture of the objects which he saw. The Impressionists were in some ways the forerunners of this subjectivity. Georges Seurat, for example, studied the separation of white light into its component colors and found that color mixing could be done by the eye as well as directly on the canvas; thus his pointillism consisted of putting small spots of pure color on the painting and letting the observer's eye and brain carry out the fusion. Analysis of the observer's role in the visual process was carried even further by Van Gogh, particularly in his last pure-color pictures of 1888-90. The subjective trend then went through the French Fauvists (wild beasts), like André Derain, to the German Expressionists like Marc, Kandinsky, and Ernst L. Kirchner, and the Italian Futurists like Umberto Boccioni and Gino Severini. It has continued with the Cubists like Pablo Picasso, Georges Braque, and Fernand Leger and on to Bauhaus painters like Klee and Fein-

◄ **Fig. 15.1** *Lyrisches* by Wassily Kandinsky (1911). (Photo courtesy of Museum Boymans-van Beuningen, Rotterdam.)

inger. Contemporary with the latter painters is the art-artisan movement of the Bauhaus following the First World War, and the architecture of Le Corbusier, Mies van der Rohe, and Frank Lloyd Wright. All these movements put more and more of the painter's subjective impressions into the paintings, in particular his reaction to the increasingly more technological surroundings. And the three movements of the Expressionists, the Futurists, and the Bauhaus are particularly interesting because they reveal the three alternate reactions of retreat, absorption, and integration.

EXPRESSIONISM

In Germany the Expressionistic movement after 1900, such as the Blaue Reiter in Munich, reacted to science and technology by retreating to an organic nature, by painting landscapes and animals with background of fantasy.

The attitude in 1912 of the Russian-born painter Kandinsky (Fig. 15.1) may be characterized by his concern with the human soul:

> On the basis of a deeply felt criticism of the materialistic structure of the contemporary world, he strove to ferret out and combat every form of materialism in art. The modern sciences had transmuted the material substance of things into symbols of energy; in painting Matisse had liberated colour from its function of signifying objects and giving it a spiritual significance. Picasso had done the same for form. For Kandinsky these were 'great signs, pointing to a great goal.' From all this he drew his own conclusion: 'The harmony of colours and forms can be based on only one thing: a purposive contact with the human soul.' The expressive resonance of pure coloured forms provided the painter with a means of making visible the inner resonance of things, their vibration in the human soul. The vibrations of the soul can be raised to the surface and made visible by pure pictorial harmonies uncluttered by objective or metaphoric images, just as they are made audible by the pure sounds of music. . . . These were the ideas that moved Kandinsky's friends to cast off their ties with the images of the visible world and to discern the reflections of a higher world in the responsive stirrings of their psyche. For these ideas did not revolve exclusively round 'art,'

Fig. 15.2   Jumping Ponies by Franz Marc (1913). (Photo courtesy of Bernard S. Myers.)

but were embedded in a religious intimation of an encompassing Being, at the centre of which, between the earthly things of nature and the transcendent realities above them, stood man, endowed with antennae that enabled him to enter into communication with the whole. (Ref. 15.5, p. 117)

So Kandinsky retained a sense of fairy-tale fantasy, combined it with the resonances of colors in the soul, and by 1914 was able to break away completely from any representational content in his paintings.

Marc was even more strongly motivated by a dread of the technological world, by a fear of losing any bonds with the reality of nature. So to him the key symbols were animals; he felt that animals were embedded in the great rhythms of nature (Fig. 15.2). The colors of his animals, as in the *Tiger* or the *Blue Horses*, always represented the spiritual essence of their nature. As his paintings became more abstract, nature and world were not excluded, but rather transposed into the wider dimension of the whole modern spirit. Along with Marc at Verdun in 1916, the whole Expressionist movement in painting died in World War I. But its spirit continued in many other fields, particularly in architecture, as will be pointed out later.

FUTURISM

The Italian parallel to Expressionism was Futurism, lasting from about 1908 to 1914. "The Futurists were not only the first artists to take cognizance of the dynamism of a technological society, but they also produced works of art of extraordinary emotional impact. They translated the kinetic rhythms and the confused, intense sensations of modern life into potent visual form." (Ref. 15.1, p. 7.) Fillippo Tommaso Marinetti in Milan in 1909 wrote the founding manifesto, which cried in part "burn the museum," "drain the canals of Venice," as a protest against the older styles of painting. Beyond this protest was a new ideal in art. The modern world was to be typified by the automobile with its violently pulsing, noisy life; the staggering speed of this mechanical achievement was to replace the classical characterizations of the mythical horse Pegasus. As Marinetti put it:

We declare that the world's splendour has been enriched by a new beauty; the beauty of speed. A racing motor car, its frame adorned with great pipes, like snakes with explosive breath ... a roaring motor-car, which looks as though running on shrapnel, is more beautiful than the *Victory of Samothrace*. ... We shall sing of the great crowds in the excitement of labour, pleasure and rebellion ... of bridges leaping like gymnasts over the diabolical cutlery of sunbathed rivers ... (From the Sackville exhibition catalog, London, March 1912, as quoted in Ref. 15.1, p. 124.)

The painter Severini said:

We choose to concentrate our attention on things in motion, because our modern sensibility is particularly qualified to grasp the idea of speed. Heavy powerful motor cars rushing through the streets of our cities, dancers reflected in the fairy ambiance of light and color, airplanes flying above the heads of the excited throng. ... These sources of emotion satisfy our sense of a lyric and dramatic universe, better than do two pears and an apple. (From the Marlborough Gallery catalogue, London, April 1913, as quoted in Ref. 15.1, p. 11.)

And Boccioni:

We cannot forget that the tick-tock and the moving hands of a clock, the in-and-out of a piston in a cylinder, the opening and closing of two cogwheels with the continual appearance and disappearance of their square steel cogs, the fury of a flywheel or the turbine of a propeller, are all plastic and pictorial elements of which a Futurist work in sculpture must take account. The opening and closing of a valve creates a rhythm just as beautiful but infinitely newer than the blinking of an animal eyelid. (Translated by R. Chase, as quoted in Ref. 15.1, pp. 131–132.)

The Italian Futurists were fighting estrangement from the world—the lonely isolation of the individual that was not only the inheritance of the artist but a common threat to modern man. They wanted their art to restore to man a sense of daring, an assertive will rather than submissive acceptance. "We want to re-enter life," they said, and to them life meant action. "Dynamism" was the magic word to them. The Futurists wanted to put the spectator in the center of the picture. "We Futurists," said Carlo Carra, "strive with the force of intuition to insert ourselves into the midst of things in such a fashion that our 'self' forms a single complex with their

identities." This is like the Expressionists, but with more emphasis on the mechanical innovations rather than on an escape into the animal world. And their works bear such titles as *Cyclist*, by Boccioni (Fig. 15.3), *Abstract Speed—Wake of Speeding Automobile*, by Giacomo Balla, *Expansion of Lights*, by Severini, and *The Street Light—Study of Light* (Fig. 15.4), by Balla. Dynamic action is indicated by multiple images, by rays of light interrupted by action, and by the conflict of separated colors. Balla, who was interested in all scientific matters, was so fascinated by astronomy that the vision of the planet Mercury passing before the sun as it might be seen through a telescope served in 1914 as inspiration for one of his happiest series of paintings. "The form/force," said Boccioni, "is, with its centrifugal direction, the potentiality of real form"; obviously the language of the Futurists itself owes debts to the sciences. The confrontation with technology is direct; man clearly must bend technology to his own will.

This attempt by the Futurists to absorb technology into art also came to an end with World War I. To them in 1914 the war promised to be the ultimate awakening and unifying force. Several of them signed up in the bicycle messenger corps; and some died in the war, terminating the movement, a movement which in any case could by its very nature probably not have survived the postwar period.

THE POSTWAR BAUHAUS MOVEMENT

After the war, there was a great confrontation of society with cruel reality; in Germany, for example, by 1924 it took a wheelbarrow full of billion-mark bills to buy a loaf of bread. In this atmosphere there could no longer be a complete retreat from technology. And an institution developed in 1919—the Bauhaus, or House of Building—which attempted to unite the arts and industry/technology. The Bauhaus was founded by Walter Gropius in Weimar, the residence long before of Goethe, and the place where the constitution of the new German Republic was drawn up after the war. Although the Bauhaus movement included many artists, such as Kandinsky and Klee, who had

◄ **Fig. 15.3** *Study for Dynamic Force of a Cyclist II* by Umberto Boccioni (1913). (Photo courtesy of Yale University Art Gallery, gift of Collection Société Anonyme.)

Fig. 15.4 *Street Light* by Giacomo Balla (1909), oil on canvas, 68-3/4 ×
45-1/4″. (Photo courtesy of the Collection of the Museum of Modern Art,
New York, Hillman Periodicals Fund.)

been involved in the Expressionist movement before the war, it was started by Gropius to become a consulting art center for industry and the trades. In every subject the students were to be trained by two teachers, an artist and a master craftsman. And these students, once familiar with science and economics, quickly began to unite creative imagination with a practical knowledge of craftsmanship, and thus to develop a new sense of functional design.

Not that the Bauhaus was the first to try the combination of art and design. There were, for example, in the middle of the 19th century attempts in Great Britain to provide this kind of synthesis. But those were failures because the products were not mass-producible. Somehow the genius of Gropius avoided this problem at the Bauhaus. The artistic instruction included the theory of form and color, mathematics, and physics; rigorous analyses of lines and planes and space were attempted by Klee, Kandinsky, and Laszlo Moholy-Nagy. The technical skills were produced both by workshops and by industrial experience. The students were not just idealists, but included many veterans of the war who were searching for a meaning of life. It is this contact with reality, through industrial work, for example, which made the Bauhaus so successful.

The fate of the Bauhaus was symbolic of its time. In 1925, when the political climate in Germany was particularly bad, the Bauhaus left conservative Weimar and moved to Dessau. In 1928 Walter Gropius left; in 1933 overnight the Nazi regime locked the doors. The impact of the Bauhaus—of the fusion of art with science/technology—is, however, still with us. Our modern tubular metal chairs are frequently based on Bauhaus designs, as are many of our advertisements, fabrics, and much of our architecture.

OTHER EXAMPLES OF SCIENCE AND ART

There are many other interesting traces of the sciences in art and architecture during the postwar period. Worthy of special note are three:

1. There is the Expressionistic architect Erich Mendelsohn, who in the period 1917–1920 constructed the Einstein tower near Potsdam as an observatory to run tests on the general theory of

relativity, fusing Expressionism with the grandeur of the Einsteinian concept (see Fig. 16.1.).

2. There is the architect Rudolf Steiner, who in his younger years
   edited Goethe's works and whose views were hence strongly
   colored by Goethe's views on science. These viewpoints are incorporated into Steiner's Expressionistic buildings Goethenaum I
   and II.

And, finally,

3. Le Corbusier took mathematical proportions along the lines of
   Pythagoras, and the idea of modularity from crystallography, to
   form his concept of a modulator—a series of proportional sizes
   based on man to build up all dimensions of buildings. While he
   used technological products, Le Corbusier's architecture was very
   much man-oriented.

Note the parallel in the interest of Goethe as a poet-scientist and in
Einstein as a philosopher-scientist.

We could also speak of Cubism in painting, with its attempts to
modularize the areas of paintings, which then led to the work Mondrian
and his squares and rectangles. As a final example there is the painter
Leger. Before the First World War he tried many styles of painting,
none of which seemed satisfactory. Then came his wartime service
in an engineering unit, where he came in close contact with men who
felt at home with technology. Their optimism about the machine
world inspired him:

> He felt that as an artist his task was to discover forms of expres-
> sion appropriate to modern life. The shining, precise, abstract
> beauty of the machine provided a visual point of departure. He
> understood that the mechanical thing possessed a representative
> value as the truest creation of modern civilisation and that the
> images derived from it could become evocative emblems of the
> modern industrial world. (Ref. 15.5, p. 253)

After the war he integrated industrial objects into his art as motifs
to evoke modern esthetics. The gleaming machine, the concreteness
of wheels, and the dynamism of repeated motion—all these are
reflected in Leger's works (Fig. 15.5).

Fig. 15.5 Three Women by Fernand Léger (1921), oil on canvas, 72-1/4 × 99″. (Photo courtesy of the Collection of the Museum of Modern Art, New York, Mrs. Simon Guggenheim Fund.)

SUMMARY

We might sum up this chapter as follows. Adding to the whole atmosphere of the period 1900 to 1933 was a confrontation between the individual artistic intellect and science/technology. This confrontation profoundly influenced the arts of the period. Some artists, like the German Expressionists, rebelled against technology by retreating to a more organic view of nature, by making something fairy-tale-like of the technology; for example, in Expressionist pictures, railroads always look like toys. Other artists, like the Italian Futurists, tried to absorb technology rather than confronting or avoiding it; for example, the Futurist's railroads look like dynamic machines. Neither of these cases necessarily involved a deep understanding of the basic scientific trends. Nonetheless, these were profound cultural reactions to the new science-based industrial age. The third, and most successful approach, was the attempt by the Bauhaus to totally integrate the arts and industry. The resultant impact is still enormously visible in all of industrial designing. Nonviolent confrontations of the two cultures can indeed be quite productive.

REFERENCES

Prime references

15.1 J. C. Taylor, *Futurism*, New York: The Museum of Modern Art, distributed by Doubleday and Co. of Garden City, New York, 1961. Many of the illustrations are Futurists' paintings.

15.2 D. Sharp, *Modern Architecture and Expressionism*, London: Longmans, Green and Co., Ltd., 1966; Chapters IX and XI have Expressionist architecture illustrations, including the Goethenaum I and II.

Interesting reading

15.3 B. S. Myers, *The German Expressionists*, New York: Frederick A. Praeger, 1966. Has many Expressionist illustrations.

15.4 A. Scharf, *Art and Photography*, London: Allen Lane, 1968. Discusses how photography modified art.

15.5   W. Haftman, *Painting in the Twentieth Century*, Vols. I and II, New York: A Praeger, 1965. Has Expressionist illustrations.

15.6   H. Bayer, W. Gropius, and I. Gropius, Eds., *Bauhaus 1919–1928*, Boston: C. T. Bransford Co., 1959, 3rd printing.

15.7   G. Kepes, *Language of Vision*, Paul Theobald and Co., 1959.

15.8   G. Kepes, Ed., *Module, Proportion, Symmetry, Rhythm*, New York: George Brazillier, 1966.

15.9   W. Scheiding, *Crafts of the Weimar Bauhaus*, New York: Reinhold Publishing Co., 1967.

15.10 L. Hirschfeld-Mack, *The Bauhaus*, Groyden, Victoria, Australia: Longmans, Ltd., 1963.

QUESTIONS FOR DISCUSSION

1. It has been suggested that the impression we have of people's faces is actually a time average, and that this is the reason why paintings are better portraits than photographs (which record one instant). Is this indeed the difference?

2. Painters use such words as "resonance" and "vibration." Do they know the scientific meaning of what they are saying? Does it matter whether they understand these words?

3. What is Op art? Does contemporary art include a response to science?

4. Is the artist's response primarily to science or to technology?

5. Should we make artists study physics?

6. Why do artists continually refer to the science of Goethe rather than to that of Newton? Why do artists such as Dali make portraits particularly of Einstein?

16 | SCIENCE AND POLITICAL IDEOLOGIES

By an application of the theory of relativity to the taste of the reader, today in Germany I am called a German man of science and in England I am represented as a Swiss Jew. If I come to be regarded as a "bête noire" the description will be reversed, and I shall become a Swiss Jew for the Germans and a German for the English.

Albert Einstein

The interaction between science and the political ideologies in Germany between 1914 and 1945 is examined, with the impact on Einstein as an illustrative example. The intellectual migration of 1933-38 out of Germany is described and discussed.

INTRODUCTION

During a recent campus crisis about the political activism of the university as a whole, a history professor maintained that any institutional political activity was inappropriate. As support for this argument he cited the example of the German universities, whose political involvement after World War I appeared to him to have been instrumental in Hitler's rise to power. Other knowledgeable people have argued exactly the opposite; namely, that there was not enough involvement by the universities in the German political process. Exactly the same charges can, and have been, leveled at the operation of science before and during the Nazi era. Scientists became too involved in conflicts about political ideology without an adequate understanding of real political processes. This led to disastrous consequences for both science and politics.

Such interactions between science and politics are, of course, not restricted to the Nazi period. In the United States, science is coupled to the political-economic system. There was the McCarthy period in the 1950s, when a significant portion of science was hampered in its normal activities (see Chapter 21); that was, however, primarily due to an attack on the political beliefs of individual scientists rather than on their scientific ideas. A prime example of a disciplinary interaction between science and a political doctrine has occurred in the Soviet Union. Marxism was founded in the 19th century as a scientific-political ideology, primarily for use in economics, but the concept of dialectical materialism has been applied even to physics. This will also be considered somewhat further in Chapter 21.

But the most impressive case of repression of the sciences by a political ideology occurred in 1933 when Germany came under the control of Adolf Hitler and his Nazi party. There took place then a great intellectual migration, which included a larger number of excellent physicists such as Einstein. Both Great Britain and the United States have benefited greatly from this migration, and Germany has taken longer to recover from these losses than from the physical destruction of the Second World War. Such concepts as Germany physics (as opposed to Jewish physics) were introduced, and special political adjustments had to be made to allow the use of Einstein's mass-energy-equivalence formula in calculations related to physical phenomena. And this all came about because science attempted to insert itself into political ideology, with the consequence that the political system in turn had to control science.

SCIENCE AND POLITICS IN WORLD WAR I

It will be profitable to start the examination of interactions between science and the Nazi ideology by picturing the political atmosphere in Europe, and particularly in Germany, prior to the Nazi takeover. A very illuminating illustration of this atmosphere will be the treatment Einstein received after he accepted an appointment in Berlin in 1913.

When the First World War broke out in 1914, the intellectual communities of the warring nations began to attack each other with "intellectual weapons" through propaganda. To emphasize the illegality and atrocity of the German invasion of Belgium, the Allies developed the contrast between the artistic Germany of Goethe and the military Germany of Bismarck. In response, 92 leading German representatives of the arts and sciences signed a manifesto which included the declaration "German culture and German militarism are identical." Roentgen, for example, signed the statement; and when Einstein refused to sign it, he was considered almost a traitor.

This intellectual conflict ruined the internationalism of the community of science. For example, a group of German physicists circulated a memorandum to their colleagues in which they urged them to avoid citing the work of English physicists except when absolutely necessary; the claim was that the scientific work of all Englishmen was on a very low level. There were attempts to prove "scientifically" that there existed national characteristics in physics and that there should consequently be as little exchange of knowledge as possible to keep these national unities and purities intact. German science was claimed to be particularly thorough and profound in contrast to the rationalistic sophistries of the French and the empirical shallowness of the British. In exchange, the French felt that the so-called German thoroughness was in fact pure pedantry. Even the British were quite upset about the willingness of German scientists to associate themselves with militarism. This kind of character assassination in science was to profoundly influence discussions of Einstein's relativity theories after World War I.

EINSTEIN AND POLITICS

The period after World War I was depressing in Germany, where the loss of the war combined with political turmoil and disastrous inflation. German science, in additon, suffered from an international boycott. In an effort to stabilize their lives, more and more people were driven to search for a metaphysical basis for their views of the world. And, somehow, Einstein's theory of relativity became very much involved in this drive, in this pessimistic outlook which prevailed in Germany.

There were many nationalists in Germany who opposed the theory of relativity for a variety of reasons. Some made Einstein one of the scapegoats for the German defeat in World War I. After all, weren't the bolshevistic Jews and the pacifists responsible for the "stab in the back" which ended the war, and didn't Einstein come out strongly for Jewish Zionism? Representative of the views of the group which complained of the war loss was an article entitled "Bolshevistic Physics":

> Hardly had it become clear to the horrified German people that they had been frightfully duped by the lofty politics of Professor Wilson and swindled with the aid of the professorial nimbus, when a new professorial achievement was again being commended to the simple Germans with the greatest enthusiasm and ecstasy as the pinnacle of scientific research. And unfortunately even highly educated people fell for this—all the more so since Professor Einstein, the alleged new Copernicus, numbers university teachers among his admirers. Yet, without mincing words, we are dealing here with an infamous scientific scandal that fits very appropriately into the picture presented by this most tragic of all political periods. In the last analysis one cannot blame workers for being taken in by Marx, when German professors allow themselves to be misled by Einstein. (As quoted in Ref. 16.1, p. 160.)

A second group involved in such anti-Einstein campaigns was composed of several physicists who had a reputation for precise experiments and who could not understand how someone could become famous for only a creative imagination. Such an imagination began to be considered un-Aryan. This group acquired some respectability and force through the support of the Nobel prize physicist Phillip Lenard (an early member of the Nazi party). Lenard was so nationalistic that he even forced all the laboratories at the University of Heidelberg to rename the unit of electric current, named an Ampere after a Frenchman, to a Weber after a German.

The third group of anti-Einsteinians consisted of philosophers whose systems were in disagreement with the theory of relativity; who read into it metaphysical implications which were not really

Fig. 16.1 Einstein Tower, Potsdam, Germany, 1920–21. An astronomical observatory designed by Erich Mendelsohn. (Photo courtesy of the Akademie der Künste, Berlin.)

there. Here again the idea was that the Nordic-Aryan philosophers investigated the more profound aspects of nature rather than presenting mere superficial viewpoints.

Einstein was disturbed by this atmosphere; when asked whether he might leave Berlin, he answered:

> Would such a decision be so amazing? My situation is like that of a man who is lying in a beautiful bed, where he is being tortured by bedbugs. (As quoted in Ref. 16.1, p. 162.)

However, at the request of the Prussian Minister of Education, he became a German citizen as a gesture of support for the constantly threatened federal government. It is hard to describe this atmosphere adequately. For example, in 1922 the German Foreign Minister Rathenau was assassinated by rightists; he had been stamped as a Jewish Bolshevist for concluding the Rapallo peace treaty with the Soviet Union. For his burial, a day of mourning was declared, but Lenard insisted on holding his classes—with student rioting as a consequence. In the eyes of many, the fight against Einstein's theory of relativity became associated with the struggle against the Republic. And rumors spread that Einstein was marked for future assassination by the extreme rightists. Even Einstein's travels resulted in nothing but controversy. When he gave talks in France, he became a symbol in the Dreyfus controversy, and in addition, was labeled as one "whose people killed our sons." Then, when he returned to Germany, he was attacked for being conciliatory toward the French. And, if we keep in mind that his theory had been characterized as Bolshevism in physics, it is not surprising that a tremendous uproar arose after it was reported that he was planning to give a talk in Moscow.

THE INTELLECTUAL MIGRATION

In January of 1933 Hitler and his Nazi party took power in Germany. For science the handwriting had long been on the wall concerning the plans of the new regime. As E. Krick, a German pedagogical leader had said:

> It is not science that must be restricted, but rather the scientific investigators and teachers; only scientifically talented men who have pledged their entire personality to the nation, to the racial conception of the world, and to the German mission will teach and carry on research at the German universities. (As quoted in Ref. 16.1, p. 228.)

The purge started just as soon as a definition of non-Aryan could be practically developed (i.e., less than three months later). The book *The Intellectual Migration* tells some of the unbelievable tales of those days; the experience of Hans Bethe of Cornell University is only one of many possible examples:

> On the first of April [1933] they had the first boycott of Jewish stores and about the same time they published a law according to

which anyone who had one Jewish grandmother could not hold an official appointment. Well, since I had a Jewish mother, not only a grandmother, it was clear that this meant me and that sooner or later I would have to leave. I didn't expect it to be quite so soon. I had a somewhat interesting experience one day in April when I got a letter from one of the two people who were taking their doctor's degree with me, saying that he had read in a small town paper in Wuerttemberg that I had been dismissed —and what should *he* do? This was the first news I had.

Then I wrote a letter to the professor of experimental physics who had been very friendly to me and who had indicated that he liked my work and would like me to remain there. I got back a very stiff letter saying that presumably the lectures in theoretical physics would have to be arranged differently the next term. About a week after the first letter from the student, I finally got a letter from the minister of education of the state of Wuerttemberg, saying that I was dismissed according to the law effective the first of May but that the salary for May could still be paid to me, and that was that. (As quoted in Ref. 16.3, p. 203.)

On May 19, 1933, the newspaper the *Manchester Guardian* could already devote one full page to a list of 196 professors dismissed from their posts in Germany due to race or politics, a list which was a veritable Who's Who. By 1936 the list contained more than 1600 names (Ref. 16.4). Hitler felt that if the dismissal of Jewish scientists meant the annihilation of contemporary Germany science, then Germany would have to do without science for a few years.

Einstein himself in 1933 accepted a post at the Princeton Institute for Advanced Studies. He resigned from the Prussian Academy of Sciences, saying that "a tolerant respect for any and every individual opinion" no longer existed in Germany. There followed an exchange of letters between Einstein and the Academy, which included such expressions as "atrocity-mongering," "anti-Semitism," "slandering," and "relapse into barbarism" (see Ref. 16.5, pp. 173-184).

Committees were set up in many countries to help the escaping intellectuals. They went primarily to Great Britain and the United States, but some made temporary stops along the way in France, Denmark, or Turkey, before the war forced them onward. There are some very revealing letters on record concerning these migrations, particularly one exchange in the journal *Nature* in 1934 between

Johannes Stark (a German Nobel prize physicist) and A. V. Hill (an English physiologist). Stark attempted to explain the reasons for the actions against Jewish scientists in Germany:

> The National-Socialist Government has introduced no measure which is directed against the freedom of scientific teaching and research; on the contrary, they wish to restore this freedom of research wherever it has been restricted by preceding governments. Measures brought in by the National-Socialist Government, which have affected Jewish scientists and scholars, are due only to the attempt to curtail the unjustifiable great influence exercised by the Jews. In Germany there were hospitals and scientific institutes in which the Jews had created a monopoly for themselves and in which they had taken possession of almost all academic posts. There were in addition, in all spheres of public life in Germany, Jews who had come into the country after the War from the east. This immigration had been tolerated and even encouraged by the Marxist government of Germany. (*Nature*, February 24, 1934, quoted for example in Ref. 16.6, pp. 222–224.)

The reply by Hill said in part:

> It is a fact, in spite of what he says, that many Jews, or part-Jews, have been dismissed from their posts in universities. . . . They have found it impossible . . . to carry on their work in Germany. Men of high standing do not, without cause, beg their colleagues in foreign countries for help. Whether they were "dismissed," or "retired," or "given leave," or merely forbidden to take pupils or to enter libraries or laboratories is another quibble: the result is the same. It is inconsistent with that "freedom of scientific teaching and research" which the German Government apparently is seeking to restore. (*Nature*, February 24, 1934, quoted for example in Ref. 16.6, pp. 222–224).

These refugees were not always received with total kindness. After all, this immigrant intellegentsia did not do any physically constructive work, and there was the economic crisis of the depression in 1933, with an inevitable competition for jobs. There were even attempts to discredit the refugees as immoral:

> How dare the 'nudist' [Bertrand] Russell and the 'refugee'

Einstein interfere in the family life of the United States? (As quoted in Ref. 16.1, pp. 276–277.)

But on the whole, the refugees fitted well, wanted to contribute, and were prepared to stay permanently and become an integral part of the host country.

THE NAZI ATTITUDE TOWARD SCIENCE

The basic attitude of the Nazi government toward science led to a condemnation of Einstein and allowed the definition of Jewish physics as opposed to a German physics; but it did permit technological applications of a discredited theory to remain and be fostered. It was a basically contradictory attitude. For example, Einstein was condemned on totally opposing grounds. On the one hand, his physics was too theoretical and not precise enough. In the foreword to his basic physics text, *German Physics* (Ref, 16.7), Lenard said:

> "German Physics?" one will ask.—I could just as readily have said Aryan physics or physics of the Nordic Race, physics of the founders of reality, of the truth seekers, physics of those who have founded the sciences.... Science is ... something fixed by race, by blood.

To Lenard, Jewish physics was characterized by Einstein, whose relativity theory was supposedly inconsistent with reality—as were the Jewish theories in general. (Incidentally, the publisher of Lenard's *Deutsche Physik* turned down my request for permission to quote several longer excerpts from the foreword to that book. He felt that these comments were made in the spirit of that time and now seemed ridiculous; that to publish these remarks would only serve to harm the reputation of a Nobel prize-winning physicist.) This alleged preference of the Jew for theoretical deliberations was contrasted with the striving of the Aryan German for concrete action. The Prussian Minister of Education, Rust, said in 1934: "National Socialism is not hostile to science, but only hostile to theories." There was the demand that German science restrict itself to service to the state and shy away from any philosophical generalizations which might interfere with the party philosophy.

But to the average Nazi philosopher, who understood little

physics, somehow Einstein's theories appeared to be materialistic and hence connected with Marxism. A lecturer to the National Socialist Student Association said:

> Einstein's theories could only have been greeted so joyfully by a generation that had already been raised and trained in materialistic modes of thought. On this account it would likewise have been unable to flourish in this way anywhere else but in the soil of Marxism, of which it is the scientific expression, just as this is true of cubism in the plastic arts and of the melodic and rhythmic barrenness of music in recent years. (As quoted in Ref. 16.1, p. 253.)

As Dr. Dietrich, one of the leading Nazi propagandists, said: "We require that the mechanistic world picture be replaced by the organismic world picture." The world "force" (or "Kraft" in German), as a romantic all-pervasive concept, was very much in use by the Nazis; and the Jews were accused of attacking the concept of this word. An article in the *Journal for General Science* said:

> The concept of force, which was introduced by Aryan scientists for the causal interpretation of changes in velocity, obviously arises from the personal experience of human labor, of manual creation, which has been and is the essential content of the life of Aryan man. The picture of the world that thus arose possessed in every detail the quality of visual clarity, from which arises the happy impression that it produces on related minds. All this changed fundamentally when the Jew seized the reins in natural science to an ever increasing degree.

> The Jew would not be himself if the characteristic feature of his attitude, just as everywhere else in science, were not the disintegration and destruction of Aryan construction. (As quoted in Ref. 16.1, p. 255.)

These are certainly conflicting comments on Einstein and his physics, and perhaps the beginning of Lenard's foreword (Ref. 16.7) tells the real tale; the Jews were simply incapable of being physicists:

> Einstein's theory of relativity offers us the clearest example of the dogmatic Jewish type of theory. It is headed by a dogma, the principle of the constancy of the velocity of light. In a

vacuum the velocity of light is supposed to have constant magnitude independent of the state of motion of the light sources and the observer. It is falsely asserted that this is a fact of experience. (As quoted in Ref. 16.1, p. 256.)

THE NAZI PRESERVATION OF APPLIED SCIENCE

The Nazi attack on theories specifically included the theory of relativity and, by implication, the equation $E = mc^2$, which is so useful in nuclear physics. Clearly the Nazi party philosophers had to do something to preserve applied science. This was accomplished in a manner which is very odd but which is in a general way similar to the means by which the Communist party in the U.S.S.R. solved its equivalent problem (Ref. 16.8). The compromise solution was worked out at two special conferences, held in 1940 and 1942, of party philosophers and scientists (Ref. 16.10). There theoretical physics was admitted to be an indispensable part of physics and the special theory of relativity was acknowledged as an experimentally verified fact. However, the credit for the theory was transferred as much as possible to earlier Aryan scientists; and the speculations on space and time were reserved for the party philosophers. In order to preserve the Nazi creed, some of the speculative cutting edge of science was dulled.

CONCLUSIONS

The period of 1914 to 1945 in Germany demonstrated how science may be faced with the demand that it conform to a political ideology. In this particular case, it appears that the scientists, as a part of the whole German intellectual community, had directly invoked the political ideology of nationalism. Somehow the concept of a nation as an organic whole produced a feeling of a political consensus among all the participants in such an idealistic political development. Consequently, it was difficult to become also involved in the compromises and nonconsensus decisions of the practical politics of a functioning republic. The constant walks in the woods (organic nature) which the German scientists were so fond of taking, the memberships in nationalistic youth movements where a spirit of an organic unity predominated, the many no-compromise splinter parties which made practical politics so difficult—all these indicated an inability of scientists, as well as other intellectuals, to engage in meaningful German politics. The result of the Nazi takeover was a control of science. It was a control in clear violation of the public-knowledge criterion of science. Instead of asking whether the science of a man was correct, the question became one of whether the science of a man agreed with the politics of the government. Since the politics were local, the science was inevitably forced into a local mold as well. This prevented any possible international consensus. In some sense, the scientists were then forced to be socially responsible to the political welfare of their respective nations.

REFERENCES

Prime references

16.1 P. Frank, *Einstein: His Life and Times*, New York: Alfred A. Knopf, 1957.

16.2 J. Haberer, *Politics and the Community of Science*, New York: Van Nostrand, 1969; Chapter 6, "The Politics of German Science in the Weimar Republic: 1918–1932," and Chapter 7, "Leadership and Crisis: The Response to National Socialist Policy: 1933–1938," pp. 103–162.

Interesting reading

16.3 D. Fleming and B. Bailyn, Eds., *The Intellectual Migration: Europe and America, 1930–1960*, Cambridge, Mass.: Harvard University Press, 1969.

16.4 E. Y. Hartshorne, Jr., *The German Universities and National Socialism*, Cambridge, Mass.: Harvard University Press, 1937.

16.5 A. Einstein, *The World as I See It* (translation by A. Harris of *Mein Weltbild*, 1933), New York: Covici-Friede Inc., 1934, pp. 173–184.

16.6 A. V. Hill, *The Ethical Dilemma of Science*, New York: Rockefeller Institute Press, 1960, pp. 205–235.

16.7 P. Lenard, *Deutsche Physik*, Munich: J. F. Lehmanns Verlag, 1936; Foreword.

16.8 B. Barber, *Science and the Social Order*, Glencoe Ill.: Free Press, 1952; "Science in Modern Society; Its Place in Liberal and in Authoritarian Society," pp. 60–83.

16.9 L. Fermi, *Atoms in the Family: My Life with Enrico Fermi*, Chicago: University of Chicago Press, 1954.

16.10 S. A. Goudsmit, *Alsos*, New York: Henry Schuman, 1947.

16.11 J. Needham, *History Is on Our Side*, New York: Macmillan Co., 1947, pp. 162–189.

16.12 A. Vavoulis and A. W. Colver, Eds., *Science and Society*, San Francisco: Holden-Day, 1966; Philip Frank, "Philosophical Uses of Science," pp. 141–155.

16.13 R. W. Clark, *Einstein: The Life and Times*, New York: The World Publishing Co., 1971.

QUESTIONS FOR DISCUSSION

1. Do we still have nationalism attached to science? After all, we go to the moon, and build high-energy accelerators to keep up with the Russians. Is this nationalism bad for science?

2. How can the theory of relativity be attacked by people of all political persuasion?

3. Why did Einstein particularly suffer political attacks? Should he have kept out of all political activities, such as Zionism, in order to protect his physics?

4. Is it possible for a government to selectively destroy basic science and yet maintain applied science and technology?

5. Did Nazi Germany accomplish the separation of basic science from applied science successfully?

6. Is there really something unscientific about viewing a nation or the world as an organism?

17 | THE SCIENTISTS GO TO WAR: BUILDING THE ATOMIC BOMB

Here [at Los Alamos] the government has assembled the world's largest collection of crackpots.

General Leslie R. Groves

I believe your people actually want to make a bomb.

Enrico Fermi to J. Robert Oppenheimer at Los Alamos

If the radiance of a thousand suns were to burst into the sky, that would be like the splendor of the Mighty One.

Quotation from *Bhagava-Gita*, remembered by Oppenheimer on seeing explosion of the first atomic bomb

In this chapter the why and how of the scientists' push for the atomic bomb is discussed. The history of the Manhattan Project to the explosion of the first nuclear weapon in 1945 is presented.

INTRODUCTION

Unquestionably the Second World War induced a very significant change in the relationship between science and society, and particularly between physics and the military establishment. For the first time, scientists both proposed and designed major weapon systems. Not only were these proposals brought all the way to fruition within the short period of the war; they (particularly radar) also helped the Allies win the war. These successes brought with them the entry of scientists into the high councils of the nation and changed the public view of science.

Two major trends will appear in the course of looking at, particularly, the atomic-bomb project. Both are related to the disciplinary interaction of science and society. First, it seems that whenever the scientists had to step outside their specialized fields of study (when, for example, they had to act as administrators), they frequently showed an inability to compromise. This sometimes actually held back progress on technological developments. The success of J. Robert Oppenheimer seems to have been due to an ability to overcome this problem. Secondly, the scientists were directly responsible for the development of the atomic bomb, including the very act of proposing the weapon, as well as building it, all in secret. Both these aspects raise the question of the extent to which the "atomic scientists" were acting as scientists in this project and whether there was something in their training which made it difficult for them to step outside their scientific role—which made it difficult for them to understand the administrative necessity for technological, economic, and political compromise.

SCIENCE IN EARLIER WARS

To appreciate the character of the changes which took place in World War II, it might be interesting to look at the role of science in World War I. That war also was a gigantic affair. And since it came in the middle of the modern scientific revolution, one might have expected science, and particularly physics, to have been mobilized for it. But this was not the case. Perhaps the most telling comment on the attitude of the war departments was the reply made in 1916 by the American Secretary of War when the American Chemical Society volunteered its services in the cause of democracy; he turned down the offer with, "We already have a chemist." The First World War was characterized by technologies which tried to take advantage of industrial skills rather than scientific skills. Edison was representative of the type of person who could make contributions to that war; he also made an antiscientific comment when one solitary physicist was added to a naval consulting board of which he was chairman: "We might have one mathematical fellow in case we have to calculate something out." Edison was certainly conscious of both science and technology, but he approached them largely from an empirical viewpoint.

Perhaps the biggest change in World War I was in supplies and sanitation, because for the first time huge armies could be moved and supplied with ease and could be kept alive and reasonably healthy. The developments from Pasteur onward allowed food preservation; and diseases could be prevented with innoculations. This made an enormous difference. In Napoleon's 1813 campaign, for example, his army was initially made up of 500,000 men. After three battles, only about 170,000 men were left; the estimate is that there were 107,000 battle casualties (33%) and 219,000 disease casualties (67%). In the Crimean War, an estimated 38% of all deaths were due to wounds, 62% due to disease. In the American Civil War in the federal armies 44,238 men were killed in battle, 49,205 died of wounds, and 186,216 died of disease (Ref. 17.2). In World War I, at least on the Western front, this situation was very different. There was, for example, virtually no typhus (i.e., there were no lice) due to careful sanitation. The slaughtered soldiers were mainly direct casualties of the battles.

The other major innovations in World War I were similarly technological in nature. There was the large-scale nitrogen fixation process, and the gadgets like the tank, the aeroplane, and the submarine. Here it was primarily a matter of "force-feeding" development, since most of the basic knowledge had already existed for a long time. And there was the problem of convincing the military organization to accept this technology; it was obviously difficult to persuade a cavalry officer that machine guns and tanks made the horse charge obsolete and suicidal.

SCIENTIFIC CONTRIBUTIONS OF WORLD WAR II

World War II saw the entry of scientists into the war effort on a day-to-day basis; they proposed weapons, designed them, and showed the military how to use them. There was, of course, the atomic bomb. But perhaps a more important development was the use of radar, particularly in connection with aerial warfare. Some comments have already been made about this in Chapter 4 in connection with the Lindemann-Tizard controversy. Beyond this early commitment by the British air force to radar for their whole aerial defense, the whole war consisted of a see-saw competition between the radar experts of the two opponents. One example of the results of a temporary advantage by one side is the famous Hamburg bombing raid in 1943 in which "window" was used for the first time. Window consisted of strips of aluminum which were scattered in the sky and then hid the radar images of the bombing planes. The German radar technicians also had discovered window independently, but had not built up any defenses against it for fear of revealing the secret to the Allies. The result was utter chaos that night. In appreciation of the results, Americans considered one of the greatest wartime gifts from Great Britain to have been the *resonant cavity magnetron* for producing very short wavelength radar signals.

Other developments included the proximity fuse and operational research in which detailed analyses of operations were carried out to maximize their efficiency. And, finally, there was the other major new weapon, the missile, which has now combined with the atomic bomb to change the world. Here, too, the scientists proposed the development; they wanted to go to the stars but ended up dropping explosives on England with their V-2's (Ref. 17.10).

THE NATURE OF THE ATOMIC BOMB

The most revolutionary scientific invention of World War II was, however, the atomic bomb. Its development presaged a new kind of interaction of science and politics, not so much during the war itself as afterward. And the development is full of ironies, conflicts, and unexpected social implications.

The discovery of the atomic bomb, or rather of the fission chain reaction, had its origins in the transmutation of the elements. Once the neutron was discovered in 1932, it was found to be particularly effective for nuclear transmutations since it is electrically neutral and hence is much better able to penetrate into the nucleus. So from 1934 on, physicists such as Italy's Enrico Fermi literally mass-produced new isotopes through systematic neutron bombardment of all the elements. Fission could have been discovered anytime after 1934; many scientists actually had it occurring in their laboratories without recognizing it as such. When Fermi was asked why he missed the discovery, he replied, "It was a thin piece of aluminum foil, three mils thick, that stopped us all from seeing what took place." This foil was always placed in front of the detector monitoring the reactions and was designed to filter out the lower-energy particles from the decays of the uranium atoms. But in the process, it also absorbed the much more energetic charged particles emitted in the fission reactions. Two Swiss physicists once accidentally left this foil off their detector and saw tremendous spikes on their oscilloscope screens from the fission process. "The damned instrument is sparking," they said, and replaced the detector with a new one—with the foil in place. And in retrospect, Fermi was glad that he had missed this discovery in 1934, since in that case Hitler would have had four additional peace-time years in which to try to produce an atomic bomb.

The actual discovery of fission represents an irony in the context of the political situation preceding World War II. In Berlin, Otto Hahn, Lise Meitner, and Fritz Strassman had been working on the radioactive isotopes produced in the bombardment of various elements by neutrons. Although she was Jewish, Miss Meitner had been allowed to keep working in Germany after 1933 because of her Austrian citizenship. But when Austria was annexed by Germany in March of 1938, she became subject to the German anti-Semitic laws and was dismissed from her post. And it was while she was in exile in Stockholm that Hahn and Strassman concluded that barium, lanthanum, and cerium were produced when uranium was bombarded by neutrons; and it was there that she and her nephew, Otto Frisch, interpreted the data as demonstrating fission. It was clear that a large amount of energy was given off in each fission process.

And on March 3, 1939, the physicists Leo Szilard and Walter Zinn found that several neutrons were also emitted in each fission process. This meant that a chain reaction was feasible—that one fission reaction could lead to several further reactions. The thought of the atom bomb was then obvious. Szilard had been thinking about chain reactions ever since 1933, when he was inspired by reading H. G. Wells' book *The World Set Free* (a book written in 1914, in which nuclear war was predicted for 1956). The chain reaction for an atomic (fission) bomb was in fact so obvious that it was even recognized by the newspaper writer William L. Laurence (Ref. 17.1). His article in the *Saturday Evening Post* for September 7, 1940, was the last public comment on the possibility of an atomic bomb.

The basic idea of the bomb is simply that one U^{235} atom can be fissioned by a neutron into several lighter nuclei plus two to three neutrons plus a large amount of energy. The reaction is a fantastically efficient source of energy: about 0.1% of the total mass of the U^{235} atom is converted into energy. In a typical chemical reaction about

20 million times as much material has to react in order to release an equivalent amount of energy; i.e., one pound of fissioning U^{235} is equivalent to 20,000 tons of exploding TNT.

However, the actual production of such a bomb was not so simple. Natural uranium is made up of two isotopes: 0.7% is U^{235} and 99.3% is U^{238}. In an atomic bomb, fairly pure U^{235} is required to produce a fission chain reaction which is rapid enough to lead to a "satisfactory" explosion. The problem thus is how to separate the desired U^{235} from the undesired U^{238}; since they are both isotopes of the same element, no chemical reaction can distinguish between them. An alternative method of producing a fission bomb became available when the physicist Edwin M. McMillan discovered the element plutonium, which not only fissions well, but which is produced when U^{238} is irradiated by neutrons. This alternative required the development of a nuclear reactor to produce neutrons in a controlled manner. Natural uranium could be used for such a reactor if only a means could be developed for slowing down the fission neutrons with some moderator to ensure their being efficiently absorbed by the small amount of U^{235}. Once the U^{235} chain reaction was controlled, then some of the neutrons could be used to produce Pu^{239} from U^{238}. Finally, the new plutonium could be separated from the uranium by relatively easy chemical techniques.

SELLING THE IDEA OF THE BOMB

After the possibility of the bomb was recognized, it then was the interaction of physics and politics which became the determining factor. As the news leaked out that the Germans were working on the problems related to a fission bomb, it was the foreign-born physicists like Szilard, Eugene P. Wigner, Edward Teller, Victor F. Weisskopf, and Fermi who stimulated government activity in the United States. Fermi tried to persuade the Navy to do something on March 16, 1939 (the day Germany occupied Czechoslovakia). His English was not the best, and legend has it that, after Fermi left the discussion, one lieutenant commander said to another, "That wop is crazy." Finally, that strong pacifist, Albert Einstein, was persuaded to send a letter to President Roosevelt on August 2, 1939:

> In the course of the last four months it has been made proba-
> ble ... that it may become possible to set up a nuclear chain

reaction in a large mass of uranium, by which vast amounts of power and large quantities of new radium-like elements would be generated. Now it appears almost certain that this could be achieved in the immediate future.

This new phenomenon would also lead to the construction of bombs, and it is conceivable—though much less certain—that extremely powerful bombs of a new type may thus be constructed. A single bomb of this type, carried by boat and exploded in a port, might very well destroy the whole port together with some of the surrounding territory. However, such a bomb might very well prove to be too heavy for transportation by air. (Quoted for example in Ref. 17.1, p. 57.)

This letter was delivered two months later in October 1939 by Alexander Sachs, an economic consultant to the White House. However, there was no large-scale commitment toward building an atomic bomb until 1941, when Great Britain offered to share with the U.S. all the experience she had accumulated in the nuclear field. Even then, by 1943 the total sum spent on nuclear research toward the bomb was only $300,000, to be compared with the final total cost of the bomb project of $2 billion.

THE FIRST NUCLEAR REACTOR

With the first government grant of $6000, Fermi purchased graphite for a fission reactor; graphite was thought to be suitable for slowing down neutrons to increase the probability of fission, without absorbing too many of them. And on December 2, 1942, the first controlled self-sustaining chain reaction took place in the squash court underneath the University of Chicago football stadium. Control was achieved by means of cadmium and boron rods which absorbed neutrons. By withdrawing them slowly from the interior of the reactor, the extent of the fission chain reaction could gradually be increased in a controlled manner. And as a precaution, a fire brigade of several young physicists was stationed at the top of the reactor with buckets full of a solution of cadmium to quench the reaction in the case of a disaster. With success came the historic telephone conversation in which Dr. Arthur H. Compton (the director of this "Metallurgical Lab" in Chicago) informed Harvard president, Dr. James B. Conant, in Cambridge, Mass., of the success:

... The Italian navigator has just landed in the New World ... the earth was smaller than estimated and he arrived several days earlier than he had expected. . . . [The natives] were indeed [friendly]. Everyone landed safe and happy. (Quoted for example in Ref. 17.7, p. 144.)

In other words, the reactor was operating, it was smaller than calculated, and it did not blow up Chicago. And the event was celebrated with a bottle of Chianti, produced by Dr. Wigner; controlled fission had become a reality.

U^{235} SEPARATION TECHNIQUES

Even before Fermi achieved the controlled fission reaction in his reactor, it was clear that a fission bomb would work if only uranium could be enriched in U^{235}. This enrichment problem was, however, a formidable one; and unfortunately there were several possible approaches, all equally difficult. The resulting conflicts between the scientists promoting the different separation techniques were large. There was the gaseous diffusion approach proposed by J. R. Dunning. Since U^{235} is slightly lighter than U^{238}, it diffuses slightly faster through a semipermeable membrane; i. e., if one takes ordinary uranium in gaseous form and diffuses it through a barrier, the uranium coming through will be slightly enriched in U^{235}. However, the only gaseous uranium compound is uranium hexafluoride, which is very poisonous and corrosive; and more than 5000 consecutive stages are needed to reach a satisfactory enrichment. An alternative was a centrifuge method proposed by Harold Urey. Here natural uranium is spun in a centrifuge, and the slightly lighter U^{235} tends to float to the top. Again many consecutive stages are required. And when the conflict between these two competing processes became too ascerbic, Ernest O. Lawrence entered the competition by proposing to use cyclotrons as mass spectrometers to separate these two isotopes. Few believed this electromagnetic separation technique would work; but Lawrence was very energetic, a real promoter. A power structure was set up for science in 1941; Vannevar Bush became the "Czar" of all science by being put in charge of the Office of Scientific Research and Development, and Conant became his representative for uranium research. This structure had the interesting effect of putting Harold Urey in charge of the diffusion process and of Dunning, and Urey liked neither. "He made life miserable for this young engineer," said Dunning. And the centrifuging approach was put under Eger Murphree from Standard Oil, who was not healthy at that moment. And the very dynamic Lawrence was pushing the least promising approach. In some sense this situation is a study in the conflicts which arise when consensus scientists are forced to do technology. (See, e.g., Ref. 17.3 for further discussions of these conflicts.)

THE FATHER OF THE ATOMIC BOMB

The design group for the bomb was first located in Chicago. It took shape in anxiety about the German nuclear threat; one leading refugee even balked at being fingerprinted: "If the Germans win, they'll use these prints to track us down and kill us all." Initially this section included many subsidiary operations at various university and research laboratories throughout the country, an approach which turned out to be too scattered to be effective. Then in June of 1942, J. Robert Oppenheimer took over this section. In a sense he symbolizes what scientists had to do to be successful at the game of progressing in physics and technology simultaneously. And because of his success, Oppenheimer is frequently called the "father of the atom bomb." It is interesting to see what sort of person Oppenheimer was and how he ran this project; it is interesting because he was able to combine a tremendous knowledge of physics with the ability to obtain agreement on technological compromises.

After all that has been written about him, J. Robert Oppenheimer still remains something of a mystery. Considering how important a person he was, it is, for example, astonishing that there can even be a debate about his first name. The Atomic Energy Commission and Nuel P. Davis in Ref. 17.3 think that the J. stands for Julius; his brother Frank contradicts this. After receiving his undergraduate degree from Harvard in 1925, Oppenheimer studied theoretical physics at various European universities until 1929, when he joined Lawrence on the faculty of the University of California at Berkeley. Although he never won a Nobel prize, he was world-famous as a scholar and teacher. He liked to read Dante and Proust; he studied Sanskrit and liked the mountains of New Mexico; and he ruined the stomachs of his friends with hotly spiced food.

This was the complex man who in 1942 took over the bomb design section. He received a rude introduction at the first general conference under his chairmanship. First Teller suggested the possibility of using the tremendous heat released by the fission bomb to trigger a fusion bomb; this was the "Super" which was later to become reality in the form of the hydrogen bomb. And then someone estimated that if the heat calculations were right, there was a chance of three-in-a-million that the fission bomb might trigger the fusion of the whole earth atmosphere. But Oppenheimer handled these challenges well, and began to try to unify all the small subcontractors in their far-away laboratories.

In September of 1942, Brigadier General Leslie R. Groves was placed in charge of the atomic-bomb project—the so-called Manhattan District (he had just finished constructing the Pentagon). Groves was to build and run whatever plants the scientists told him to build. The trouble was that none of the scientists was prepared to tell him what to build. Except for Lawrence: Groves was impressed with Lawrence and his lab and his claims and his promises. So in spite of the advice of other scientists to drop the idea for electromagnetically separating U^{235}, Groves supported it to the extent of $544 million out of the $2 billion total for the whole Manhattan Project. This was a clear-cut case of "personality" having an impact on technological choices. And, in fact, something similar happened when Oppenheimer met Groves. With no personal axes to grind in these technological choices, Oppenheimer quickly became Groves' personal advisor, functioning like a marvelous encyclopedia. To Groves he appeared capable of separating the science of a question from the social and political implications.

To help get all the scattered bomb design section together, Groves built for Oppenheimer a new laboratory at Los Alamos in New Mexico. There all the strands from the other Manhattan Project subdivisions met. Los Alamos was unique in several ways. Oppenheimer there did something unheard of; instead of following the "need-to-know" policy of most secret wartime research, he let everyone know everything. Orientation lectures were given describing even quantitative details. There was to be a 33-pound U^{235} bomb, 17 feet long, less than two feet thick—the "Thin Man;" and it was to be a gun affair, with a pellet shot into a larger mass to bring together a critical mass of U^{235}, such that the number of fission neutrons would exceed the number of neutrons lost from and absorbed in the bomb material, such that a multiplying chain reaction would take place. How fast would the trigger have to work? The Thin Man ultimately was cut in half and renamed the "Little Boy." There was also to be an 11-pound Pu^{239} bomb named the "Fat Man," in which explosives would squeeze the plutonium together to make the mass critical. And both bombs were to be designed around U^{235} and Pu^{239} which would become available only at the very end of the program. By strategies such as his openness, Oppenheimer was able to keep the secret lab from appearing unscientific to its "crackpot" participants, and was able to instill an *esprit de corps* which led to an acceptance of compromises.

The comments which the members of the Los Alamos group of that period make about Oppenheimer's contribution are monotonous in their use of the word "magnificent." They emphasize the point that he was able to create an apparent scientific atmosphere of consensus on most topics. Raemer Schreiber said:

[At the earlier lab] I'd spent a year measuring tritium-beryllium cross sections without knowing what for. When I got here in July of 1943, Oppenheimer handed me a copy of the Primer that explained it.

Morris Bradbury, who himself later became a director of the lab, said:

Here I have seen him deal incredibly well with what looked like dead-end situations technically speaking. It was not that his decisions were always correct. But they always opened up a course of action where none had been apparent. They were made with a sense of dedication which moved the whole laboratory.... They felt that what he had decided they had decided and that therefore the official course of action deserved all their support.

Robert Serber discussed Oppenheimer's ability to achieve a consensus:

One thing I noticed: he would show up at innumerable different meetings at Los Alamos, listen, and summarize in such a way as to make amazing sense.

Hans Bethe said:

He worked at physics mainly because he found physics the best way to do philosophy. This undoubtedly had something to do with the magnificent way he led Los Alamos.

And the present-day director of the U.S. fusion-reactor program, James Tuck, sums it up:

> At the very start Oppenheimer killed the idiotic notion prevalent in other laboratories that only a few insiders should know what the work was about and that everyone else should follow them blindly. . . . Oppenheimer had to concert the fullest effort of the best minds of the Western world. . . . It required a surpassing knowledge of science and of scientists to sit above warring groups and unify them. A lesser man could not have done it. Scientists are not necessarily cultured, especially in America. Oppenheimer had to be. The people who had been gathered here from so many parts of the world needed a great gentleman to serve under. I think that's why they remember that golden time with enormous emotion. (As quoted in Ref. 17.3, pp. 183–187.)

Clearly one of Oppenheimer's biggest contributions was to extract agreement from these physicists who were all used to giving consent to a scientific answer only after long-term investigations.

THE ATOMIC BOMB

Things began to come together. At Hanford, Washington, 60,000 inhabitants of a tar-paper city built plutonium-producing nuclear reactors. At Oak Ridge, Tennessee, both the electromagnetic-separation and the gaseous-diffusion plants (see Fig. 17.1) were constructed by a working force of 25,000. There were many last-minute problems, such as how to get Fat Man to implode quickly enough; but they were solved in time. And so on July 16, 1945, the atomic age (or more precisely, the nuclear age) began with an explosion 125 miles southeast of Albuquerque, at a target area named Trinity. It was a test of the plutonium bomb, both because it was easier to mass-produce, and because this design was the more dubious one.

There was a betting pool established prior to the explosion—a pool in which a hundred physicists guessed the power of the bomb in terms of an equivalent number of tons of TNT. The calculated prediction was 20,000 tons; but no one was that optimistic, other than certain atmospheric-ignition enthusiasts. The highest estimate by anyone was the 18,000-ton bet by Isodor I. Rabi, who came too late to be able to choose his preferred value of zero. Oppenheimer bet

Fig. 17.1 The K-25 Oak Ridge Gaseous Diffusion Plant as it looked in 1945. (Photo courtesy of the United States Atomic Energy Commission.)

on a relative fizzle of 300 tons. When the explosion took place at 5:30 a.m., there were very contrasting responses. Oppenheimer remembered passages from the *Bhagava-Gita*:

> I am become Death, the shatterer of worlds, from Sri Krishna, the Exalted one, lord of the fate of mortals.

General Groves, on the other hand, was far more down-to-earth:

> The war's over. One or two of those things, and Japan will be finished.

The explosive force turned out to be exactly as calculated.

Fig. 17.2   General Leslie Groves (right) and Dr. J. Robert Oppenheimer (left) at the remains of the test tower for the first atomic bomb explosion in 1945. (Photo courtesy of United Press International.)

SUMMARY

To sum up, the Second World War saw the utilization of scientists on a gigantic scale. Scientists proposed weapons, developed them, and saw them used—the atomic bomb included. The physics behind the atomic bomb was actually rather simple, so simple in fact that this weapon could even be forecast in a scientific sense as early as 1933. All the scientific discoveries leading to it were more-or-less inevitable; to suppress them would have required great modification in the very nature of science. There was, however, not quite this inevitability in the actual acceptance of the proposed new weapon in the high political and military circles. In fact, the scientists had to do quite a bit of "selling" to achieve this acceptance, because they seemed to be the only individuals who were prepared to understand the whole potential of the bomb. Of course, it would have been better, and under the consensus criterion far more scientific, to have the decision to build the bomb made after public discussion, but this was impossible under wartime conditions.

Qualitatively the biggest difference in the interaction of the scientists with this war was in the way that they entered in their trained capacities, i.e., as physicists rather than just as technologists. They investigated the same kinds of phenomena they might have studied had they stayed at their universities; they used the same equipment, and at least at Los Alamos they had the same kinds of discussions with fellow physicists as they might have had if there had been no war. Yet there was a difference. The scientists now had a purpose in their research, and they had to channel their curiosity into looking at only the relevant phenomena. At times they had to stop short of a complete understanding once they had learned enough about a subject to help build the bomb. Compromises had to replace certainty; their work was not meant to convince, but rather to produce results; there was only limited criticism possible of any scientific effort. By the public-knowledge and consensus criterion of science, the nuclear physicists of the Manhattan Project were *not* acting as scientists during World War II.

Scientists in World War II for the first time entered the halls of real power. One day they worried about a $5 electron tube, a year later they spent $1 million with no second thoughts (at times with very poor judgment, particularly when a technological compromise was difficult to attain). They became advisors whose advice was sought by the military and by politicians. All the presently influential scientists were there—Kistiakowsky, DuBridge, Wiesner. . . . There was then superimposed upon the exponential growth of science an abrupt change in the influence of science. By influencing not only governmental scientific choices, but political choices as well, scientists began to go at times far beyond their consensus status as pure scientists.

REFERENCES

Prime reference

17.1 W. L. Laurence, *Men and Atoms*, New York: Simon and Schuster, 1962; pp. 3–133.

Interesting reading

17.2 H. Zinsser, *Rats, Lice and History*, Boston: Little, Brown and Co., 1935.

17.3 N. P. Davis, *Lawrence and Oppenheimer*, New York: Simon and Schuster, 1968.

17.4 R. Jungk, *Brighter Than a Thousand Suns*, New York: Harcourt, Brace and Co., 1958; pp. 82–155.

17.5 D. Fleming and B. Bailyn, Eds., *The Intellectual Migration: Europe and America, 1930–1960* (Ref. 16.3).

17.6 L. Fermi, *Atoms in the Family: My Life with Enrico Fermi* (Ref. 16.10).

17.7 A. H. Compton, *Atomic Quest: A Personal Narrative*, New York: Oxford University Press, 1956.

17.8 J. Baxter, IIIrd, *Scientists Against Time*, Boston: Little, Brown and Co., 1946.

17.9 J. B. Conant, *Modern Science and Modern Man*, New York: Columbia University Press, 1952.

17.10 W. Dornberger, *V-2* (in German, *The Shot in Space*), New York: Ballantine Press F273K, 1954.

17.11 L. R. Groves, *Now It Can Be Told: The Story of the Manhattan Project*, New York: Haper and Row, 1962.

QUESTIONS FOR DISCUSSION

1. Why were the foreign scientists the prime movers in the proposal and development of the atomic bomb?

2. Would it have been proper for the nuclear scientists to have voluntarily suppressed articles on fission before World War II? Would it have been scientific?

3. How could a pacifist like Einstein justify to himself writing the letter to Roosevelt proposing the atomic bomb?

4. Is there such a thing as an acceptable risk of blowing up Chicago in order to try out the first nuclear reactor? Was it OK to accept the three-in-a-million chance that the atomic bomb might set off the atmosphere in a fusion reaction?

5. Is it appropriate for a scientific advisor to restrict himself to acting as a marvelous encyclopedia, with no perspective of self-interest?

6. The need-to-know technique does not work well with scientists. Why?

7. How can there be such a thing as an atmosphere in a laboratory which might lead to a greater acceptance of the bomb?

18 | THE DECISION TO DROP
THE ATOMIC BOMB

... the physicists felt a particularly intimate responsibility for suggesting ... and ... for achieving the realization of atomic weapons. ... In some sort of crude sense, which no vulgarity, no humor, no overstatement can quite extinguish, the physicists have known sin; and this is a knowledge which they cannot lose.
J. Robert Oppenheimer in *The Open Mind*, p. 80

Some of the military, political, and emotional background to the decision to use the atomic bomb is presented. The interaction of the views of the nuclear physicists with those of the military and the President is discussed.

INTRODUCTION

In 1941 the nuclear scientists proposed the atomic bomb, in 1945 some of them were opposed to its use, and now there are those who consider the use of the bomb to be the event wherein scientists for the first time tasted sin. In this chapter we will examine the scientific, emotional, and military-political background behind the decision of the United States to actually use the atomic bomb as a weapon in the Second World War.

This was a particularly interesting decision for at least two reasons. First, in the United States the atomic bomb was proposed by scientists primarily because of fear of German militarism. Yet it was finally used against an enemy who would have been easily defeated without it. Secondly, the bomb was proposed and built by scientists who were trained to think in terms of a consensus. Yet because of the secrecy of the Manhattan Project, only a very select group of persons was in a position to influence the final decision concerning use of the bomb—a group which did not even include the members of Congress.

We shall begin by considering the basis for the fear of a German atomic bomb. Then the attitudes of the scientists toward the use of the bomb on Japan will be outlined. Finally, the military and political situation which led to its use will be compared with the consequences of its use. Hopefully this review will make clear the resulting ambivalence in the attitude of the scientific community toward this mixture of great scientific, technological, and organizational achievement combined with the horror of its wartime usage.

THE FEAR OF THE SCIENTISTS

The original motivation of the scientists in the United States for proposing the atomic bomb as a weapon was fear. The immigrant scientists had tasted Hitler's Germany firsthand; they knew the oppression which an Axis victory would bring. Even Einstein, though basically a pacifist, knew there would be circumstances intolerable enough to negate his pacifism; and he knew that a war against Nazism was one of these.

But beyond this general fear, the immigrant nuclear scientists had the more direct fear that Germany would be the first to build an atomic bomb and use it to win the war. This fear was the reason Einstein wrote his letter to President Roosevelt; his primary purpose was to get the President to convince the Belgians not to let Hitler capture their stock of uranium, and to thereby delay the Germans as long as possible in building the bomb. This fear led to the overriding concern of the scientists that the Allies should be the first to possess the bomb; until the German surrender this was the specter haunting the Manhattan Project. There was, in fact, so much fear at the end of 1942 that some scientists convinced themselves that Hitler would attack Chicago with the radioactivity from a reactor (on Christmas day, of course); they so convinced themselves that they sent their families to the country.

THE GERMAN ATOMIC BOMB

It is interesting to examine this specter a little closer in order to see how substantial it may have been. When the curtain of wartime secrecy shut off contact between the two scientific camps, the Germans were rapidly moving toward building the atomic bomb. Not only had fission first been observed in Berlin by Hahn, but in April of 1939 a first meeting concerning an atomic bomb had already been held under the official auspices of the Reich Ministry of Education. There had also been a bomb proposal to the War Office; even the Postal Ministry began to perform nuclear research with such a bomb in mind. By September 1939, more than a fortnight before Sachs could obtain an interview with Roosevelt to transmit Einstein's letter, nine German nuclear physicists had met in the Army Weapons Office and drawn up a detailed program of research. The Uranium Club was then formed, with Heisenberg (the discoverer of the Uncertainty Principle) as head; and the Kaiser Wilhelm Institute for Physics in Berlin was made the club's Scientific Center. Negotiations were begun for all the uranium and radium from the Joachimsthal mines in Czechoslovakia; a 3500-ton supply of uranium was captured when Germany overran Belgium; and when Norway was taken over by Germany, the Germans captured the world's only large-scale plant for manufacturing the heavy water which would make a nuclear reactor an easy thing to build. As far as the Americans and the British could see, the Germans had then a two-year headstart toward an atomic bomb, had all the natural advantages, and were clearly moving rapidly in the right direction. This was a self-feeding fear. The lack of any nuclear-progress spy reports after 1939 surely meant simply that supersecrecy was instituted to hide tremendous German achievements. And when the V-2 rocket construction started, the worry arose that, since the V-2 was too small to have much effect with ordinary explosives, it must be intended to deliver nuclear warheads.

The fear of the German atomic bomb evoked three different responses. First the British and later the American atomic-bomb programs were pushed with great vigor. Secondly, the Norwegian heavy-water plant was bombed and sabotaged. The plant was promptly rebuilt; this indicated to the Allies that the German atomic-bomb program must have very high priorities. The third part of the response was the "Alsos" mission. ("Alsos" is Greek for "grove;" the mission was presumably named in honor of General Groves.) Alsos was an intelligence group which included physicists whose assignment was to pick up German scientific secrets as Axis laboratories and universities were captured by the Allies. The scientific chief of this operation was Dr. Samuel Goudsmit (now editor of the *Physical Review Letters*, perhaps the most prestigeous physics journal in the West). This group went along with the Allied armies (sometimes even ahead of them) and examined the files at the universities and laboratories for hints about the nuclear operations. As the story uncovered, it became clear that not only was there no German atomic bomb, there wasn't even an operational nuclear reactor.

There were many factors contributing to the German failure to build an atomic bomb. The first was the competition among the scientists participating in the program. Although Berlin had been set up as the center for the Uranium Club, most of the physicists preferred to do their work in their own institutes. There was constant competition between the three agencies supporting the groups working on the bomb—between the Educational Ministry, the War Office, and the Post Office. When the Postal minister informed Hitler about his bomb project, Hitler joked, "Look here gentlemen, while you experts are worrying about how to win the war, here it is our Postal Minister who brings us the solution." In the United States a similar problem was finally terminated by Oppenheimer when he set up the centralized laboratory at Los Alamos. In Germany, however, the competition continued, and its results were manifold. There were constant fights as to who was to be allowed to use the limited amounts of pure uranium and heavy water; even in the last days of the war these materials were still being shuttled from one laboratory to another, with no group ever having enough to run a conclusive reactor experiment. Splits between those groups came out also in discussions of separation processes, and as a result the priorities for programs were usually determined by the pecking order; in part as a consequence of this, no separation process had made any significant progress by the end of the war.

One of the more powerful brakes on the program was a purely technical mistake. Very early in the war a measurement was carried out which indicated that carbon in the form of graphite could *not* be used as a moderator in a fission reactor using natural uranium.

Presumably the carbon used in this measurement had impurities in it; after all, Fermi in the United States successfully built a graphite reactor in 1942. As a consequence of this error, the German physicists thought they needed heavy water for a reactor, and hence made themselves totally dependent on that captured Norwegian heavy-water plant. The Allied sabotage and bombings of this plant then completely upset the program.

Another significant reason for the lack of progress toward the bomb was the very nature of the German Nazi state and ideology. As indicated in Chapter 16, by 1937 nearly 40% of the German university professors had been dismissed, and many more had fled. Between 1932 and 1937 the number of university students in mathematics and the sciences had dropped to 36% of its former level. It was only in 1942, when it became clear that the end of the war was not imminent, that the government began to recognize this problem. Then Goering said:

> What the Führer abhors is any strict regimentation of science, with results like this: "This invention may indeed be vital— extremely vital to us, and would bring things a long way for us; but we can't touch it because the fellow's got a Jewish wife, or because he's half-Jewish himself. . . ."

> I have discussed this with the Führer himself now; we have been able to use one Jew two years longer in Vienna, and another in photographic research, because they have certain things which we need and which can be of the utmost benefit to us at the present. It would be utter madness for us to say now: "He'll have to go. He was a magnificent researcher, a fantastic brain, but his wife is Jewish, and he can't be allowed to stay at the University, etc." The Führer had made similar exceptions in the arts all the way down to operetta level; he is all the more likely to make exceptions where really great projects or researchers are concerned. (As quoted in Ref. 18.3, p. 126.)

And, as was pointed out in Chapter 16, political meetings had to be called to decide what physics was consistent with the party philosophy. This not only was discouraging to any real scientists; it further was very encouraging to all scientific quacks who were party members.

But the final and perhaps most decisive reason for the failure of the German atomic-bomb program was the attitude of the German scientists. They felt no fear; they were not worried about an American atomic bomb; after all, German science was superior. The prompt rebuilding of the Norwegian hydro plant after the sabotage and bombing and the prompt production of pure uranium made it clear that German industry and the war offices were prepared to support an atomic-bomb program. But the scientists never learned to ask for money; from either a lack of confidence or of desire, they never pushed the program very forcefully. When the scientists had a talk with the sympathetic Armaments Minister Speer, they asked for so little money that he was embarrassed. The German scientists themselves claim that they never really wanted to build an atomic bomb (e.g., Refs. 18.1 and 18.5). To them the program was an opportunity to preserve some German science for the postwar period; by doing defense work they were able to keep away from the front and to maintain a semblance of university teaching and research. Doubts have been expressed as to the correctness of this after-the-fact explanation (e.g., Ref. 18.3), but in any case, fission research was not pursued in Germany with enough energy to lead to significant progress.

THE ATOMIC BOMB AND JAPAN

The Alsos mission and the surrender of Germany in May of 1945 ended any fear of a German atomic weapon on the part of American scientists in the Manhattan Project. And Japan clearly had not the facilities, the resources, or the scientific establishment necessary to build such a weapon. Once the fear motive was removed, American nuclear scientists could then think about the longer-term implications of the bomb and specifically about its possible application to the war with Japan. Should it be used, and if so, how? And what would happen to nuclear research and nuclear information once the war was over? To the military, including the man in charge, General Groves, there was no question that the weapon would be used if built; the only worry was that it might not be finished in time. So any change of plans had to occur at the very top; only the President could decide the ultimate use of the bomb.

There were attempts to influence Roosevelt on this issue. Alexander Sachs, who had passed the Einstein letter to him, debated the question with him in December of 1944 and later claimed that Roosevelt at that time agreed to a rehearsal demonstration of the atomic bomb before international and neutral witnesses prior to any wartime use. But this agreement, if it indeed existed, was never mentioned to Secretary of War Stimson, who on March 15, 1945, had his last talk on the subject with Roosevelt:

> I went over with him the two schools of thought that exist in respect to the future control after the war of this project, in case it is successful, one of them being the secret close-in attempted control of the project by those who control it now, and the other being international control based upon freedom of science. I told him that those things must be settled before the projectile is used and that he must be ready with a statement to come out to the people on it just as soon as that is done. He agreed to that. (Quoted for example in Ref. 18.1, p. 175.)

A report by Szilard on the scientists' feelings about the bomb was lying on Roosevelt's desk when he died. After Roosevelt's death, any changes in the decision about the use of the bomb required convincing the new President, Harry S. Truman, who had never heard of the weapon while he was Vice President.

THE SCIENTISTS' VIEWPOINT

The most general and wide-ranging discussions about the use of the bomb took place among the nuclear scientists in Chicago, where toward the end of the war there was not so much pressure since the production processes had already passed on to industry; this stood in contrast with Los Alamos where everyone continued to work at fever pitch until the very end to meet the bomb-construction and testing deadlines. It was in Chicago that the Jeffries Report, *Prospectus on Nucleonics*, was prepared—a report which contained discussions of a possible future armaments race as well as of the future applications of nuclear fission. Early in 1945 several of the Chicago scientists became convinced that international control of nuclear knowledge would be the best way to ensure open dissemination of this new information. As James Franck put it in April of 1945:

We read and hear about all the efforts which the best statesmen devote to peace planning in Dumbarton Oaks, San Francisco, etc., and we hear about plans to control industries, etc. in the agressor states, but we know in our hearts that all these plans are obsolete, because the future war has an entirely different and a thousand times more sinister aspect than the war which is fought now. How is it possible that the statesmen are not informed that the aspect of the world and its future is entirely changed by the knowledge that atomic energy can be tapped, and how is it possible that the men who know these facts are prevented from informing the statesmen about the situation? One of the grave political decisions which will soon have to be made is how and when to inform the public, since in a democratic country effective political steps cannot be taken without enlightened public opinion. (As quoted in Ref. 18.2, pp. 294–295.)

A "Committee on the Social and Political Implications of Atomic Energy" was formed under Franck. It completed the Franck Report in early June of 1945, a report which was promptly classified. A quotation from the preamble to this report is appropriate here because it shows that the scientists were aware that they could speak about the implications only as well-informed citizens, not as experts:

The scientists on this Project do not presume to speak authoritatively on problems of national and international policy. However, we found ourselves, by the force of events, during the last five years, in the position of a small group of citizens cognizant of a grave danger for the safety of this country as well as for the future of all the other nations, of which the rest of mankind is unaware. We therefore feel it our duty to urge that the political problems, arising from the mastering of nuclear power, be recognized in all their gravity, and that appropriate steps be taken for their study and the preparation of necessary decisions. We hope that the creation of the Committee by the Secretary of War to deal with all aspects of nucleonics, indicates that these implications have been recognized by the government. We believe that our acquaintance with the scientific elements of the situation and prolonged preoccupation with its world-wide political implications, impose on us the obligation to offer to the Committee some suggestions as to the possible solution of these grave problems. (As quoted in Ref. 18.2, p. 302.)

The objections raised in the report to the use of the atomic bomb were that it would be likely to induce an armaments race and thus reduce the possibility of an international control agreement. While the report was signed by all seven members of the committee, there were other scientists who felt that an all-out attack on Japan by the atomic bomb would significantly shorten the war. There were petitions and counterpetitions. A poll was carried out July 12, 1945, among 150 out of the 250 nuclear scientists at the Chicago Metallurgical Lab. The following alternatives were presented:

Which of the following five procedures comes closest to your choice as to the way in which any new weapons that we may develop should be used in the Japanese war:

1. Use them in the manner that is from the military point of view most effective in bringing about prompt Japanese surrender at minimum human cost to our armed forces.

2. Give a military demonstration in Japan to be followed by renewed opportunity for surrender before full use of the weapon is employed.

3. Give an experimental demonstration in this country, with representatives of Japan present; followed by a new opportunity for surrender before full use of the weapon is employed.

4. Withhold military use of the weapons, but make public experimental demonstration of their effectiveness.

5. Maintain as secret as possible all developments of our new weapons and refrain from using them in this war.

The results were as follows:

Procedure indicated above	1	2	3	4	5
Number voting	23	69	39	16	3
Percent of votes	15	46	26	11	2

(As quoted in Ref. 18.2, p. 304.)

Clearly there was concern among the scientists, but there was no unanimity; some scientists wanted the weapon to be first demonstrated before being used in combat in Japan, but this view was not universal; there was concern about the moral and political aspects of being the first nation to use this weapon, but it was the concern of private individuals.

The new President, Truman, did ask for advice about the way to use the bomb; near the end of April 1945 he appointed the so-called Interim Committee. It included Stimson, Secretary of War; George L. Harrison, Stimson's assistant; James F. Byrnes, future Secretary of State; Ralph A. Bard, Undersecretary of the Navy; William L. Clayton, Assistant Secretary of State; Dr. Bush; Dr. Karl T. Compton, president of M.I.T; and Dr. Conant. A panel of four scientists was appointed to advise the committee: A. H. Compton, Fermi, Lawrence, and Oppenheimer. According to Stimson, after discussions with the scientific panel, the committee unanimously adopted the following recommendations:

1. The bomb should be used against Japan as soon as possible.

2. It should be used on a dual target—that is, a military installation or war plant surrounded by or adjacent to houses and other buildings most susceptible to damage, and

3. It should be used without prior warning [of the nature of the weapon]. One member of the committee, Mr. Bard, later changed his view and dissented from recommendation.

In reaching these conclusions the Interim Committee carefully considered such alternatives as a detailed advance warning or a demonstration in some uninhabited area. Both of these suggestions were discarded as impractical. . . . (As quoted in Ref. 18.2, pp. 296–297.)

Since President Truman ultimately followed the advice of this committee, a critical point is whether indeed all possible alternatives had been considered or whether the agreement was not just an act of rubber-stamping. Apparently many different alternatives were considered, such as a nighttime airflash several miles above Tokyo, the demonstration bombing of a forest area in the vicinity of Tokyo, or at least a detailed advance warning. But all the alternative uses of the bomb were rejected because they would not be impressive enough or their results could be hidden through military secrecy or they could be negated by moving prisoners of war into the area. The consensus in the committee was not quite as total as implied by Stimson. The scientific panel, for example, only advised; it did not vote on the recommendations. And Mr. Bard had never heard of the Manhattan Project prior to this meeting; consequently, his agreement was so forced that he subsequently withdrew his consent to the recommendations and a month later resigned his naval post to emphasize his opposition to the bombing (feeling that the Navy was quite able to bottle up Japan and that the Army just wanted to share in the glory of the final victory). There is, however, no question that Truman received the recommendation from this high-level committee (with a large representation from science and technology) that only a bombing of a live target would be convincing to the Japanese. The scientists certainly were not unanimously against the usage of the bomb.

THE MILITARY SITUATION IN JAPAN

In the meantime, the war situation was as follows. Okinawa had been invaded in a very bloody battle with suicidal kamikazi plane missions taking place on a large scale. On March 9, 1945, 325 B-29's bombed Tokyo with 2000 tons of incendiaries. The resulting fire storm killed approximately 100,000 people, flattened 16 square miles, and destroyed 250,000 buildings. In five months of bombing, the 21st Bomber Command had paralyzed 66 metropolitan centers and had made eight million Japanese homeless. Hunger was a constant torture; rice rations were down to one-fourth of the prewar level. And overriding all this was fear; as the B-29's and the planes from the carriers dominated the people's very movement, the civilian population of Japan was on the edge of desperation.

Attempts to negotiate concerning a surrender began as early as May, 1945—through Switzerland, over radio propaganda broadcasts, and even through Russian intermediaries (since Russia still had not declared war on Japan). But the Japanese military was not prepared to surrender. The plans for the defense of the homeland were to kill as many invaders as possible and thus to shatter American morale enough to lead to a negotiated peace in place of the demanded unconditional surrender. And the American military plans still called for an invasion of Japan; casualty estimates were hundreds of thousands of Americans, plus many more Japanese. The Potsdam Conference was going on at this time, and on July 24 Truman "casually" told Stalin that the U.S. had a new weapon of unusual destructive force. The Russian premier showed no special interest in this weapon. He only said that he was glad to hear it and hoped the U.S. would make "good use of it against the Japanese." He never asked a question about it. In the Potsdam Declaration of July 26 there was an ultimatum threatening complete destruction of Japan. For the Japanese the biggest stumbling block in the way of surrender was Point 6 of this declaration. This point said: "There must be eliminated for all time the authority and influence of those who have deceived and misled the people of Japan into embarking on world conquest." They interpreted this as requiring the abdication of the Emperor, which was an unacceptable condition. In his radio response to the Potsdam Declaration, Premier Suzuki tried to say that the government would "withhold comment," but he accidentally used the words meaning to "take no notice of, treat with silent contempt, ignore." Truman could only interpret this as a refusal to surrender, so he authorized the use of the atomic bomb. On August 6 the B-29 named "Enola Gay" took off. The weather was good, so at 8:15 a.m. local time, the "Little Boy" was dropped on Hiroshima. (The city of Kyoto had been struck from the original target list since it had been the ancient capital of Japan and was a shrine of Japanese art and culture.) Truman made a public statement: "It is an atomic bomb." Three days later, one day after Russia entered the war, a plutonium bomb was dropped on Nagasaki. As part of this flight, a letter was dropped by parachute, addressed by Professors L. Alvarez, R. Serber, and P. Morrison to their former colleague at Berkeley, Professor R. Sagane at the Imperial University of Tokyo:

> We are sending this as a personal message to urge that you use your influence as a reputable nuclear physicist, to convince the Japanese General Staff of the terrible consequences which will be suffered by your people if you continue in this war.
>
> You have known for several years that an atomic bomb could be built if a nation were willing to pay the enormous cost of preparing the necessary material. Now that you have seen that we

Fig. 18.1   Remains of the Nagasaki Medical College after the A-bomb drop on August 9, 1945. (Photo courtesy of the United States Atomic Energy Commission.)

have constructed the production plants, there can be no doubt in your mind that all the output of these factories, working 24 hours a day, will be exploded on your homeland.

Within the space of three weeks, we have proof-fired one bomb in the American desert, exploded one in Hiroshima, and fired the third this morning. We implore you to confirm these facts to your leaders, and to do your utmost to stop the destruction and waste of life which can only result in the total annihilation of all your cities if continued. As scientists, we deplore the use to which a beautiful discovery has been put, but we can assure you that unless Japan surrenders at once, this rain of atomic bombs will increase manyfold in fury. (See, for example, the facsimile in Ref. 17.7, p. 258.)

The number of dead due to these two atomic bombs is not very accurately known, but is on the order of 150,000. Official Japanese statistics placed the number of dead at Hiroshima (out of a population of 400,000) at 70,000 up to September 1, 1945, and the number of wounded at 130,000 with 43,500 severely wounded. The supreme Allied Headquarters announced in February of 1946 that the casualties in Hiroshima were:

$$\begin{aligned}
\text{dead} &- 78,150; \\
\text{missing} &- 13,983; \\
\text{seriously wounded} &- 9,428; \\
\text{slightly injured} &- 29,997.
\end{aligned}$$

The horror of those days has been often described (as in Refs. 18.12 through 18.15); the survivors still bear psychological scars (Ref. 18.15).

Even after the atomic bomb was used, the Japanese cabinet was still split on whether to surrender or not; one man who was basically committed to the policy of trying to get better surrender terms by bleeding the Americans on the beaches was the War Minister Anami, spokesman for the Army and the most powerful man in Japan. But finally Emperor Hirohito saved face for everyone by taking the onus of surrender on himself: ". . . the time has come when we must bear the unbearable." On the 10th August, Japan offered to surrender. Members of the Army briefly tried to rebel and to destroy the Emperor's recording of the planned surrender radio broadcast; but Anami vacillated and the uprising failed. Included in the brief 300-word announcement of August 15 (nine days after the first atomic bomb) were the following statements:

> ... the war situation has developed not necessarily to Japan's advantage. ... Moreover, the enemy has begun to employ a new and most cruel bomb, the power of which to do damage is indeed incalculable, taking the toll of many innocent lives. Should we continue to fight, it would not only result in an ultimate collapse and obliteration of the Japanese nation, but would also lead to the total destruction of human civilization. (Quoted for example in Ref. 18.7, p. 182.)

SUMMARY

In fear of a German atomic bomb, the U.S. scientists proposed such a weapon and built it. But then they lost control of it, as it inexonerably was used in defeating Japan. President Truman had to make the final decision concerning its use, and it is questionable whether he ever had any major doubts in his mind about the correctness of his ultimate choice. The bomb may or may not have significantly shortened the war, but now the world must live with that memory.

For the scientists there is much irony in the course of events related to the atomic bomb. First, the fear of Germany was groundless insofar as the bomb ultimately was not necessary for the winning of the war. Secondly, the designing of the bomb was a technological feat, but it was not science since it was product-oriented. In fact, this wartime contact with secrecy and its consequent hampering of scientific activities impressed the participating scientists tremendously, and colored all their future political attempts at arranging the course of science. And finally, the instincts of the scientists were right when they tried to get the broadest possible audience for the discussions on the bomb's use—when they asked for a more general public consensus. Perhaps it would have been the very best possible thing if the discussion could have been made totally public; only in that way could the most socially responsible decision have been reached. But this was impossible under wartime secrecy, a secrecy which perhaps was not necessary but which did exist. The decision to drop the bomb could, therefore, in no sense be called a scientific decision. This whole exercise brought home to the nuclear scientists the difference between science and politics, a difference which they have had to continually relearn. They discovered that no consensus was possible in the latter field.

REFERENCES

Prime references

18.1 R. Jungk, *Brighter Than a Thousand Suns*, (Ref. 17.4); pp. 156–210.

18.2 A. K. Smith, "Behind the Decision to Use the Atomic Bomb, Chicago 1944–45," *Bulletin of the Atomic Scientists* **14**, 288–312 (1958).

Interesting reading

18 3 D. Irving, *The German Atom Bomb*, New York: Simon and Schuster, 1967; also published as *The Virus House*, London: William Kimber and Co., Ltd.

18.4 S. A. Goudsmit, *Alsos*, New York: Henry Schuman, Inc., 1947.

18.5 W. Heisenberg, *Encounters and Conversations*, (Ref. 13.2).

18.6 W. L. Laurence, *Men and Atoms*, (Ref. 17.1); pp. 134–185.

18.7 W. Craig, *The Fall of Japan*, New York: Dell Publishing Co., 1968.

18.8 J. Toland, *The Rising Sun*, New York: Random House, 1970.

18.9 E. Fogelman, *The Decision To Use the Atomic Bomb*, New York: C. Scribner's Sons, 1964.

18.10 M. Amrine, *The Great Decision: The Secret History of The Atomic Bomb*, New York: Van Rees Press, 1959.

18.11 H. Feis, *The Atomic Bomb and the End of World War II*, Princeton, N.J.: Princeton University Press, 1966.

18.12 J. Hersey, *Hiroshima*, New York: Alfred Knopf, 1946.

18.13 R. Jungk, *Children of Ashes*, New York: Harcourt, Brace and World, 1961.

18.14 M. Hachiya, *Hiroshima Diary: The Journal of a Japanese Physician, August 6-September 30, 1945*, Chapel Hill, N.C.: University of North Carolina Press, 1955.

18.15 R. J. Lifton, *Death in Life: Survivors of Hiroshima*, New York: Random House, 1968; it is the survivors who feel guilty for having been part of the complete social collapse which took place in the hours after the blast of the bomb.

18.16 F. Dürrenmatt, *The Physicists*, New York: Grove Press, 1964; a play about scientists without social responsibility.

18.17 K. Vonnegut, Jr., *Cat's Cradle*, New York: Dell Publishing Co., 1963; a satirical book about scientific social responsibility.

QUESTIONS FOR DISCUSSION

1. Was it right for the German nuclear physicists to want to preserve some German physics (as opposed to some physics for Germany)?

2. Do the reasons given seem to adequately explain the failure of the German atomic bomb as compared to the success of the American program?

3. Can we say with hindsight that the decision to use the bomb was wrong? Is it not good that the world saw a demonstration of the effects of such a weapon?

4. To whom belongs the glory of this magnificent achievement? To whom belongs whatever guilt may be associated with it?

19 | NUCLEAR MEDICINE

Cells are sensitive to radiation in proportion to their proliferation activity and in inverse proportion to their degree of differentiation.
The Law of Bergonie and Tribondeau, 1906

The effects of radiation on living tissue are examined, and the uses of radioactive isotopes in medical diagnosis and therapy are discussed. The technological impact of nuclear physics on medicine has led to improvements in both the quantity and the quality of life.

INTRODUCTION

The nuclear age began with two bangs in 1945, when nuclear physics in a sense saddled itself with a debt of about 150,000 lives. The nuclear-physics community has been trying to repay this debt ever since, particularly through technological developments arising out of the large-scale availability of radioactive isotopes. In this chapter we will discuss some of the ways in which the medical use of radioactive materials has helped to improve human life.

To begin, the rise of nuclear technology will be considered, with the ultimate question being whether the Manhattan Project was a significant stimulus to this rise. In examining what makes radioactive isotopes so generally useful, we will illustrate the effects of radiation on living tissue by means of some examples of medical uses of isotopes in both diagnosis and therapy. Finally, there will be some thoughts on the nature and significance of this particular technological interaction of science and society.

THE PRODUCTION OF RADIOACTIVE ISOTOPES

Radioactive isotopes were, of course, discovered long before the Manhattan Project of the Second World War. Radium had already been extensively used in therapy. The impetus toward a more general nuclear medicine was, however, provided by the large-scale production of artificial radioactive isotopes in the cyclotron of Ernest O. Lawrence. From the beginning, he and his brother John were quite conscious of the effects of radiation on living tissue. For example, to check on how safe it was near their cyclotron when it was in operation, the physicist Paul C. Aebersold imprisoned a rat in a box on the side of the machine. When after five minutes the box was opened, the rat was dead. Everyone was very concerned until it was discovered that Aebersold had forgotten to put breathing holes in the box. And just as soon as the radioactive isotopes which were produced in cyclotron irradiations were discovered, radiation diagnosis and treatment in places far from cyclotrons became a reality. George von Hevesy in Sweden, who received a Nobel prize for his tracer work with radioactive substances, wrote: "I could not have worked without those wonderful shipments of radioactive phosphorus." Lawrence ran his cyclotron night and day to try to keep up with the demand. Wealthy people like Lewis Strauss and William Donner, who saw close relatives die of cancer, helped Lawrence build the Donner Laboratory at Berkeley to investigate medical aspects of radiation—a lab which is still a leader in the field of nuclear medicine.

But the widespread use of radioisotopes had to wait for the development of nuclear reactors. Inside these reactors it is much easier to produce isotopes in large quantities at relatively low cost. Some of the isotopes, such as iodine-131 (I^{131}), are automatically produced in the fuel elements when the uranium fissions into elements of lower atomic mass. Some other radioisotopes, such as gold-198 (Au^{198}) and cobalt-60 (Co^{60}), are produced by inserting nonradioactive samples into the reactor to be irradiated by neutrons for periods of time varying from hours to months. Much of the momentum for this work was provided by the several hundred nuclear physicists who switched into this field of radiation biophysics from the Manhattan Project. It is they who ensured that the full technological benefits of their wartime activities reached the public.

THE USES OF RADIOACTIVITY

To some extent, the usefulness of radioactive substances is related to that of x-rays. As with x-rays, it is the great penetration ability of the emitted radiation which makes radioactive isotopes so useful for exploring solid materials and for producing changes deep inside them. But here there is the added fact that the source of the radiation can be incorporated directly into the substances of interest. It then becomes possible to study internal dynamic processes by tagging some chemical with a very small number of radioactive tracer atoms and tracing these as they flow along with the chemical. And with the large number of isotopes now available, it is possible to select one that is particularly suitable for a given experiment with respect to its lifetime and the energy of the emitted radiation.

A brief list of nonmedical uses of radioactive isotopes will give an indication of possible applications. For example, how might one test the wear on a tire to substantiate the 40,000-mile claims of its manufacturer? One could, of course, drive the tire for 40,000 miles and measure the remaining tread, but that takes a long time. The easy way is to make the tire slightly radioactive and then see how much of the radioactivity is left on the road per foot of travel. Since one can detect a very minute number of radioactive atoms by their radiations, one can determine the tire wear in minutes rather than in weeks. In this application use is made of the fact that a few million radioactive atoms are quite enough to trace such a process, whereas chemical tests for the deposited rubber would require at least a billion times as many atoms.

Suppose a pipeline is used to transport a variety of petroleum products. How could one let the engineer at the receiving station know that he should be ready to switch the flow of a new liquid to a different storage tank? By inserting a slight amount of a radioactive isotope at the interface between the two liquids, a Geiger counter at the receiving station can be activated to throw the switch at the appropriate time. This represents the use of a radioactive tracer to reveal itself from deep inside a sample.

A producer of plastic films wants to maintain the constant thickness of his product without repeatedly interrupting his presses for quality checks. He solves this problem by placing a radioactive source on one side of the film and a radiation detector on the other side. The film absorbs a certain fraction of the radiation passing through it—a fraction which depends on the film thickness. If the film becomes too thin, then the count rate in the detector increases; if it becomes too thick, the count rate decreases; and these changes in count rate can be used to automatically adjust the operation of the machinery to maintain the desired thickness. In this case the known absorption rate for the radiation is used to measure a thickness which might otherwise be very hard to determine in a continuous way.

An agriculturalist claims that a lot of money is being wasted because some components of certain fertilizers are never utilized by plants. This can be tested by simply adding some radioactive carbon to the suspect component and then seeing whether any of this radioactivity appears in plants treated with this fertilizer. If it does not, then the agriculturalist is right. This application hinges on the fact that the chemical processes in plants cannot distinguish between stable and radioactive carbon.

When food is stored, it spoils due to organisms contained in it; irradiation with gamma rays can therefore prolong the shelf life of foods tremendously by killing these organisms. Pork can, for example, be treated with radiation to kill the helmithic parasites which cause trichinosis; at the same time, the radiation does not significantly damage the already dead pork meat. And lately there has been much concern about the ill effects of the widespread use of pesticides. One way of avoiding this problem in some cases is to disturb the breeding cycle of the insects. The trick is to breed in captivity large populations of males of these species, sterilize them by exposure to radiation, and then release them. These males will compete with wild males in the mating process, but will lead to no offspring. It has been found possible in several instances to drastically reduce insect populations by such techniques. In this example the high sensitivity of living cells, and particularly of the reproductive organs, to radiation is the key to the application.

RADIOACTIVE ISOTOPES IN MEDICAL DIAGNOSIS

The above examples give a feeling for the wide range of applicability of radioactive isotopes, as well as illustrating their main attractive features. But the most fascinating uses for such isotopes are probably in medicine; and since medicine is directly concerned with preserving life, those uses provide the most direct contrast with the taking of life with nuclear weapons. These uses are essentially twofold; one is diagnostic, the other is therapeutic (concerned with treatment). The diagnostic techniques consist in somehow getting a radioactive isotope to indicate an abnormality in the animal or human tissue by abnormal concentrations of the isotope (by either its excess or absence). The radiation emitted by radioactive substances then allows nondestructive detection of these abnormal concentrations simply by using a radiation detector outside the body. The therapy involves getting a localized concentration of the radioactive material to somehow produce a desirable change in the abnormality by irradiation of the involved tissue.

The use of radioactive iodine in connection with the thyroid gland is a case which actually illustrates both the diagnostic and the therapeutic aspects of nuclear medicine. The thyroid gland is located at the base of the neck in the front of the body; it controls a variety of body functions including growth and activity. This gland is subject to being overactive (hyperthyroid) and underactive (hypothyroid); for example, the latter condition might be due to a cancerous growth occupying some of the space normally filled by the thyroid gland. The thyroid gland concentrates body iodine; any iodine ingested accumulates in it quite rapidly. One way of characterizing the effectiveness of this gland is by the "24-hour uptake;" i.e., by the percent of ingested iodine which accumulates in it within one day. Typical values for this percentage are as follows:

	24-hour uptake	24-hour excretion
Hypothyroid (inactive)	16%	58%
Normal	34%	48%
Hyperthyroid (overactive)	65%	24%

Studies with radioactive iodine can supply this information very readily. Many different isotopes of iodine can be used for this purpose, including I^{131}. As already mentioned, I^{131} is one of the byproducts of fission processes in a reactor, it has a halflife of 8.3 days; it can be very readily purchased from the Atomic Energy Commission after proper

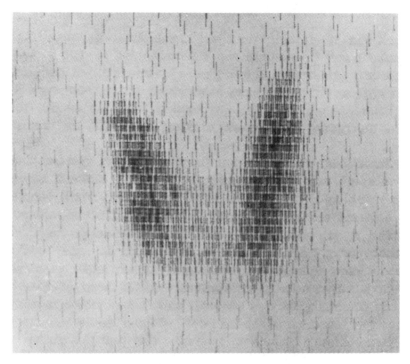

Fig. 19.1   Scan with a scintillation counter of a thyroid gland 6 hours after ingestion of radioactive Iodine-123. (Photo courtesy of Prof. William G. Myers.)

licensing. Typical shipments consist of 10 millicures (mCi) of I^{131}, where a mCi of a radioactive element is that amount in which 37 million atoms decay per second (an amount which poses a considerable threat to a human being). Each I^{131} atom decays into xenon-131 by emitting both an electron and an energetic gamma ray; this gamma ray is in fact energetic enough so that it can penetrate all the way through the body tissue overlaying the thyroid gland. To diagnose the health of the gland, one therefore gives the patient an "atomic cocktail" containing a known quantity of I^{131} to drink. Then, 24 hours later, a detector for gamma rays is placed a standard distance away

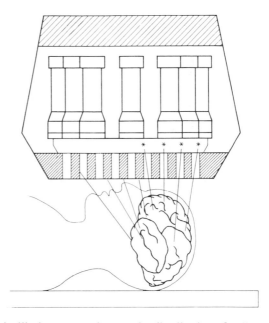

Fig. 19.2   The Anger scintillation camera images the distribution of radio-activity. The gamma rays are collimated by lead, photomultiplier tubes detect these gamma rays, and the signals are then processed and displayed on an oscilloscope screen.

from the neck and the count rate of gamma rays emitted from the gland is taken. This count rate then gives directly the percent up-take.

It is possible to obtain even more detailed information about a thyroid gland or any other organ by taking its picture using the radi-ation as "light." The field of view of the detector is made very narrow by means of a collimator made out of lead with a narrow hole in it, and the organ is scanned by moving the detector over it. Whenever the detector sees a "hot" or "cold" spot in the distribution of radiation, the count rate rises or falls off at that point in the scan. Figure 19.1 shows

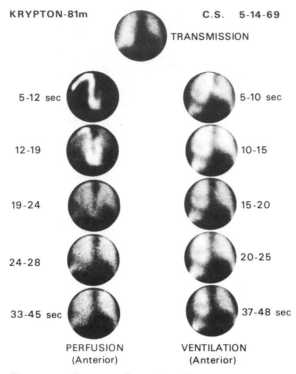

KRYPTON-81m   C.S.   5-14-69   TRANSMISSION

5-12 sec   5-10 sec

12-19   10-15

19-24   15-20

24-28   20-25

33-45 sec   37-48 sec

PERFUSION   VENTILATION
(Anterior)   (Anterior)

Fig. 19.3 Lung studies with radioactive Krypton-81 m (with a halflife of 13 sec). In the perfusion study the radioactivity was infused into a vein; in the ventilation study the patient inhaled air containing the radioactivity. These studies show poor ventilation and perfusion into the right lung. (Photo courtesy of Prof. Yukio Yano; see Ref. 9.5, p. 674.)

such a scan of a normal thyroid gland taken with radioactive iodine, in this case I^{123}. There are more modern techniques of getting this whole picture instantaneously. This involves the apparatus resembling a pinhole camera shown in Fig. 19.2. A piece of lead with a very small hole is used to view the radioactive sample. The radiation falls on a big crystal which emits light wherever struck by the gamma rays. The distribution of radioactivity in the sample is then reproduced as light spots in the crystal; this light distribution in turn is converted by some photomultiplier tubes (light detectors) coupled to complex electronic circuitry into electrical pulses which display these dots on an oscilloscope screen where they can be photographed. Because the whole picture can be acquired in a short time, it then becomes possible to study dynamic processes, such as a radioactive compound moving through an organ, as shown in Fig. 19.3. In all this, the overriding objective is to get information with a minimum of exposure of the patient to radiation, and nuclear technology is constantly increasing the efficiency of data gathering.

EFFECTS OF RADIATION ON MAN

Of course, diagnosis is only the first step. Once a defective thyroid gland has been detected, it is often possible to treat the abnormality by means of radioactive isotopes; in this case there is a very specific treatment in which the skin and the rest of the body are relatively unaffected by any radiation. If the patient is given a large dose of radioactive iodine, it will again accumulate in the thyroid gland and irradiate the thyroid tissue. If part of the tissue is cancerous, then, by careful selection of the dosage, that part may be destroyed, while leaving the healthy tissue alive.

Effects of radiation on living tissue had, of course, first been observed in the pioneers playing with the (then) new x-rays. And even now, x-ray specialists suffer from the effects of radiation. In a study of the causes of death of 82,441 physicians as reported in the period 1930–1954, it was found that radiologists died on the average 5.2 years younger than do other physicians. Relevant to this point is the book *American Martyrs to Science Through the Roentgen Rays* (Ref. 19.3) concerning some of the pioneers in the field of radiology. Just one short excerpt will indicate the terrible consequences to physicians of using their hands to calibrate their fluoroscopes or of remaining in close proximity to patients during their exposure in order to reassure them. One of these pioneers was Benjamin Franklin Thomas. He was a physics professor at the Ohio State University when x-rays were discovered, and he promptly repeated and extended Roentgen's studies.

> He was quick to perceive . . . that the practical future of the x-rays was within the field of medicine. . . . In the autumn of 1896,

before American roentgenology had completely emerged from its "premedical" era—in other words, an era when the number of medical men attacking its study with anywhere near the system and thoroughness of the physicists was far from being "enough to go around," Doctor Thomas was called on to make a radiographic record of the vertebral bone structure, at the lower thoracic and upper lumbar levels, in an adult patient of a local medical practitioner. In order to spare the patient the annoyance of an additional visit or of possible repeated exposures in the effort to determine the proper exposure-time in this deeply seated structure, he instituted an inquiry based on a series of experimental exposures on himself over the corresponding anatomic region. To reveal even the contour of the "shadows" of the vertebrae with the primitive Crookes tube of that day, whereof the penetration would drop rapidly with the inception of heat production, was a tremendous task. With his own body as the control, Doctor Thomas's first exposure lasted "roughly two hours," and was followed by several others progressively shorter!

The result, in about two weeks, was an area of localized dermatitis four or five inches square involving the anterior abdominal wall, an area which promptly broke down, with sloughing of the subcutaneous tissues until the peritonaeum was denuded.

For a number of years Doctor Thomas's life was spared, but he was spared neither physical distress nor disability. The extensive wound would show a tendency to heal under the assiduous care it received, only to break down at remarkably regular periodic intervals. With this handicap and that of the internal derangement engendered by it, he carried on his teaching work with increased periods of very necessary rest. The pre-occupation of work, as with so many of these roentgen martyrs, had a certain analgesic effect on him. His death, when ultimately his strength failed him, was not the type of metastatic death usually recorded in their history, but was due rather to a slow process of interstitial visceral degeneration in the immediate vicinity of the structures involved in the initial roentgen-disorganization. Two other similar instances have been recorded among the pioneers herein considered. (Ref. 19.3, pp. 101–104.)

Since then our understanding of the effects of radiation on tissue has improved somewhat. It is appropriate here to give the vocabulary

Table 19.1
Symptoms of radiation sickness from observations made in Japan. (Data from
Ref. 19.1, p. 135.)

Time after exposure	600r (lethal dose)	400r (median lethal dose)	200r (moderate dose)
	Nausea and vomiting after two hours	Nausea and vomiting after two hours	
First week	No definite symptoms		
	Diarrhoea, vomiting, inflamation of throat	No definite symptoms	No definite symptoms
Second week	Fever, rapid emaciation leading to death (100 percent)		
Third week		Loss of hair begins Loss of appetite General malaise Fever and pallor leading to rapid emaciation and death for 50% of the population	Loss of hair Loss of appetite Sore throat Pallor and diarrhoea Recovery begins (no deaths in absence of complications)
Fourth week			

necessary to obtain a feeling for the magnitudes of irradiation involved in medicine, as well as in the exposures from nuclear bombs
and fallout. Radiation exposure is talked about in terms of the Roentgen (r), the radiation unit (rad), or the Roentgen-equivalent-in-man
(rem). They all represent essentially the same radiation dose (in terms
of an energy per volume; the difference among them has to do with
their relative effectiveness in damaging human-body tissue. The
following will give an idea of the magnitude of these units: for a single
whole-body exposure of 400r of gamma rays, 50% of the population of
an average sample of human beings will die. The data in Table 19.1
comes from observations made in Japan following the nuclear ex-

Table 19.2
Radiation dose necessary to kill 50% of the population (LD50). (Data from Ref. 19.1, p. 110.)

Mammals	200–1,000r
Goldfish	700r
Frog	700r
Tortoise	1,500r
Newt	3,000r
Snail	10,000r
Yeast	30,000r
Bacterium coli	10,000r
Fruit fly (adult) and other insects	60,000r
Amoeba	100,000r
Paramecia	300,000r

plosions at Hiroshima and Nagasaki. The table does not include any longer-range effects such as a shortening of life due to induced cancer or due to a lowering of the body's ability to resist disease. For comparison, we list typical dosage from medical x-rays (note that in these cases the radiation does not irradiate the whole body, this reduces the total damage done by it):

Chest x-ray: as little as 0.05r, as much as 1r if poorly done.
Chest fluoroscopy: as much as 130r if poorly done.
Gastrointestinal series: 15r, as much as 200r if poorly done.
Lumbro-sacral series: 7r to 24r.
Dental x-rays: full mouth 70r, as much as 500r if poorly done.

And finally, the average lifetime dose from various background radiations (such as cosmic rays) is on the order of 10r of whole-body irradiation. So, clearly, the Roentgen unit is the relevant one for the exposures we might experience over our lifetime. For a discussion of the effects of very weak long-term exposures, see Chapter 20.

If we ask more specifically just how radiation damage in tissue is correlated to dosage, we must consider the following facts. One observation is the relative radiation sensitivities of different animals and microanimals as shown in Table 19.2. The sensitivity of isolated mammalian cells in tissue cultures also varies greatly: while the lymphocytes in blood may be killed by as little as 300r, some cells from the skin may survive as much as 5000r. One of the most easily detectable

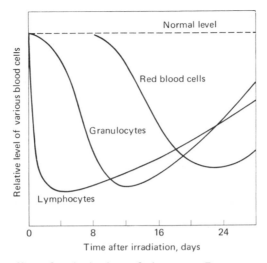

Fig. 19.4 Effect of a single dose of about 300 Roentgens of x-rays on the different cells in blood. (Data from Ref. 19.1.)

changes induced by nonlethal doses is a hold-up in cell division as shown in Fig. 19.4. For high dosages the cultures never completely recover from the irradiation. Radiation can also break chromosome linkages; in that case the radiation sensitivity depends on the phase of the mitotic cycle, with the highest sensitivity occurring at the moment of chromosome division. In general, these data can be summarized in the Law of Bergonie and Tribondeau as quoted at the beginning of this chapter. There are, of course, some exceptions to this rule; the most notable ones are the lymphocytes (the white blood cells), which are quite incapable of division at the end of their mitotic cycle, yet are highly radiosensitive. Figure 19.5 shows the effect of a single dose of x-rays of 300r on the different cells of the blood; clearly the white lymphocytes are most quickly eradicated, while the blood-clotting red cells survive the longest. These lymphocytes can be affected by radiation dosages as low as 25r.

While the Law of Bergonie and Tribondeau does not tell us exactly how cells are affected by radiation—whether by ionization of

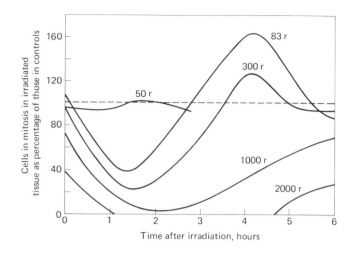

Fig. 19.5 Effects of increasing x-ray dosage on the rate of cell division. Up to 30or, there is only a temporary depression, with a compensatory recovery. For higher doses, mitosis is fully suppressed for a time and never recovers completely. (Data from Ref. 19.1.)

water, or whatever—it does show why radiation can both produce and destroy cancer. On the one hand, radiation induces cancer by causing mutations in cells by ionizations and by chromosome destruction. It is particularly dangerous to rapidly dividing tissue as in a foetus, while it affects the dormant skin much less. The stomach lining consists of cells which reproduce very rapidly, and much of the diarrhoea and loss of appetite observed in the atomic bomb victims was due to the complete destruction of this lining. On the other hand, radiation can destroy cancer because cancer consists of very rapidly growing cells which are then abnormally sensitive to radiation effects.

THE RADIATION TREATMENT OF CANCER

The treatment of cancer by means of radioactive isotopes thus hinges on getting the radiation dose to the cancerous cells without killing the normal cells. In a few cases, as for the thyroid gland, the cancerous area selectively takes up some chemical compound like iodine. If this is not the case, other techniques must be used. It is, for example, possible to beam the radiation into the body from the outside in a teletherapy unit. By irradiating natural cobalt in a reactor, curies of Co^{60} can be produced. This Co^{60} can then be installed inside a lead housing with a narrow exit port through which the high-energy gamma rays emitted by the Co^{60} are directed at the cancer. To reduce skin damage, the patient may even be rotated about an axis passing through the tumor, so that the beam traverses various parts of the body while always striking the tumor. Another example of external irradiation is the use of strontium-90 (Sr^{90}) for the treatment of skin cancers. This source of electrons is placed directly against the skin; since these electrons never penetrate deeply enough to damage the underlying tissue, a radiation dose is given only to the cancerous surface skin cells.

If external irradiation is for some reason undesirable, then it is possible to deliver the radiation dosage more directly to the cancer. One can, for example, make small pellets of radioactive gold and insert these directly into the cancerous tissue. Not only is the gold chemically inert, so that it remains in location with no side effects, but furthermore, with a halflife of 2.7 days, its radiation soon dies out completely, so that the gold can be safely left in place after the treatment. Alternatively, some radioactive pellets can be put into nylon tubing which is then sewn into the cancer in the desired pattern and can later be withdrawn.

CONCLUSIONS

This has been a necessarily very sketchy review of some aspects of nuclear medicine. Obviously there could have been a much longer discussion of various potentially useful radioisotopes and their relative merits. We could have discussed the diagnosis of breathing functions by means of oxygen-15, which has a halflife of only two minutes, so that some hospitals are installing cyclotrons in their basements just to produce it on the spot. We might have talked of long-lived yttrium-87 "cows" (solutions), where the Y^{87} constantly decays to Sr^{87}, which can be "milked" (separated) from the Y^{87} and then used in bone studies. In the treatment section we could have analyzed the tremendous advantages of some of the newer isotopes over the old radium and radon techniques with respect to lower patient exposures for the same diagnostic information. We could also have discussed the more specific character of radiation damage in cells, by talking about the production of hydroxyl ions and excited water ions. But the point is clear: the use of radioactive isotopes has made a large contribution to medicine. There are two questions that might be asked: Were these developments a scientific or a technological interaction (i.e., can science take any credit for the benefits)? And was it necessary to produce and use the atomic bomb in order to obtain the impetus toward nuclear medicine?

DISCUSSION

This interaction between science and society seems to take place primarily on the technological level. That is not to say that there are no scientists involved in these developments; on the contrary, there are several hundred bona fide nuclear physicists who have gone into this field and have made tremendous contributions. But to some extent they are motivated by a social sense of responsibility for the applications of nuclear physics, and they do the work for a social purpose. It usually comes down to a question of the possible; i.e., what isotope can be produced right now in large enough quantities, and at a low enough price, which will do the job? There are many feasibility studies, much gadgetry, and ultimately much salesmanship, but there comes out relatively little addition to nuclear physics in a very basic sense. Of course, there were scientific contributions to medicine, but there again it was frequently a matter of overcoming the inertia of the medical profession rather than of producing scientifically convincing data. If this is indeed a technological interaction, then we must raise the question whether nuclear medicine has led to an improvement in both the quality of life as well as in the quantity of life. About the latter there is not much question; just to cite an example—the cancer survival rates have essentially doubled from 1940 to 1960. But in the same sense as there are now being raised some questions about the overall value of heart transplants, one can ask: have these advances in medical technology not at times led to an unnecessary preserving and prolonging of life at the expense of not only much money but also of great agony? And are perhaps some bad genes being retained in the world genetic pool which would otherwise mercifully die out? These questions are perhaps somewhat farfetched in this context, but they are not totally irrelevant.

Finally, has nuclear medicine repaid any possible debt accrued at Hiroshima and Nagasaki? There is no doubt that the nuclear reactor, as well as other developments of the atomic bomb program, were necessary for these great developments. This in some sense reduces that question to whether the nuclear reactor and these other developments would have come about at anywhere near the actual rate without the Manhattan Project. Could a group of "socially responsible" nuclear scientists have squelched the atomic bomb without delaying or losing the medical benefits? One could apply a cost-effectiveness approach by considering the fact that the origin of many of these hundreds of ex-nuclear physicists lies in the Manhattan Project, and that their motivation in part may have been a guilt feeling, and that these nuclear scientists pushed for public benefits from the AEC after the war. Then one might be inclined to believe that indeed the atomic-bomb project has paid for itself; if for no other reason than as an object lesson in "social responsibility." But that is a rather cold-blooded approach.

REFERENCES

Prime references

19.1 P. Alexander, *Atomic Radiation and Life*, Baltimore: Penguin Books, 1957; the introductory quotation is on p 66.

19.2 J. Schubert and R. E. Lapp, *Radiation: What It Is and How It Affects You*, New York: Viking Press, 1957; Chapters 3–5, pp. 32–107.

Interesting reading

19.3 P. Brown, *American Martyrs To Science*, (Ref. 12.6).

19.4 G. L. Brownell and R. J. Shalek, "Nuclear Physics in Medicine," *Physics Today* **23**, 32–38 (August 1970).

19.5 Y. Yano, J. McRae and H. O. Anger, "Lung Function Studies Using Short-Lived ^{81m}Kr and the Scintillation Camera," *Journal of Nuclear Medicine* **11** (#11), 674 (November 1970). See other issues of this journal for further relevant articles.

QUESTIONS FOR DISCUSSION

1. Are doctors scientists?

2. All persons liable to be exposed to harmful radiation must wear film badges to record the dosage they have received. These are then processed by a radiation-safety office, and if the recorded dosage exceeds certain standards, the person is not allowed to work with radiation for some time. Some radiologists deliberately forget to wear these badges whenever they know that they will be exposed to large doses of radiation, since they feel their contributions to mankind should not be halted just because some old fogy in an office says so. Is this a reasonable attitude? Is it right to deliberately sacrifice your life for others?

3. Figures are not easy to obtain, but the savings in lives through nuclear medicine by now have far exceeded the number of lives lost in Hiroshima and Nagasaki. Is such a cost-accounting a reasonable technique for a technological assessment of the atomic bomb?

4. At what point should doctors stop trying to prolong the life of suffering patients?

20 | THE HYDROGEN BOMB AND FALLOUT

Sweet and lovely and beautiful.

J. Robert Oppenheimer about the technical breakthrough which
made the fusion bomb feasible

The history and the development of the hydrogen bomb is presented, with emphasis on the political context in which the scientific/technological decisions were made. The implications of the radioactive fallout associated with bomb tests are discussed.

INTRODUCTION

Ernest Sternglass, a radiological physicist at the University of Pittsburgh, has suggested (Ref. 20.3) that radioactive fallout is responsible for 375,000 infant deaths in the United States during the period 1951–1966. He argues that there is a correlation, as shown in Fig. 20.1, between changes in the infant mortality rate and local accumulations of Sr^{90} fallout. He arrives at this number by evaluating the difference between the decrease in the infant-mortality rate extrapolated from prebomb times and that which actually occurred. This suggestion has, of course, provoked a tremendous controversy; its implications are obviously extremely far-reaching with respect to nuclear weaponry.

This chapter will present the scientific and political facts behind the development of the hydrogen (or fusion) bomb. It is the radioactive fallout from the test programs associated with this development which so concerns Sternglass. Therefore we shall examine the charac-

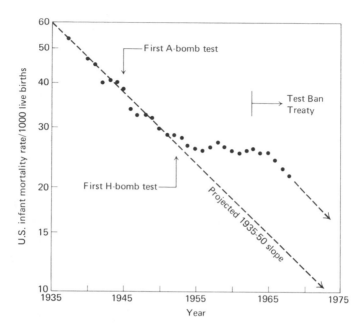

Fig. 20.1   Infant mortality per 1000 live births. Projected slope is fitted to the data of the period 1935–50, assuming that continued improvement in the mortality rate would have happened if there had been no nuclear weapon tests. (Data from Ref. 20.3.)

teristics of this fallout, both to clarify the debate and to indicate the power of the fusion process and the magnitude of that new weapon. But ultimately, the most interesting aspect of the fusion-bomb program will be the way in which the political and historical context impinged on the scientific and technological developments.

THE FUSION PROCESS

In the fission process very heavy nuclei, such as uranium, are induced by neutron bombardment to split into two more-or-less equal smaller atoms. The reaction is an easy one to initiate, since the bombarding neutrons are not repelled by the nucleus which is to be split. The energy released in the fission reaction is on the order of 0.1% of the total fissioned mass. Fusion is exactly the opposite process. Two light nuclei fuse together to form a heavier nucleus. This process takes place much less readily than fission, since the charged nuclei repel each other, energy must be supplied to start the reaction by bringing them into contact with each other. The reaction of this type which is the easiest to initiate takes place between deuterium and tritium and leads to a helium nucleus plus a proton plus a large quantity of energy. To make even this reaction go requires a bombarding energy equivalent to a temperature on the order of 100,000,000 degrees centigrade. The amount of energy released in such fusion processes is enormous; it can in fact be as much as 0.7% of the total mass of the fusing nuclei; i.e., fusion can be seven times as efficient as fission. But the biggest advantage of the fusion process is the ready availability of the components involved. Deuterium, for example, exists in all ordinary water to the extent of one part in 6700, so the supply is essentially unlimited.

THE HYDROGEN BOMB

These facts about the fusion process were well known before the Second World War. Consequently it is not too surprising that the building of a fusion bomb (the "Super") was proposed by Edward Teller in 1942, early in the U.S. atomic bomb project. The high ignition temperatures were to be provided by the fission bomb, once it was completed. However, so many technical objections were raised at the time against building such a bomb, particularly by Oppenheimer, that it was not very actively pursued. And since an atomic bomb was required as a trigger, the A-bomb project obviously required the highest priority. But even after the end of the war, Teller was not able to overcome all of the objections which made the fusion bomb seem unfeasible. For example, the tritium for the bomb would have to be made from lithium by neutron bombardment in a reactor. This placed it in direct competition with the production of plutonium; one pound of tritium required as many neutrons as 80 pounds of plutonium. A fusion bomb could seemingly be made only at the expense of many fission bombs. Furthermore, to make the fusion bomb feasible, the deuterium-tritium mixture would have to be very closely packed; the only feasible way to do this appeared to be to liquefy the mixture by cooling it to a very low temperature in a huge refrigerator. So seemingly a fusion bomb would never be small enough to be carried in an airplane. A final difficulty lay in the enormously complex calculations which would be necessary to design such a bomb. Of course, Teller argued that this would be a fantastic weapon, of virtually unlimited potential; and that if enough people would work in such a development program, then such problems would surely be solved by someone.

But until 1949 no great effort was invested in Teller's "Super." Then in September of that year President Truman announced that the Russians had exploded an atomic bomb. This was a great shock, since this had not been expected to happen before 1955. Immediately in January of 1950 Truman ordered the Atomic Energy Commission to proceed with the development of the hydrogen bomb. It still appeared that the best hope was to coat the fastest possible fission bomb with successive layers of frozen tritium and deuterium to the amount of about a cubic yard. There was in fact a test of such a bomb in 1951 at Eniwetok Atoll; it did not work. Then Stan Ulam and Teller came up with a technically sweet idea (an idea which is still classified), and the first hydrogen bomb, "Mike", was set off in November 1952. Its three megatons caused the Atoll of Elugelab to vanish. In 1953 came another shock when Russia announced its first explosion of an airplane-dropped hydrogen bomb. The final reduction in size of the bomb came about when the bomb was made out of the crystalline material lithium hydride (Li^6H^2). In a fusion bomb made out of this compound, the required tritium is produced on the spot from the lithium by the neutrons from the fission trigger. No refrigeration is necessary. The first dry U.S. hydrogen bomb was set off on March 4, 1954. (But note that no transportable hydrogen bomb was available to the U.S. until 1956.) A large contribution to this bomb was made by the ENIAC and MANIAC computers.

THE BIKINI HYDROGEN BOMB ACCIDENT

The most controversial fact about this first "dry" U.S. hydrogen bomb was the accident involved in its explosion; the most significant fact was the nature of the resulting radioactive fallout. This bomb was mounted on a test tower on the edge of Bikini Atoll in the Marshall Islands. There were several nearby islands (where "nearby" meant less than 150 miles, but more than 50 miles; see Fig. 20.2). But these were essentially eastward of Bikini, and the bomb was to be set off only if the wind were guaranteed to be at least NE. In addition the

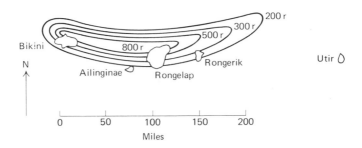

Fig. 20.2 Bikini bomb fallout pattern from the 1954 20-megaton hydrogen bomb. (After Ref. 20.4.).

area downwind for many miles had been checked for intruding boats; so everything appeared to be quite safe with respect to possible fallout.

Then three things happened: At 20 megatons the bomb was about twice as powerful as expected; the wind changed to an easterly direction; and a Japanese tuna trawler, the *Lucky Dragon #5*, was fishing undetected within 100 miles North of Rongelap. The explosion blew a lot of debris into the air, primarily from the surrounding coral. The *Lucky Dragon* was not damaged by the blast, but three hours later flecks of grayish-white dust settled on the boat and on the 23 men on board. The dust also settled on those not-so-nearby islands. While their populations were evacuated as soon as possible, the natives went about their normal work outside for up to 48 hours and received considerable radiation exposures, ranging as high as 175r. Figure 20.2 shows clearly that if the wind had shifted just a little more, people as far as 150 miles away from the blast could have been killed. When the *Lucky Dragon* returned home two weeks later, some of the men were immediately diagnosed to be suffering from radiation sickness. Checks of the boat indicated that the men had received a radiation dose estimated at 200r. The victims suffered nausea the night of the blast, then swelling and reddening of the face, neck, and hands, complete loss of hair, and within three months 17 cases of jaundice were reported; seven months after the blast, the radio operator of the *Lucky Dragon* died from a liver disorder brought on perhaps by a blood transfusion which replaced blood damaged by the radiation. A panic swept over Japan when it was found that a sizable amount of the Japanese fish catch made at the time was radioactive. Some of the fish had clearly concentrated the fission radioactivity from the sea water to as much as 100,000 times above the background level.

In the process of detailed analysis of data related to this contamination, it became clear that the amount of fallout was far larger than expected. The fission-bomb trigger should have produced relatively little fallout because of its small size, while the fusion process is relatively "clean". Then a Japanese physicist found U^{237} in the fallout, which could only have been produced by the inclusion of natural uranium (U^{238}) in the bomb. From such data it became evident that the Bikini shot must have been a three-stage blast: a fission trigger which set off a fusion bomb, which in turn emitted enough neutrons to convert an outer layer, made up of about one ton of natural uranium, into a further huge fission device. For only $35,000, the price of this ton of uranium, the power of this bomb was almost tripled. This made the sky the limit in bomb power—and in fallout, since such an enormous fission bomb is very "dirty" with respect to producing radioactivity.

THE NATURE OF FALLOUT

The existence of this bomb, and its ability to unleash an unlimited amount of radioactivity from cheap uranium onto the earth, has certainly changed the world. The doomsday machine of *Dr. Strangelove*, which releases enough radioactivity to kill off mankind, is probably possible. In fact, the scenario for such a possibility is contained in the book and movie *On The Beach*. We will now briefly consider both the pattern and the nature of present and potential fallout. This will provide a scale of measuring the significance of this weapon.

A hydrogen bomb is an unbelievable weapon. A one-megaton fusion process will be completed in less than one millionth of a second. After 1/100th of a second, the fireball will be about 440 feet in diameter, and at a distance of 300 miles will be as bright as the noonday sun. In 10 seconds it will have expanded to a $1\frac{1}{2}$-mile diameter and will be rising at 300 mph. After six minutes it will be 14 miles high and will be a cloud of condensed particles, first red because of 5000 tons of nitric acid, then white. About 50% of its energy will go into blast or pressure waves, 35% into heat radiation, and 15% into radioactivity. The range of devastation of such bombs increases as the cube root of their energy; this blast will destroy buildings at two miles, or about

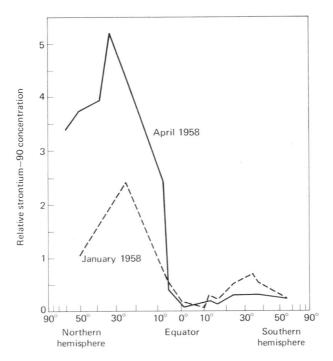

Fig. 20.3 Strontium-90 content of the air, as measured in air samples collected by the U.S. Naval Research Laboratory. (Data from Ref. 20.5.)

four times as far away as did the 20-kiloton bomb dropped on Hiroshima. Third-degree burns are possible as far away as 13 miles.

The radioactivity produced by this megaton bomb is fantastic. One hour after the explosion, the gamma radiation is equivalent to the radioactivity from 300,000 tons of radium. Some of this radioactive material settles very quickly, some rides the dust for weeks, and some will rise into the stratosphere. It is the very long-lived isotopes which are of long-range concern, since they have the chance of being spread all over the globe via the stratosphere. And the two most important isotopes in this kind of fallout are Cs^{137} and Sr^{90}, with halflives of 33 years and 28 years, respectively. Of these two, Sr^{90} is the most dangerous because of its chemical resemblance to calcium. This one-megaton bomb produces an amount of Sr^{90} equivalent in gamma radiation to 400 pounds of radium.

The distribution of fallout from a nuclear bomb depends on its power. A small bomb will drop most of its products a few miles down-wind, while the megaton bomb will drop contaminants as far away as several hundred miles via the troposphere. If the bomb is even more powerful, then a large part of the debris will be thrust into the strato-sphere, where it will participate in the global air circulation pattern. Globally the air circulates separately in the Southern and Northern Hemispheres, going up near the equator and down near the poles in both cases. This means that there should be relatively little mixing of northern air and southern air; only 10% of all radioactivity released north of the equator should ever get into the southern circulation cycle. Figure 20.3 supports this conclusion. This phenomenon, in fact, forms the basis for the temporary survival of the Australian popula-tion after the nuclear war in *On The Beach*. This circulation pattern also correctly predicts that Russian fallout from their far-north tests will come to ground very quickly; and it predicts that fallout will be strongest in late winter when the increased cold in the arctic leads to increased circulation.

THE EFFECTS OF FALLOUT

Most of the Sr^{90} and Cs^{137}, produced in the approximately 1000 megatons of nuclear explosions to date, has settled to the ground. The Sr^{90} has been mixed with natural calcium. It is now being taken up by the roots of plants along with this calcium and is being passed on to the leaves. From there it can go into human beings directly via lettuce, milk, or meat. There is generally a certain amount of dis-crimination by plant and animal tissue against strontium, as opposed to calcium, so that the relative concentration of strontium in plants and animals may ultimately be reduced by as much as a factor of 10. This is, however, not a universal rule; both rice and fish seem to actually prefer strontium over calcium.

Once the strontium is inside the human system, it is incorporated into the bones as they grow, thus particularly affecting children. And it tends to be trapped there with a biological halflife of about 10 years.

The strontium in the bones is in a position to do real damage. Not only is it strongly localized in the bone per se; it furthermore tends to accumulate at the specific point where the bone is growing. In addition, the strontium emits electrons when it decays, and since these have only a very short range in tissue, they lead to very intense local irradiation of the bone marrow. Finally, the Sr^{90} is bad because this bone marrow in turn is extrasensitive to radiation, since it is constantly producing blood. The lifetime radiation dose from Sr^{90} to this marrow in the United States is an estimated average of 1 to 6 roentgens, which compares to a natural background dose of about 6r (due to cosmic rays, brick walls, etc.) and a typical lifetime x-ray dose of 3 to 7r. (See, e.g., Fig. 13 on p. 62 of Ref. 20.5.)

The other long-lived contaminant, Cs^{137}, is not quite so dangerous. It does not concentrate nearly as much as strontium; it has a relatively short biological halflife of 20 days, and its radiation is energetic gamma rays which produce irradiation of the whole body. The special danger of Cs^{137} is its irradiation of the genes, which presents a potential hazard to man's heredity. The total lifetime dosage from Cs^{137} fallout is only about 0.1r, small compared to other background contributions.

The Atomic Energy Commission feels that, since the dosages from fallout are smaller than other unavoidable irradiation, we must therefore accept fallout as part of the price of national security. And, in fact, there is much debate on whether or not the fallout should be of concern. The debate hinges to a large extent on whether or not there exists a threshhold to radiation damage. It might be that small continuous exposures to irradiation actually give the body time to recover continuously; in that case these small fallout doses might cause no harm at all. However, as indicated at the beginning of this chapter, some scientists believe that low-dose irradiations of many people are just as harmful as large doses given to few people. In the latter case it is possible to estimate the effects of fallout. There are guesses that in the United States, fallout shortens the average lifespan by somewhere between one-half to six days and has resulted in one to two thousand additional leukemia cases. Sternglass has tried to establish even more far-reaching effects of this fallout. As Fig. 20.1 shows, there occurred a leveling off in infant mortality rates in the U.S. after 1950. Most scientists ascribe this effect to improvements in health-reporting and to the lack of further significant improvements in maternity health after the wonder drugs were mass-produced following World War II. Sternglass, however, tries to show that there is a correlation between changes in these actual infant and foetal mortality rates and specific bomb-testing events and fallout distributions. He assumes that without fallout the mortality would have kept dropping after 1950 in the same way as between 1935 and 1950. The differences between the expected and the observed rates, when multiplied by the number of births, leads then to this grim figure of 375,000 deaths induced by fallout in the U.S. While these estimates are not generally accepted (see Ref. 20.3), the mere possibility that *some* deaths may be attributable to fallout is disquieting.

SUMMARY

As with the atomic bomb, the scientific aspects of the hydrogen or fusion bomb were public knowledge before World War II, and there was similarly an agreement about its feasibility—a general technological consensus which in this case said "not readily." As long as only a few scientists like Teller tried to counter this "no," then most scientists were able to resist the construction of the "Super," citing in part moral grounds for their resistance. The decision to build the hydrogen bomb was ultimately a political decision, but even then it took that (classified) flash of scientific (technological?) genius to make most of the nuclear scientists work on the project with a reasonable amount of enthusiasm.

The political decision to build the fusion bomb was based primarily on fear of Russia, a fear induced by the explosion in 1949 of the first Russian atomic bomb. This fear may have been self-induced; nonetheless, it was there. The resulting military secrecy concerning the bomb ultimately prolonged the general ignorance about harmful fallout radiation effects. While the above-ground test moratorium has now led to a stoppage of the atmospheric pollution by radioactive materials, such contaminants as Sr^{90} are now incorporated into all plant and animal tissue. The extent of the resulting health hazard is very much subject to debate, with estimates of resulting fatalities ranging from negligible to many hundreds of thousands. In any case, the critical question always comes down to the matter of national security, a topic where scientific consensus is not very relevant.

REFERENCES

Prime references

20.1 J. Schubert and R.E. Lapp, *Radiation: What It Is and How It Affects You*, (Ref. 19.2); pp. 212–253.

20.2 R. Jungk, *Brighter Than a Thousand Suns*, (Ref. 17.4); Chapter 16, "Joe I and Super," Chapter 17, "Dilemma of the Conscience," and Chapter 18, "In the Sign of the MANIAC," pp. 260–312.

Interesting reading

20.3 E. J. Sternglass, "Infant Mortality and Nuclear Tests," *Bulletin of the Atomic Scientists* **25**, 18–20 (April 1969); see also replies to this article in the issues of October 1969, December 1969, and May 1970.

20.4 E. Teller and A. Latter, *Our Nuclear Future*, New York: Criterion Books, 1958.

20.5 J. M. Fowler, Ed., *Fallout: A Study of Superbombs, SR-90 and Survival*, New York: Basic Books, Inc., 1960.

20.6 W. L. Laurence, *Men and Atoms*, (Ref. 17.1); Chapters 22–25, pp. 189–210.

20.7 R. E. Lapp, *The Voyage of The Lucky Dragon*, New York: Harper, 1958.

20.8 N. P. Davis, *Lawrence and Oppenheimer*, (Ref. 17.3); pp. 293–355.

20.9 G. Peter, *Red Alert*, now the movie *Dr. Strangelove: or How I Learned to Stop Worrying and Love the Bomb*, any one of several editions under either title; the use of a nuclear doomsday machine.

20.10 N. Shute, *On the Beach*, New York: Signet Book D1562, 1958; on the consequences of a nuclear war.

QUESTIONS FOR DISCUSSION

1. From 1953 to 1956 the U.S. had no hydrogen bombs which could be used, but Russia did. Can any traces of this apparent imbalance be found in external and internal U.S. policies, such as McCarthyism?

2. What should have been the role and approach of scientists in developing the fusion bomb? Of the military? Of the government?

3. A neutron bomb would wipe out all human life without destroying buildings. Would this be an immoral weapon?

4. The death rates from all fallout are presumably small even if not necessarily zero. What rates would be an acceptable cost of a bomb-test program?

5. Can bomb-testing in any sense be compared to enforced fluoridation?

21 | SCIENTIFIC HERESY, SECRECY, AND POLITICS

It was further reported that in the autumn of 1949 and subsequently, you strongly opposed the development of the hydrogen bomb: (1) on moral grounds, (2) by claiming it was not feasible, (3) by claiming there were insufficient facilities and scientific personnel to carry on the development, and (4) that it was not politically desirable.

24th charge in the accusation which led to Oppenheimer's being declared a security risk

Any scientist, participating in what has become a moving crap game, must expect to get slugged occasionally.

Norbert Wiener

A comparison is made between various examples of political control of scientific beliefs, both in the U.S.S.R. and in the U.S. The examples presented include the case of Kapitsa, the Lysenko affair, the *Scientific American* censorship, and the Oppenheimer affair.

INTRODUCTION

One of the more successful recent off-broadway plays in New York was the production of Heinar Kipphardt's, *In the Matter of J. Robert Oppenheimer* (Ref. 21.11). As suggested earlier, Oppenheimer is the tragic hero of the scientific establishment, and this play presents a version of the 1954 security-clearance hearing which put him in this role by attaching a political label to his scientific advice.

The Oppenheimer affair indicates that political interference in scientific activities was not unique to the Nazi regime. Both in the U.S. and in the U.S.S.R. events have taken place in which scientific activities were challenged on political grounds. This chapter presents several examples of such political interference. In Russia the question was generally one of loyalty to the ideological basis of the government; this will be illustrated by the examples of the physicist Peter Kapitsa and by the Lysenko affair in genetics. In the U.S. the problem was more one of loyalty to the political-military beliefs of the government; this can be illustrated by the examples of the 1950 censorship of the journal *Scientific American* and by the Oppenheimer case.

MARXISM AND SCIENCE

In considering the interaction of Soviet science and Soviet politics, one of the most fascinating aspects is the reevaluation that our viewpoint has undergone since the Second World War. In 1949, for example, Lewis Feuer still felt he could say:

> Perhaps the failure of Soviet physics to achieve the Western successes in atomic theory and invention are partially due to wasteful influence of the philosophy of dialectical materialism. (Ref. 21.1, p. 114.)

But then came the Russian atomic bomb, the hydrogen bomb, and finally Sputnik in 1957; so we now know this was an improper accusation; Soviet physics has certainly had enough achievements to satisfy anyone. So what actually is the interaction of science and politics in the U.S.S.R.?

Marxism is, by its very nature and origin, of particular interest as an example of the interaction of science and politics. After all, when Karl Marx and Friedrich Engels wrote their major works in England in the middle of the 19th century, it was in an atmosphere saturated with applied science and technology; Engels particularly was an avid reader of scientific works. Their revolt was not against science and technology, but rather against their misuse. As a result, the contemporary Soviet theory of knowledge is most accurately classified as a species of pragmatism, with a strong emphasis on usefulness. Whereas Plato held that only those statements which are useless can really be "true," the Soviet theory holds that only statements which are useful are really "true." This attitude attacks the concept of basic research by transforming the reasonable statement "we desire knowledge which will be of immediate practical value" into the unreasonable statement "knowledge consists of propositions which have an immediate practical value." The communistic concept of a dialectical materialism—of opposites, of struggle—also restricts the scope of theories of truth. It means that all scientific work must lead to some sort of victory—that Soviet science must be superior in defeating nature. In some sense this turns all scientific work into a technological effort to overcome nature rather than to understand her.

As a result of philosophical objectives for all Soviet science, there arose inevitably the demand that scientists should apply the dialectical materialism to science and at the same time not let science in any way do anything except substantiate this philosophy. The science-philosophy interaction was pictured as a one-way street.

PETER KAPITSA

In examining the science-politics relationship in Russia, there is the difficulty that the ideological impact is at times confused by the impact of pure power politics. In fact, the suggestion has been made (Ref. 21.6, p. 101) that the difficulties lie not in any incorrectness of dialetical materialism, but rather with political (not philosophical) misinterpretations. An example of this mixture of philosophy and power politics is the case of the Russian physicist Peter Kapitsa. Born in Russia in 1894, he went to Cambridge in 1921 to work under Rutherford. His field of specialization was the properties of materials at very low temperatures, particularly of liquid hydrogen and helium. He was so well thought of as a physicist that Rutherford had a laboratory built just for him. In addition, he was unique because his engineering background allowed him to make the mental switch from small-scale laboratory experiments to large-scale engineering production.

In the late 1920s and early 1930s, the Soviet government waged a campaign to lure back gifted emigrés; and Kapitsa clearly was one they wanted. But he had no desire to return. Then in 1934, he was invited back to Russia for a visit, and Stalin personally promised that he could leave again. However, once Kapitsa was inside Russia, his exit visa was canceled so that he had to stay. Stalin gave him all he needed; much of the equipment from his lab in Cambridge was bought by the Russian government; Kapitsa was made director of the Institute of Problems of Physics; and his favorite English tobacco was imported. So Kapitsa did the work which was expected of him; he discovered the superfluidity of liquid helium, and he built up an industry for liquifying gases. But it is reported that he refused to help evolve or improve the Russian atomic and hydrogen bombs. Supposedly Stalin, not daring to shoot or even exile the great scientist, had him confined by house arrest for several years. After Stalin's death, Kapitsa was reinstated in his position, and since then has acted as an elder statesman of Russian science.

It is tempting to say that here is an example of interference of communist philosophy with science. But actually the impact seems to have been primarily one of Stalin's power politics on Kapitsa's personal preference for living in England.

PHILOSOPHY AND SCIENCE IN THE U.S.S.R.

There are, however, some clear-cut cases where there was a direct impact of communist philosophy on science. Victims of philosophical attacks included the fields of relativity and quantum mechanics (attacks which we saw earlier in Nazi Germany) and cybernetics. Soviet philosophers frequently claimed that some parts of bourgeois science were rotten to the core, and the theory of relativity was definitely in that category. In 1953 A. A. Maksimov published the following remarks in a major Russian philosophical journal:

> ... we consider it right, not only to reject the whole conception of Einstein, but also to substitute another name for the name expressed by words "theory of relativity" as applied to problems of space, time, mass, and movement for great velocities. (As quoted in Ref. 21.3, p. 184.)

As a consequence, for a long time only the strictly technical applications of this theory were recognized in Russia, just as in Nazi Germany.

The field of quantum mechanics also inevitably came into conflict with dialectical materialism. After all, the Copenhagen school of quantum mechanics feels that no observable quantity has a unique value before a measurement of it has been made. This view conflicted at least in spirit with Lenin's contention that a dialectical materialist must recognize the existence of matter separate and independent from the mind. Once again Maksimov was in the forefront of this attack, as he accused scientists such as Bohr of not only committing grievous mistakes in the interpretation of science, but even of factual mistakes. As he put it:

> Only a decisive rejection of the idealistic inventions of N. Bohr and M. A. Markov [the Soviet defender of quantum mechanics], ... can lead our philosophical organ out of this blind alley into which it attempted to lure several sections of our intellegentsia, those inclined to waver on the basic questions of Marxist-Leninist ideology. (As quoted in Ref. 21.5. p. 390.)

Although Maksimov represented pseudoscience, he was successful enough to prevent for some time any consistent application of the Principle of Complementarity in Russian quantum mechanics, a principle which is very useful in connecting quantum-mechanical behavior with that predicted by classical Newtonian mechanics.

In the third interaction of physics with Marxism, in the field of cybernetics, where economic policy and even governmental structure were involved, Kapitsa himself gave a summary of the problem in 1962:

> *The Philosophical Dictionary* (1954 edition) [said]: "Cybernetics ... is a reactionary pseudo science, which emerged in the U.S.A. after the Second World War and spread widely in other capitalistic countries as well; a form of modern mechanism." ... philosophers should look ahead and see what is coming and not merely record a stage already passed. (As quoted in Ref. 21.4, p. 201.)

Cybernetics was originally found objectionable because it had close connections with the mechanistic view of such fields as psychology, pedagogy, biology, and econometrics, all of which were under strict control of the communist ideology. It was also associated with Western capitalistic attempts to replace the proletariat by automation. But in more recent years, cybernetics has had a dramatic rise in popularity in Russia. This is at least in part due to the fact that computers promise to make possible a centrally planned economy which still allows enough local administration to make the system efficient.

THE LYSENKO AFFAIR

In the above three examples there is a clear retardation of science by ideology. But these are minor cases compared to the Lysenko-Vasilov controversy in genetics. N. I. Vasilov directed agricultural research in the U.S.S.R. after the revolution, and by 1935 he had placed Soviet genetics in the forefront of world science. Then the geneticist, T. D. Lysenko, attacked him on the grounds that his work was inconsistent with dialectical materialism. He demanded that Vasilov should "come closer to life, to practice." And he accused him of "bowing slavishly before foreign science." As a result of this attack, Vasilov was ultimately exiled to Siberia, where he died in 1942. In this case, Lysenko used dialectical materialism to argue that "there can be no stable, hereditary characters, independent of the environment; no so-called 'pure lines,' or constant varieties of crops." All matter is, after all, in a constant state of flux. So Lysenko claimed that nurture must take charge of nature, that new breeds can be obtained by careful handling rather than by selection. For this school of thought, the accident of mutation is the enemy of ideology.

This struggle had a very practical background. Vasilov was revolutionizing Soviet agriculture, but this was taking time. Meanwhile the Soviet leaders were demanding immediate results. And Lysenko promised immediate results. One of the biggest agricultural problems in Russia at that time was the production of potatoes. The overriding desire in Russia then was to make each region of the country self-sufficient. However, this plan was not working in potato production, where healthy seed tubers could be produced in only one restricted area. So when Lysenko promised that it was possible to let each area produce its own tubers simply by changing the potato planting time and by increasing the loving care taken with the potatoes, he was publicly applauded by Stalin. Lysenko declared degeneration to be not the result of infectious diseases but instead an "aging" or "enfeeblement" of the plant due to excessive heat. In the Lysenko version of genetics, induced characteristics could be inherited. By publishing only the best results in experiments and rejecting the bad results as due to inefficient management, he was able to maintain this interpretation for many years. But contrary to juggled statistics, this policy led to an increase of only 10% in the yield per acre of potatoes in the U.S.S.R. from 1925 to 1958 (a period in which the U.S. output grew by 130%). Lysenko's theory was finally rejected in 1965, but this interference of political ideology with science did have very costly effects, far beyond just forcing scientists to subscribe to some cant or rhetoric.

CENSORSHIP OF SCIENTIFIC AMERICAN

We need now to ask the question whether the United States has done any better in this respect. And we can indeed find political interference in scientific activities, but it is an interference on the military-political level rather than in a philosophical-political manner. But since the military argues that it is engaged in preserving our philosophy and our way of life, this difference may not be so great.

One example of political interference with science in the U.S. occurred in 1950. As indicated in Chapter 20, in January of that year President Truman had directed that work should proceed on the hydrogen bomb. And in the middle of March, the Atomic Energy Commission asked all those concerned in that work to refrain from any public discussion of "the thermo-nuclear reactions of the commission's thermo-nuclear weapons development program" irrespective of whether or not the technical information was unclassified. The AEC explained that its objective was

> ... to avoid the release of technical information—which even though itself unclassified may be interpreted by virtue of the project connection of the speaker as reflecting upon the commission's program with respect to the thermo-nuclear weapons. (As quoted in Ref. 21.2, p. 8.)

Some weeks earlier, the physicist Hans A. Bethe had undertaken to write an article about the newly projected hydrogen bomb for the journal *Scientific American* as part of a special series on fusion processes. During the Second World War, Bethe had been Chief of the Theoretical Physics Division at Los Alamos, and in 1950 he was still employed as contract consultant by the AEC. Needless to say, he was careful not to reveal any classified information in this article. Yet in March, the AEC asked that several sentences be deleted from this article and that the 3000 copies of the magazine already printed be destroyed. The expurgated version then was published. The censored sentences said the following.

1. Bethe explained that heavy hydrogen (deuterium or tritium), rather than ordinary hydrogen, would be used in such a bomb. This information had been published in the 1930s long before fission was known; and the editors of *Scientific American* published it in another article of this series as a table derived from the public literature.
2. Bethe pointed out that a fission bomb was necessary to start the fusion process. This was an obvious fact from the published knowledge that enormous ignition temperatures were required to trigger fusion. For example, the Austrain physicist Hans Thirring in 1946 had published a book pointing this out.
3. Bethe also stated that an exploding H-bomb would release a flux of neutrons roughly in proportion to its power. This information also was published as part of a table prepared from public information.
4. Finally, the AEC crossed out some pessimistic comments made by Bethe in projecting that the research and development of the fusion bomb would take years rather than months.

The justification given by the AEC for this censorship was that it was not the information itself which was significant, but rather the source of it. The AEC argued that since Bethe worked for them, his comments would be taken seriously and might be thought to represent the AEC viewpoints and that these comments would therefore be revealing. This is the reason that the same information was not censored when presented by the editors in a separate table. One must ask whether this actually was the reason for the censorship. After all, the Russians surely were aware of this information. The actual reason seems to have been the tremendous controversial questions that raged around the AEC at that moment. Should the hydrogen bomb be built at all? What would be the gains and losses accrued to the United States by it? Was this the time to engage in a crash program? It appears that besides overriding the technical and moral judgments of scientists like Bethe, the AEC also muzzled them to keep them from taking the controversy to the public. By keeping the real experts from making authoritative information available to the public, the decision about the building of the hydrogen bomb was kept essentially internal to the Truman administration. This was, therefore, a case of avoiding a public decision by preventing informed public debate; no constructive criticism was possible—only an uninformed hysteria; under the guise of military secrecy, a political secrecy was obtained.

IN THE MATTER OF J. ROBERT OPPENHEIMER

The problem of making decisions concerning the hydrogen bomb under the guise of secrecy came out again "In the Matter of J. Robert Oppenheimer." As indicated earlier, Oppenheimer was the director of the Los Alamos Laboratory during World War II, earning thereby the title "father of the atomic bomb." After the war he became a high-level advisor to the AEC by chairing the highly respected General Advisory Committee, as well as being a member of at least 34 other government committees. After the bitter internal struggles in the AEC about building the hydrogen bomb, he began to withdraw from these influential positions and to devote himself to his position as Director of the Institute for Advanced Studies at Princeton.

Then in December of 1953, he was given a letter detailing 24 charges which indicated that he was not fit to serve the AEC and that his security clearance to read top secret documents was to be withdrawn. The hearings on these charges were held for three weeks starting in April of 1954; the proceedings were then published as a report entitled *In the Matter of J. Robert Oppenheimer*. This was not a trial in the ordinary sense; the decision was only that it was not consistent with the security interests of the United States to reinstate Oppenheimer's clearance. The father of the atomic bomb was declared to be a security risk. The first 23 charges dealt with Oppenheimer's associations with communists and communist sympathizers, mainly prior to his Los Alamos appointment. As Oppenheimer himself admitted, before the war he had probably been a member of every conceivable communist-front organization, but without ever being a member of the party itself. The charges had been in the hands of General Groves when he appointed Oppenheimer, and they had also been known when the Q-clearance had originally been issued. The 24th charge reads as quoted at the beginning of this chapter and then continues:

> It was further reported that even after it was determined, as a matter of national policy, to proceed with the development of a hydrogen bomb, you continued to oppose the project and

declined to cooperate fully in the project. (As quoted in Ref. 21.14, p. 24.)

This charge grew out of the fact that Oppenheimer had been opposed to the hydrogen bomb when it had appeared technically impractical. Oppenheimer's attitude toward his role in the construction of both the atomic and the hydrogen bomb appears in the following exchange during the hearing with the AEC counsel Roger Robb:

Robb: Did you oppose the dropping of the atom bomb on Hiroshima because of moral scruples?

Oppenheimer: We set forth our—

Robb: I am asking you about "I," not "we."

Oppenheimer: I set forth my anxieties and the arguments on the other side.

Robb: You mean you argued against dropping the bomb?

Oppenheimer: I set forth arguments against dropping it.

Robb: Dropping the atom bomb?

Oppenheimer: Yes. But I did not endorse them.

Robb: You mean having worked, as you put it, in your answer, rather excellently, by night and by day for three or four years to develop the atom bomb, you then argued it should not be used?

Oppenheimer: No. I didn't argue that it should not be used. I was asked to say by the Secretary of War what the views of scientists were. I gave the views against and the views for.

Robb: But you supported the dropping of the bomb on Japan, didn't you?

Oppenheimer: What do you mean, support?

Robb: You helped pick the target, didn't you?

Oppenheimer: I did my job, which was the job I was supposed to do. I was not in a policy-making position at Los Alamos. I would have done anything that I was asked to do, including making the bombs a different shape, if I had thought it was technically feasible.

Robb: You would have made the thermonuclear weapon, too, wouldn't you?

Oppenheimer: I couldn't.

> *Robb:*   I didn't ask you that, Doctor.
> *Oppenheimer:* I would have worked on it.
> *Robb:*   If you had discovered the thermonuclear weapon at Los Alamos, you would have done so. If you could have discovered it, you would have done so, wouldn't you?
> *Oppenheimer:* Oh, yes.
>
> (As quoted in Ref. 21.14, pp. 153–154.)

He clearly considered himself a more-or-less dispassionate consultant, who gave advice and opinions when asked and who built devices without entering into policy questions. And the large majority of scientists supported him, with Edward Teller being the outstanding exception. They all felt that a man cannot be tried for his opinions. As Bush put it:

> I feel that . . . this bill of particulars, is quite capable of being interpreted as placing a man on trial because he held opinions, which is quite contrary to the American system, which is a terrible thing. And as I move about I find that discussed today very energetically, that here is a man who is being pilloried because he has strong opinions, and the courage to express them. If this country ever gets to the point where we come that near to the Russian system, we are certainly not in any condition to attempt to lead the free world toward the benefits of democracy. (As quoted in Ref. 21.14, p. 38.)

And Rabi said:

> A very unfortunate thing and should not have been done. . . . In other words, there he was. He is a consultant, and if you don't want to consult the guy, you don't consult him, period. Why you have to then proceed to suspend clearance and go through all this sort of thing—he is only there when called—and that is all there is to it. So it didn't seem to me the sort of thing that called for this kind of proceeding at all against a man who had accomplished what Dr. Oppenheimer had accomplished. There is a real positive record, and a whole series of it * * * and what more do you want—mermaids? This is just a tremendous achievement. (As quoted in Ref. 21.14, p. 235.)

But Teller testified that he did not consider Oppenheimer reliable and that Oppenheimer's negative opinions had held up progress on the hydrogen bomb. (For this testimony, Teller was for some time ostracized by his colleagues.)

The conclusion of the hearing was a recommendation to deny Oppenheimer the security clearance:

1. We find that Dr. Oppenheimer's continuing conduct and associations have reflected a serious disregard for the requirements of the security system.

2. We have found a susceptibility to influence which could have serious implications for the security interests of the country.

3. We find his conduct in the hydrogen bomb program sufficiently disturbing as to raise a doubt as to whether his future participation, if characterized by the same attitudes in a government program relating to the national defense, would be clearly consistent with the best interests of security.

4. We have regretfully concluded that Dr. Oppenheimer has been less than candid in several instances in his testimony before this Board. (As quoted in Ref. 21.14, p. 184).

And the general manager of the AEC concurred:

... following the President's decision, Oppenheimer did not show the enthusiastic support for the [Super] program which might have been expected of the chief adviser to the Government under the circumstances; that, had he given his enthusiastic support to the program, a concerted effort would have been initiated at an earlier date, and that, whatever the motivation, the security interests of the United States were affected. (As in Ref. 21.14, p. 243.)

Oppenheimer never again worked for the government. However, the national hysteria about the hydrogen bomb and about security slowly began to disappear. By 1958 the U.S. could agree to discuss with Russia the possibility of a test-ban treaty. And in 1963, on November 22, the White House announced that President Kennedy would personally present Oppenheimer with the Fermi award, this nation's highest honor in the nuclear field. And when President Kennedy was assassinated that afternoon, President Johnson himself later took over this duty, saying "One of President Kennedy's most important acts was to sign the award."

The conviction in the hearing was clearly not on the basis of factual charges, but rather on the basis of past associations and past expressed opinions. It was the vicious infighting about the hydrogen bomb which wrote the script. It was not any lack of security, but rather the fact that Oppenheimer did not "show the enthusiastic support . . . expected of the chief atomic advisor" which led to the security withdrawal. That this lack of enthusiasm had a scientific and technical basis as well as a moral basis, was irrelevant.

CONCLUSIONS

Cases of persecution of science and scientists on political grounds have occurred both in the U.S.S.R. and the U.S. The demands went so far as to ask that the facts of science conform to a philosophy or to a military situation and that certain technical and scientific results be achieved independent of whether they were possible. Once the problem went beyond a question of creating a certain technological climate—once the scientific facts themselves were attacked, then there necessarily arose a conflict with the very basis of science, namely with the consensus concept. A philosophy and military-political system by their very nature are nonconsensible, therefore they cannot modify a science without harming themselves and the science. A philosophy or a political system appears silly if it can be factually disproven. And if the science is attached to such a system, then scientists with different nonscientific commitments will possibly be unable to agree on the science as well.

In that sense, were the grounds for persecution in the U.S. so basically different from those in persecutions of Kapitsa, Einstein, or Vasilov? Not really. Even though the ideologies were not the same in these cases, in all cases the consensus concept of science was attacked under the guise of demanding a specific direction for the technological uses of science. Once scientists became technical advisors in the U.S. government, then the influence they derived thereby had a price. And Oppenheimer inevitably had to pay this price. It is this inevitability of having to pay for the Faustian power that made Oppenheimer the tragic hero of science.

REFERENCES

Prime references

21.1 L. M. Marshak, Ed., *The Rise of Science in Relation to Society*, New York: Macmillan and Co., 1964; L. S. Feuer, "Dialectical Materialism and Soviet Science," pp. 108–121.

21.2 G. Piel, *Science in the Cause of Man*, New York: Alfred A. Knopf, 1962; "Science and Secrecy," pp. 3–20, "Security and Heresy," pp. 113–133, "Science, Censorship and the Public Interest," pp. 168–177.

Interesting reading

21.3 A. Vavoulis and A. W. Colver, *Science and Society*, (Ref. 16.12); pp. 141–150.

21.4 A. Perry, *Peter Kapitsa on Life and Society*, New York: Simon and Schuster, 1968.

21.5 L. Graham, "Quantum Mechanics and Dialectical Materialism," *The Slavic Review* **25**, 381 (1966).

21.6 G. Fisher, Ed., *Science and Ideology in Soviet Society*, New York: Atherton Press, 1967; L. R. Graham, "Cybernetics," pp. 83–106.

21.7 D. Jarovsky, "The Lysenko Affair," *Scientific American* **207**, 41–49 (1962).

21.8 L. Graham, *The Soviet Academy of Sciences and the Communist Party: 1927–1932*, Princeton, N.J.: Princeton University Press, 1970.

21.9 W. R. Nelson, Ed., *The Politics of Science*, (Ref. 4.7); J. Turkevitch, "Soviet Science Appriased," pp. 396–406.

21.10 J. B. S. Haldane, *Marxist Philosophy and the Sciences*, London: George Allen and Unwin, 1939.

21.11 H. Kipphardt, *In the Matter of J. Robert Oppenheimer*, New York: Wang, 1968.

21.12 J. Haberer, *Politics and the Community of Science*, (Ref. 16.2); Chapter 10, "The Public Career of J. Robert Oppenheimer," and Chapter 11, "The Oppenheimer Case and the American Community of Science," pp. 217–298.

21.13 N. P. Davis, *Lawrence and Oppenheimer*, (Ref. 17.3); Chapters 8–10, pp. 243–358.

21.14 C. P. Curtis, *The Oppenheimer Case—The Trial of a Security System*, New York: Simon and Schuster, 1955; has extensive quotations from the hearings.

21.15 P. Michelmore, *The Swift Years*, New York: Dodd, Mead and Co., 1969.

21.16 H. Chevalier, *Oppenheimer, The Story of a Friendship*, New York: Pocket Books, Inc., 1966.

21.17 P. M. Stern, *The Oppenheimer Case: Security on Trial*, New York: Harper and Row, 1969.

21.18 G. E. Lowe, "The Camelot Affair," *Bulletin of the Atomic Scientists* **25**, 44–48 (May 1969); and I. L. Horowitz, Ed., *The Rise and Fall of Project Camelot*, Cambridge, Mass.: The M.I.T. Press, 1967; Project Camelot is another celebrated case of the interference of politics with science, in this case in the field of sociology.

QUESTIONS FOR DISCUSSION

1. "The history of science shows that an erroneous philosophic theory may, nonetheless, harbor insights which promote the development of science at a given period." And under the influence of the dialectical materialism, Russian science has indeed grown up, to the extent that it is now the challenger to the older Western science centers as led by the U.S. There is, however, the danger that "At a later stage, that same philosophic theory may become a hindrance to the further, unfettered development of science." At what stage is Russia now?

2. Are there any real differences between the repressions in the U.S.S.R. and in the U.S.?

3. The book written in 1946 by Thirring on the fusion bomb was openly available in Austria but was declared secret in the U.S. and hence nonimportable. Why?

4. There was recently circulated a proposal that all persons working at the weapons laboratories in the U.S. be excluded from professional scientific discourse. Is this reasonable?

22 | THE SCIENCE PIE, AND HOW TO SPLIT IT

Scientists . . . are more likely to make new and unsuspected contributions to the development of the army if detailed instructions are held to a minimum.

D. D. Eisenhower, 1946

In the [weapons] systems we studied, the contributions from recent undirected [basic] research in science was very small.

Project Hindsight, 1963

Using the consensus definition of science, and the Weinberg criteria for the social merits of science, the value of basic research is examined. Emphasis is placed on the relative merits of the various subfields of physics.

INTRODUCTION

In this chapter we will examine the magnitude of the present U.S. scientific effort and the justifications which are usually offered for financial support of basic research. The Ziman definition of science as a consensus activity will ensure that we concern ourselves as much as possible with that segment of research which does not have utility as its immediate justification. An examination of both Project Hindsight and the Westheimer Report will help make this distinction clearer, and will suggest that any belief in the value of basic non-utilitarian research will simply have to be an act of faith.

We shall then apply the Weinberg criteria concerning the internal and external merits of a social effort to various sections of physics. Because high-energy physics is both the most expensive and the most frontierlike subdivision of physics, we shall look at it in some detail in order to emphasize the article-of-faith nature of the arguments for the value of basic science.

THE FINANCES OF SCIENCE

In the United States the total amount of money involved in science and its technological applications is quite large—about 3% of the total GNP. Of this amount, about 71% is spent by industry, about 13% by governmental laboratories, and about 16% by universities. The federal government contributes about 75% of all of these R&D funds, and in turn about 80% of the total government contribution comes from the Department of Defense (DoD), the Atomic Energy Commission (AEC), and the National Aeronautics and Space Agency (NASA). Or put in another way: out of every $100 that is spent for R&D, $60 comes from the DoD and NASA.

What arguments can be used to get such fantastic sums of money out of Congress? If the technological part of this budget is being considered, then one might use an argument originally proposed by Jerome Wiesner while he was Science Advisor to President Kennedy (Ref. 22.7). This argument goes something as follows: Our technologically based economy should be forced to operate at nearly "full load," because this promises the largest possible material progress, and material progress is a goal intrinsic to our society. Economists say that to approach full-load conditions, R&D (research and development) investments should be increased until an additional dollar of R&D will produce only one dollar of increased productivity. While it is impossible to make detailed projections about something as complicated as the national economy, a lower limit that can reasonably be set on desirable R&D investment is the entire annual increase in the economic output due to productivity increases. After corrections for population increases and inflation, this increase has averaged to something on the order of 3.5% per year. In other words, the U.S. should be spending each year at least 3.5% of the GNP on productivity-oriented R&D. Out of the 3% which the U.S. actually commits to R&D, about 1% goes toward nonproductive research, as in weapons development. So it appears that the U.S. could profitably increase its R&D budget by at least another 1.5%, without exceeding this full-load limit.

Such a chain of arguments is a tempting one, insofar as it allows us to calculate an actual number for the desirable amount of R&D. This chain has unfortunately one major fault in that it is purely economic. The inherent assumption is that we want the economy going full blast and constantly expanding. This is an argument about technological merits, and it totally ignores the other Weinberg criteria as outlined in Chapter 3 for evaluating the merits of any efforts by society. In particular, this chain of arguments leaves out all considerations of the social desirability of an expanding economy; such consequences as automation-unemployment, overpopulation, and pollution are not included in the evaluation. And it is these consequences which are becoming major concerns of society.

SUPPORT FOR BASIC RESEARCH

The above justification is concerned with the total R&D budget. It is not really relevant to that 10% subsection related to support of basic research. If we accept Ziman's definition of science as an activity which is directed toward public knowledge and a consensus (Chapter 4), then the financing of basic or "pure" research intrinsically cannot be justified with any arguments about utility. If research intentionally aims toward usefulness, then it is more technology than basic science no matter how "scientific" the work seems to the onlooker. Ultimate economic benefits of basic research can thus be taken only as a matter of faith. Weinberg (Ref. 3.2) suggests that basic science may simply have to be considered an overhead charge on applied science, and hence on R&D in general.

The faith in basic research has been particularly strong in the U.S. since World War II. During the war the Armed Forces, Congress, and the average citizen saw what scientists could produce. So when the scientists said that basic research made it all go, and that the store of knowledge provided by basic research had been dangerously depleted during the war, they were believed. Even General Groves made provisions for basic research at the end of the war by allocating as much as possible of the left-over Manhattan Project funds to this purpose; in fact, he considered that allowing scientists to always do some basic research on the side was part of their pay. The military certainly was grateful for the scientists' help during the war, as indicated by the Eisenhower quotation at the beginning of this chapter. And it was essentially the postwar support by the military that made basic research into the present-day giant.

PROJECT HINDSIGHT

Unfortunately this faith in science has been somewhat shaken lately. Not only are there charges of irresponsibility in the uses of the resulting scientific knowledge; not only is the interest in, and support of, basic science decreasing; there is even some doubt about the ultimate usefulness of undirected basic research. It may all have started with the "infamous" study known as Project Hindsight (Ref. 22.9). In this 1964−66 study, the DoD tried to evaluate the return it was getting on its investment in basic research. It analyzed some 20 major weapons systems, such as the C-141 transport plane, to see what R&D discoveries (or *events*) in the preceding 20 years made significant contributions to their developments. The sources of these events were then separated into technology, directed science, and undirected science. The scientific community was quite shocked to read that 92% of all important events were technological, 7.6% were directed science (i.e., applied science in the sense that the research aimed toward direct usefulness), while only 0.4% were undirected science (i.e., basic or pure or real science). This study concluded that undirected research has made no significant contributions toward the needs of the DoD and that research aimed toward a specific DoD system is far more productive and efficient. There were, of course, many objections raised to these conclusions (Ref. 22.9). After all, where would technology be without Newton's laws? But certainly many myths were punctured, particularly the article of faith that basic research would pay for itself in a reasonably short time. It appears that in order to produce useful results, scientific research must be oriented toward an objective.

There were counterattempts to show that basic science does indeed more than pay for itself. Here chemistry took the lead with the 1964 Westheimer Report entitled "Chemistry: Opportunities and Needs" (Ref. 22.8; note that the Pake Report, Ref. 3.7, was patterned after this report). Basic chemistry tried to use utility as a justification for its support. It linked itself directly to the $40 billion chemical industry by showing that basic research journals predominated as sources of development discoveries. It is interesting that the engineers of Project Hindsight thought basic research worthless, while the basic chemists of the Westheimer Report concluded exactly the opposite. And financial repercussions from this loss of faith have already taken place. The 1969 DoD appropriations bill had attached to it the so-called Mansfield amendment, which required of all DoD agencies that they sponsor only research which was reasonably directly related to their specific missions.

TYPES OF SUPPORT FOR BASIC RESEARCH

To clarify further what is meant by a basic research program, it might be interesting to see how the National Science Foundation (NSF) operates. The NSF supports only basic research; it is not mission-oriented like the DoD, the AEC, or even NASA. The epitome of its basic research program lies in the "little-science" projects which account for about 20% of NSF's total budget (about $600 million for 1972). This budget is tapped, for example, by an individual professor at a university who asks for the sum of $30,000 per year to buy some equipment, to support a few graduate students, to provide necessary supplies, to help underwrite publication costs—and to pay the professor's own summer salary. All this money is to finance research which the researcher has proposed to the foundation and which several referees of the foundation (peers of the proposer) have evaluated as worth supporting. The researcher then does more or less whatever research he wants to do, related as much as possible to his proposal.

PHYSICS AND THE WEINBERG CRITERIA

Once some sum of money has been allocated for basic research, then decisions must be made between scientific incommensurables, namely between various scientific disciplines such as molecular biology, metallurgy, and nuclear physics. Such choices have, of course, constantly been made in the past by individual scientists in deciding what research to perform, by university department chairmen in hiring specialists in particular fields, and by research administrators in deciding what kinds of projects to push. But with money for research becoming less plentiful, such decisions are becoming more frequent and more painful.

The Weinberg criteria of Chapter 3 were originally developed to help in exactly this process of allocation among the various fields of science. And there is now enormous pressure from outside the scientific disciplines to make such rational decisions rather than just letting competition within the disciplines determine the financial distribution. It may be interesting to illustrate these criteria by comparing the various sections of physics. Particularly interesting will be the arguments which are put up in support of research in the field of high-energy physics, as it is perhaps the most clear-cut example of a non-utilitarian scientific discipline.

For the purpose of such a discussion, we might divide physics into six sections:

1. astrophysics,

2. atomic and molecular physics,

3. nuclear physics,

4. plasma physics,

5. solid-state physics, and

6. high-energy physics.

Astrophysics at the present has a huge budget through NASA. We will look at it again later in Chapter 24, but it is plagued by difficulties in separating the space science from the space technology. *Atomic and molecular physics*, which deals with isolated atoms and molecules, is experiencing a revival to some extent because it has led to such products as the laser. *Nuclear physics* is the study of the structure of the nucleus. Low-energy nuclear physics has led to the applications of radioactivity to medicine, etc., as discussed in Chapter 19; and it partially blends into high-energy physics. The present-day applications are largely based on fairly old information, and there seems to be no real breakthrough in sight in the theories of the nucleus. The field of *plasma physics* we will discuss in Chapter 27; through its relation to controlled fusion processes, it has great economic and social implications for the future. *Solid-state physics* is the study of aggregates of atoms in a regular crystalline array. This is today the largest subfield of physics. Work in this field is at present relatively easy to justify because of its close connection to myriads of solid-state devices. Certainly a major landmark in solid-state physics was the development of the transistor in 1948 (an event which Project Hindsight labels "applied physics," since the work was definitely aiming toward a usable product). It is a field which is ripe for exploitation, with enough capable workers in it. Scientifically, this field overlaps with many other disciplines, such as chemistry, engineering, and medicine. The social contributions consist of technologically making our lives "better" quantitatively and perhaps even qualitatively.

That leaves the hardest subfield to discuss, namely *high-energy physics*, or elementary particle physics. It is an outgrowth of the desire to understand the forces which hold together the nucleus. By bombarding nuclei with very energetic projectiles, it is possible to explore the finer nuclear structure. Additionally, new subatomic particles may be created through collisions between very energetic particles. And new ones have been produced in large numbers: *mesons, lambda particles, omega particles, hyperons,* even a whole class called *strange particles.* Classification schemes based on underlying symmetry properties have been invented, such as the "eight-fold way" of Gell-Mann. There has even been discovered a force beyond the electromagnetic, gravitational, and nuclear forces; this is the so-called *weak interaction,* and it has the interesting property of knowing right from left; because of it, if we should ever be communicating with creatures on another planet, we will be able to tell them whether they are right-handed or left-handed (unless they are antimatter creatures, in which case we don't want to shake hands with them in any case).

Is all this high-energy research appropriate and worth it? It certainly is expensive. The annual research cost per post-doctorate scientist in this field is estimated to be about $150,000, as opposed to about $30,000 in atomic physics. Much of this money goes into costly accelerators; the latest model at Batavia, Illinois (Fig. 22.1), will cost in excess of $300 million, with about another $50 million per year required to operate it. There is no question that the men in the field are competent; they are probably the best, simply because scientists have a feeling as to where the frontiers lie. The field is ready for exploitation; the technology exists to build bigger accelerators. But there is some question as to whether any other scientific disciplines are really dependent on (or waiting for) the new data from high-energy physics. In addition, there seems little promise with regard to future technology

Fig. 22.1 Aerial view of the main accelerator at the National Accelerator Laboratory, Batavia, Illinois. The main accelerator is 4 miles in circumference. (Photo courtesy of the National Accelerator Laboratory.)

(except for some spin-off) or human welfare. This leaves two supporting arguments: an almost humanistic one and another related to the social aspects of accelerators.

The "humanistic" argument has to do with the intellectual beauty of high-energy physics. High-energy physics is beautiful because of the illumination of the age-old question concerning the particulateness of nature. So many subatomic particles have been discovered by now that we must once again ask whether matter is really made up of a set of elementary particles. And, in fact, the answer may be that the question makes no more sense than to ask where the electron in an atom may be located at a given time. Because these results may threaten *ways* of thinking about nature, high-energy physics does in a way interact very strongly with neighboring disciplines, although primarily in an inspirational way. This inspiration is reflected in the way in which high-energy physicists justify their work:

> A spirit would be fostered, different from the one which created modern science, if basic questions that can be answered are left unanswered. . . . (V. F. Weisskopf, Ref. 22.3, p. 27.)

> A great society is ultimately known for the monuments it leaves for later generations. . . . We can foretell . . . that such a machine, which is on the scale of a national effort, will without question be a source of inspiration for new science and a monument to our days. (A. Pais, Ref. 22.3, p. 17.)

> If we cut back on [high-energy physics] . . . I think we will have seriously damaged the best single element we have contributed to human culture. (G. Feinberg, Ref. 22.3, p. 15.)

The other supporting argument for high-energy physics includes such social aspects as national prestige, international cooperation, and pork-barrel politics. The competition with Russia for the biggest accelerator has been very effectively used as an argument in the past by American physicists. Since these ventures are very visible, there has been hope off and on that there might result international scientific cooperation; and, indeed, the nuclear laboratory CERN in Switzerland hosts not only European physicists but also some from the U.S. and from East-bloc countries (see, e.g., Ref. 22.6). But a big part of the push for new accelerators has been a pork-barrel one. Such an installation is a tremendous economic plum. And since there exists a belief that a collection of university-type scientists is a drawing card for certain industries, such an installation is always the object of intense competition. Whether all these aspects are social merits or demerits is, of course, a subject for debate.

SUMMARY

If the basic-science parts of the R&D budget are separated from the technological parts, then the justification for the former becomes very difficult, and to a large extent simply a matter of faith in the ultimate utilitarian usefulness of nonutilitarian science. The Weinberg criteria then provide useful guidelines in considering the relative merits of various scientific disciplines. A detailed analysis of the sections of physics reveals that high-energy physics appeals to an almost humanistic argument for its justification. As a matter of fact, the overall allocation decisions are, of course, frequently made on political grounds rather than on any thoroughly rational arguments.

REFERENCES

Prime references

22.1 D. S. Greenberg, *The Politics of Pure Science*, (Ref. 4.2).

22.2 A. Weinberg, *Reflections on Big Science*, (Ref. 3.2); Section III, pp. 65–122.

Interesting reading

22.3 L. C. L. Yuan, Ed., *Nature of Matter: Purposes of High Energy Physics*, Upton, L. I.: Brookhaven National Laboratory, 1965.

22.4 D. K. Price, *The Scientific Estate*, Cambridge, Mass.: Harvard University Press, 1965; touches in general on the question of rationale and allocation.

22.5 W. R. Nelson, Ed., *The Politics of Science*, (Ref. 4.7); contains various articles on the appropriation and allocation of funds for science.

22.6 R. Jungk, *The Big Machine*, New York: Charles Scribner's Sons, 1968.

22.7 H. Wolff, Ed., *Science as a Cultural Force*, Baltimore, Md.: The Johns Hopkins Press, 1964; J. Wiesner "Technology and Society," pp. 35–53.

22.8 *"The Westheimer Report,"* *Chemistry, Opportunities and Needs*, Washington, D.C.: The National Academy of Sciences, 1964.

22.9 C. Sherwin and R. Isenson, "Project Hindsight," *Science* **156**, 1571–1577 (June, 1967); see also other issues: **154**, 872–873 (Nov. 1966), **154**, Editorial (Dec. 1966), and **155**, 397–400 (Jan. 1967).

QUESTIONS FOR DISCUSSION

1. The suggestion has been made to let the "marketplace" take care of the allocation of scientific funds. The more aggressive scientists will then get more money. Is this reasonable?

2. Does it make sense to use the Weinberg criteria to compare physics with any other disciplines such as molecular biology?

3. Why are students now going out of the physical sciences into the life sciences?

4. How reasonable is the "intellectual beauty" argument for the support of high-energy physics? How does it compare with the arguments for the Apollo moonshot program?

5. Should the science pie be cut on a geographic or demographic basis, or should the best institutions get most of the support?

6. Do you believe the conclusions reached by Project Hindsight?

23 | SCIENCE AND THE UNIVERSITY

What I wish to contend is, that the Professor of a modern university ought to regard himself primarily as a learner, and a teacher only secondarily. His first obligation is to the Faculty he represents; he must consider that he is there on his own account, and not for the sake of his pupils. The pupils, indeed are useful to him as urging him to activity of mind, to clearness of expression, to definiteness of conception, to be perpetually turning over and verifying the thoughts and truths which occupy him.

Mark Pattison, 1868

The history of the role of science in the universities is presented, with emphasis on the origins of the present-day research orientation. The relationship between university science and the federal government is then examined as one visible expression of that orientation.

INTRODUCTION

Throughout history science has played many different roles in the universities. The contemporary role is most turbulent, with the military-industrial-academic complex providing a focus for student discontent. Partly because of this discontent, there is going on at the present time a lot of soul-searching by members of the academic community, as well as by nonacademic policy makers, about the ultimate justification of the present arrangements. Critical attacks are most heavily centered on the seemingly overwhelming orientation of the universities toward research; the cry is against the publish-or-perish syndrome; the demand is for more excellence in teaching and for a vigorous recommitment to the education of beginning students.

This chapter will present a brief summary of the history of the attitude of universities toward science, with particular emphasis on the origin of the present research-oriented model. Then there will be a review of the relationship of the present-day universities with the federal government and of the nature of the military-industrial-academic complex. Finally, it will be interesting to look at the modifications that are presently taking place in the modern science-government relationship as mirrored by the new attitude toward large university-associated laboratories such as the M.I.T Lincoln Laboratory.

THE SCHOLARSHIP MODEL OF THE UNIVERSITY

In many respects our present-day universities are derivatives of the medieval concept of what a university ought to be. At that time the idea was that the university is a community of scholars whose function it is to preserve, collect, and comment on already existing work. Then the objective was the learned man, a man who knew as much as possible of what was in the storehouse of knowledge. If there were disagreements on the topic among the faculty, these were resolved by Thomistic debates about the ancient authorities rather than through the acquisition of new information. The whole approach was a persuasive one rather than a convincing one.

THE RESEARCH MODEL OF THE UNIVERSITY

But to this older scholarship model a new twist was added near the end of the Industrial Revolution. Up to that time science had been considered an integral cultural part of a gentleman's education; even 18th-century Newtonian science was of this mold of having little contact with the real world. Thus when the Industrial Revolution began, the universities initially were left out of the new expansion. The Lunar society promoted science as a respectable leisure-time activity for gentlemen; there were many public science lectures for interested laymen; and some of the academies formed in support of the sciences gave public science courses. But the universities did not share this enthusiasm; they neither taught higher-level science nor made any original contributions to scientific thought. As late as 1852 the Regius Professor of Medicine at Oxford reported that he had discontinued his lectures because there were only four students; and the Professor of Chemistry at Cambridge reported that:

> ... There is no residence, museum, library, collection, or apparatus attached to the Professorship ... and there are no funds for this purpose. There are no opportunities afforded to students for instruction in the actual manipulation of instruments. ... Hitherto the study of Chemistry has not only been neglected but discouraged in the University, as diverting the attention of pupils from what have been considered their proper academical studies. (As quoted in Ref. 23.1, p. 10.)

Only gradually did the Industrial Revolution break into the universities. It happened first in France, where in 1794 the *Ecole Polytechnique* was set up. Since, however, Britain did not see eye-to-eye with either the French Revolution or Napoleon, the new scientific spirit did not cross directly into England. Rather, it first detoured through Germany, where the appropriate climate existed in the little independent duchies: the finance, leisure, and freedom to pursue research, coupled with opportunities for scholars to associate together and to transmit ideas and techniques to their disciples. So in Germany there arose the concept that private study and research are essential qualifications for a university teacher. There developed the idea of "Wissenschaft," the objective and critical approach to all knowledge, not only in the sciences but also in the humanities. The ideal put before the students was no longer liberal humanism, but rather a fanaticism toward advancing knowledge.

It was this German model which penetrated into Great Britain. In the first half of the 19th century Britain had been preoccupied with the utility of science, since it had become the industrial leader of the world after the Napoleonic wars. But by 1851, discerning Englishmen could already see that this leadership could not last without some university participation; Prince Consort Albert, the German-born husband of Victoria, was the inspiration behind some of the early attempts at such an integration. Then in the 1860s came the electric telegraph, the synthesis of analine dyes, and the start of artificial fertilizers, all of which involved basic science. These combined with the eye-opening industrial exhibition of 1867 (where Britain won very few first prizes) to ensure that the German university model solidly took root. So in 1868, Mark Pattison set up the British system based on the premises outlined in the introductory quotation. He added:

> But we must go further than this: Even merely to be efficient as teacher, the University teacher must hold possession of so much as has to be communicated to the pupil. . . . No teacher who is a teacher only, and not himself a daily student, who does not speak from the love and faith of a habitual intuition, can be competent to treat any of the higher parts of any moral or speculative science. . . . Our weakness of late years has been that we have not felt this;—we have known no higher level of knowledge than so much as sufficed for teaching. Hence education among us has sunk into a trade, and, like trading sophists, we have not cared to keep on hand a larger stock than we could dispose of in the season. (As quoted in Ref. 23.1, p. 34.)

The poet Matthew Arnold was very deeply concerned with this problem:

> . . . Our dislike of authority and our disbelief in science have combined to make us leave our school system, like so many other branches of our civil organization, to take care of itself as best it could. . . . The result is, that we have to meet the calls of a modern epoch, in which the action of the working and middle class assumes a preponderating importance, and science tells in human affairs more and more, with a working class not educated at all, a middle class education on the second plane, and the idea of science absent from the whole course and design of our education. (As quoted in Ref. 23.1, pp. 36–37.)

The resultant rearrangement led to the establishment of the Clarendon Laboratory at Oxford and the Cavendish Laboratory at Cambridge; practical physics became a subject recognized for a degree; new universities were opened. Knowledge became an open-ended system with constant new additions; dissent became more recognized and accepted; the academic world became more democratized. The research model took a deep hold.

One might summarize (in a tongue-in-cheek way) the differences between these two university-science models by repeating the legendary distinction between Oxford and Cambridge. This distinction can be characterized by the way two of their students answered question "How many angels can dance on the tip of a pin?" on a civil service examination. The Oxford graduate wrote a long essay in which he described the medieval thinking about this problem and described the impact of this question on modern theological thought. The Cambridge man wrote only two lines; he said that to answer this question he would have to know the size of the pin, the mass of the angels, and their density. We still retain to some extent this dichotomy in our present university system, a dichotomy which smacks of the two cultures.

SCIENCE IN AMERICAN UNIVERSITIES

Somewhat parallel developments took place in the United States. All nine of the colonial colleges had included natural philosophy in their basic course of study; but science was considered an ally of religion intended to show the magnificence of the universe. There did arise in the early 19th century great interest in the applications of technology to the exploitation of vast new territories, and some of this interest led to changes in the universities. But these were on the whole only superficial changes. The many new colleges founded during this period simply did not have the faculties and facilities to make the necessary adjustments to science. Then in the late 1840s through the 1860s the increasing demand for science led to the establishment of schools of science at Harvard and Yale. And the 1860s then assured a permanent place for science in the universities by the passage of the Morrill Federal Land-Grant Act, the founding of M.I.T and Cornell, and the addition of scientific departments in 25 other educational institutions. This act was passed in the middle of the Civil War; it granted large tracts of federal land to the individual states, land which could be sold to help establish state universities with agricultural departments. The whole system of coupling basic agricultural research at the universities with direct applications through extension agents derived from this act. From then on, science in the American universities grew steadily.

The Second World War brought with it a complete revolution in this situation when the federal government became deeply involved in university science. Before the war, the support for science research at universities came from private individuals, from industry, and from the Carnegie, Ford, and Rockefeller Foundations. The federal contribution to this support in 1935–6 was $6 million, an almost negligible amount compared to the more than $2 billion of 1970. The change came about when the universities became involved in wartime defense-oriented research and the big laboratories were set up at the universities: the Radiation Laboratory for Radar Research was located at M.I.T; the Applied Physics Laboratory, at Johns Hopkins University, grew out of the proximity-fuse work performed there; the University of Chicago had the Metallurgical Laboratory; and Los Alamos Laboratory was an adjunct of the University of California. Some of the universities received huge contracts during the war: M.I.T—$117 million, Caltech—$83 million, Harvard—$31 million, and Columbia—$28 million. This money was for war-related technology, but the university scientists spent it. And these wartime-developed relationships are still with us; there are still big laboratories at these universities, and the people involved in the wartime efforts are still in positions of power and influence (as indicated in Chapter 4).

The pervasiveness of this legacy is easy to show. A 1964 study of the President's Science Advisory Committee (PSAC) revealed that of the 41 persons who at one time or another had been members of this committee, 29 had received their graduate training at the University of California, Caltech, Chicago, Columbia, Harvard, M.I.T, and Princeton. And 28 were employed by only nine different universities. The distribution of university research funds across the country have reflected this concentration of power. In the same year, out of some 2100 institutions of higher learning in the U.S., 10 universities received 38% of all federal funds for academic research; namely, the University of California, M.I.T, Columbia, the University of Michigan, Harvard, Illinois, Stanford, Chicago, Minnesota, and Cornell. Ninety percent of the federal money went to only 100 universities. Through managing large laboratories for the government, some universities have enormous fractions (as much as 80%) of their total budgets provided by the federal government.

ARGUMENTS FOR THE SUPPORT OF
UNIVERSITY SCIENCE

What arguments do the science departments in the universities use to justify receiving this much money from the federal government and for supervising such laboratories? Basically the claim is that such arrangements are good for training graduate students and for increasing the excellence of science departments. In justifying increasing requests for physics research funds, the Pake Report (Ref. 23.4) in 1964 used arguments of the following types:

> Because of the scientific importance and promise of atomic and molecular physics and quantum electronics, because of its value for PhD training, because of its suitability for research in small physics and applied science departments, and because of the great need for information in many technical missions of the government, we believe there should be a minimum annual increase of 25 percent in the federal support in the field. The great need of the government for information on atomic and molecular physics has been shown by a number of crash programs in the field.... It would be very desirable to increase the number of universities and colleges active in the field.

> Nuclear physics is a vital field of fundamental research in which current rapid progress may confidently be expected to continue; basic work in nuclear physics is an essential part of university research and is eminently suited to student training; it is also a legitimate concern of the governmental laboratories; the student population in U.S. universities will double by 1973....

> The growth of solid-state physics in the universities and colleges should be encouraged particularly because training in solid-state physics is especially appropriate for students interested in modern developments on the borderline between science and technology. Understanding of solid-state physics is of great value to students specializing in most other physical and biological sciences or in engineering. Doctoral theses in this field continue as an ample opportunity for independence and ingenuity. Unfortunately, this is no longer so in some other areas of physics. Finally, there are many significant frontier solid-state problems

that can be investigated with a small number of faculty members. The costs of equipment and operating expenses are relatively low. (Ref. 23.4, pp. 48–59)

The pattern of the justification is clear—physics is a vital field, it provides good training for Ph.D.'s, and we need more Ph.D.'s. (The validity of the last of these assumptions was discussed in Chapter 4.)

UNIVERSITY-ASSOCIATED LABORATORIES

Inevitably these large contracts with the federal government have raised the question whether the universities might not be performing research which is inappropriate for their teaching objectives. This concern recently has come to a head with the result that many of the university ties to large laboratories are being reexamined. This particular problem can be illustrated by the example of M.I.T.

M.I.T has two special laboratories associated with it. The first is the Instrumentation Laboratory originating from the gyroscope research of World War II; it performs research in vehicle guidance and control, including both the control of the Poseidon missiles for submarines and the Apollo guidance system for the moon flights; in this work it has been supported about equally by DoD and by NASA. The Lincoln Laboratory was set up in 1951 at the specific request of the federal government to do research and development related to continental air defense. Supported almost totally by the DoD, it has made extensive contributions to various radar warning systems and has built several communications satellites. It is the extensive military orientation of these laboratories which upset many students and faculty. Consequently, in April of 1969 a special panel was set up to investigate the relevance of these labs to the purpose of M.I.T.

Needless to say, there was no agreement among the panel members on all details. There was a general consensus that, while M.I.T had an obligation to perform services, this service effort should be more diversified and should not degrade M.I.T's primary function of education and research. The more-or-less noncontroversial recommendations were that the laboratories and M.I.T should try to provide more balanced research projects, that the educational interaction between the special labs and the campus should be increased, and that classification and clearance barriers should be removed as much as possible. Then came the difficult point, namely, the question of what kinds of projects were not satisfactory for a university. For military research, the panel considered various possible criteria and rejected most as implying political judgments by M.I.T:

> Is the military application offensive or defensive? Will the work contribute primarily to existing military hostilities? Is it tied directly to a capability for destroying human life? Is it justified on strategic grounds or is it an unnecessary escalation of the arms race? Do the potential civilian applications outweigh the military? Are some sponsors acceptable and others not?

> As soon as these questions are asked about specific projects, it becomes obvious that collective judgments on military and strategic policy would be necessary. The Panel believes such judgments are inappropriate for any official group at the Institute to make. This is not to say members of the Panel may not speak out as individuals on these matters.

> In addition, we believe there is an important difference between undertaking research and development and making a decision to build and deploy specific systems. Research and development may easily be justified on many grounds—to avoid technological surprise, to evaluate opponents' claims, to understand system vulnerabilities, and to be prepared for deployment if necessary even when immediate deployment itself may be very unwise. (Ref. 23.5, pp. 20–21)

The criteria finally adopted by M.I.T to evaluate the appropriateness of research were such that the development work on the man-detecting jungle radar was declared inappropriate, while the basic research leading up to it was found acceptable.

There was strong dissent to these conclusions by some of the panel members, particularly by Noam Chomsky, Professor of Modern Languages and Linguistics. He felt that "any act undertaken by M.I.T in its public service function is a political act" and that scientists cannot avoid the political responsibility for their products:

> They cannot ultimately control the social use of knowledge, but they also cannot remain blind to the question of how their contributions are likely to be put to use, under given social

conditions. It is possible, of course, to adopt uncritically the concept of "national interest" and "public service" that is defined by those in a position to allocate funds and determine public policy. To do so is, in effect, to make a particular political judgment, namely, to support the existing structure of power and privilege and the particular ideological framework that is associated with it. This decision may or may not be correct. It must be recognized clearly, however, that it is a political decision, and must not be disguised by the pretense that it is no political decision at all, but simply the non-ideological, value-free pursuit of knowledge for its own sake. In an institution largely devoted to science and technology, we do not enjoy the luxury of refusing to take a stand on the essentially political question of how science and technology will be put to use, and we have a responsibility to take our stand with consideration and care. Those who find this burden intolerable are simply complaining of the difficulties of a civilized life. To exercise this responsibility scientists must continually make political and historical judgments. (Ref. 23.5, pp. 31–32)

To Chomsky the government in its military posture has only the purpose of increasing America's overwhelming strategic nuclear superiority and its tactical counter-insurgency capability, and these are bad. He would, therefore, ask for political judgments by the university, openly derived at by the members of its community.

The attempts to civilianize these laboratories have not been very successful. With the tighter research budget situation it is difficult to find enough alternate sources of nonmilitary research funds to make such a change-over possible. The decision was finally reached that operation of the Instrumentation Laboratory, with its work on weapons systems, was inconsistent with the nature of the university; that rather than destroying the lab's usefulness, it should be totally separated from the university.

CONCLUSIONS

The discussion about the big university-associated laboratories illustrates the conflict which is aroused by the two differing models of university science. The large laboratories are an outgrowth of the research model, while, in a sense, the protestors are oriented more toward a scholarly direction; to some extent the problem here is a collision between undergraduate teaching through scholarly discussion, and graduate teaching through research. Of course, in the past the argument had always been made that faculty research was necessary for good undergraduate teaching. But this has led to the publish-or-perish syndrome and, even more important, is an assumption that has recently been seriously challenged (e.g., Ref. 23.11).

But in an even deeper sense, the laboratories are inappropriate for universities because they are somewhat unscientific in their intent. They were set up in World War II to solve specific problems under wartime conditions, and this historical fact has continued to control their problem-oriented approach. In many cases the problems to be worked on are not selected because of their suitability for graduate-student research, but rather because the problems arose out of an externally imposed need. One is left with the general impression that the research model of the university, with its need for large funds to do the research, may in its present form be ultimately nonviable, simply because it leaves too few options open in this day of almost total federal funding of research. This funding raises the specter that the universities might be losing their ability to be critical.

REFERENCES

Prime reference

23.1 E. Ashby, *Technology and the Academics*, London: Macmillan and Co., 1958; the introductory quotation is on p. 34.

Interesting reading

23.2 D. D. Van Tassel and M. G. Hall, Eds., *Science and Society in the United States*, Homewood, Ill.: The Dorsey Press; C. Weiner, Chapter 6, "Science and Higher Education," pp. 163–190.

23.3 D. S. Greenberg, *The Politics of Pure Science*, (Ref. 4.2).

23.4 The Pake Report, *Physics Survey and Outlook*, (Ref. 3.7).

23.5 *Final Report of the Review Panel on Special Laboratories*, Cambridge, Mass.: M.I.T, October 1969; and *Scientific Research* (November 24, 1969), pp. 11–12, 22–25.

23.6 B. R. Kenan, *Science and the Universities*, New York: Columbia University Press, 1966.

23.7 A. Weinberg, *Reflections on Big Science*, (Ref. 3.2); Section IV, "The Institutions of Big Science," pp. 123–174.

23.8 Lord Bowden, L. Goldberg, R. Gandry, and H. Margenau, *Science and the University*, Toronto: Macmillan of Canada, 1967.

23.9 J. Ridgeway, *The Closed Corporation: American Universities in Crisis*, New York: Random House, 1968.

23.10 J. Barzun, *The American University*, New York: Harper and Row, 1968.

23.11 J. R. Hayes, "Research, Teaching and Faculty Fate," *Science* **172**, 227–230 (April 1971).

23.12 A. Flexner, *Universities: American, English, German*, New York: Oxford University Press, 1930; a prewar evaluation of science in the university.

QUESTIONS FOR DISCUSSION

1. What are the origins of the present-day university science requirements? What should these requirements be?

2. Should research and teaching be mixed at a university? Why should a university professor have a Ph.D.?

3. Is the publish-or-perish syndrome completely bad?

4. Is it wrong for the federal government to support basic science in universities for its accomplishments rather than purely for teaching purposes?

5. Should the Department of Defense be allowed to support basic research at the universities?

6. Should we train more scientists toward applied science? Toward teaching?

24 | NASA: MAN IN SPACE

Prometheus stole the sacred flame from heaven and brought it down to earth as a gift to the human race; and on a pillar of flame man is now riding back into the abode of the gods. What other divine powers remain there for us to discover—and to exploit?

Arthur Clarke

The century would seek to dominate nature . . . would create death, devastation and pollution. Yet the century was now attached to the idea that man must take his conception of life out to the stars. It was the most soul-destroying and apocalyptic of centuries.

Norman Mailer

Some background behind the decision to go to the moon is presented, as well as the attitude of scientists toward NASA. Some future possibilities and limits of space travel are examined.

INTRODUCTION

Man has long dreamed of traveling to the moon, as can be seen from the enormous amount of literature written about the subject over the centuries. One of these many dreamers was Cyrano de Bergerac, a 17th-century poet. As told by Edmond Rostand in his 1897 play, Cyrano proposed several different ways of reaching the moon:

I scorned the eagle
Of Regiomontanus, and the dove
Of Archytas! . . .
I imitated no one. I myself
Discovered not one scheme merely, but six—

Six ways to violate the virgin sky! . . .
As for instance—Having stripped myself
Bare as a wax candle, adorn my form
With crystal vials filled with morning dew,
And so be drawn aloft, as the sun rises
Drinking the mist of dawn! . . .
Or, Sealing up the air in a cedar chest,
Rarefy it by means of mirrors, placed
In an icosahedron. . . .
I might construct a rocket, in the form
Of a huge locust, driven by impulses
Of villainous saltpetre from the rear,
Upward, by leaps and bounds. . . .
Or again,
Smoke having a natural tendency to rise,
Blow in a globe enough to raise me. . . .
Or since Diana, as old fables tell,
Draws forth to fill her crescent horn, the marrow
Of bulls and goats—to anoint myself therewith. . . .
Finally—seated on an iron plate,
To hurl a magnet in the air—the iron
Follows—I catch the magnet—throw again—
And so proceed indefinitely. . . .
[Finally] The ocean! . . .
What hour its rising tide seeks the full moon,
I laid me on the strand, fresh from the spray.
My head fronting the moonbeams, since the hair
Retains moisture—and so I slowly rose
As upon angels' wings, effortlessly,
Upward— . . .   (Ref. 24.8, pp. 123–125.)

Some of these proposed methods are impossible because there is a vacuum between the earth and the moon; some of them violate the law concerning the conservation of momentum; and the rocket idea has turned out to be basically correct. The point is that these were all quite concrete suggestions.

After all that dreaming, man finally did land on the moon on July 16, 1969. This chapter will discuss why it happened. It will present of some of the reasons why the Apollo program was started, outline some of the returns from the space program, and discuss the future of man's exploration of space. The most relevant question here is about the role of science in the Apollo decision and program. And it appears that the science and technology of the moon landing was simply a matter of lots of money and technological dedication. In contrast, the overall choices and alternatives were anything but simple: the decision to go to the moon was a political arrangement of social priorities rather than a scientific (or even a technological) choice.

HISTORY OF THE SPACE PROGRAM

One of the most concrete and inspiring fictitious descriptions of a trip to the moon is that by Jules Verne in *From the Earth To the Moon and Round the Moon*. There are many correct details in this story, as well as a few mistakes. The escape velocity to make it to the moon was right at 12,000 yards per second, as was the launching from Florida (in this case from St. Petersburg-Tampa), and the landing in the Pacific Ocean. However, the escape velocity is supposedly acquired in a cannon (named Columbiad) only 900 feet long. This would require an average acceleration inside the barrel of 20,000 times the acceleration of gravity. Picture what would happen to an astronaut who suddenly weighed 1500 tons. During the flight, the dog on board the spaceship dies and is buried in space; and Verne correctly points out that the body will keep pace with the ship. However, he errs when he has the astronauts walk first on the floor and then on the ceiling of the space capsule, rather than having them float in free fall.

The actual turning of this inspiration into reality is an inheritance from some realistic dreamers who devoted their life to it. In the United States there was Dr. Robert Hutchings Goddard, who began playing with rockets as early as 1908 (supported in part by the Smithsonian Institution in Washington). The Russian visionary was Konstantin Eduardovich Tsiliakovsky. In Germany people like Hermann Oberth and Willy Ley inspired the practical engineers who built rockets. In the case of the Germans, the financial support came from the army as early as 1930, and that program led to the very successful V-2 missile. (Incidentally, in 1944 one of the chief movers of this work, Werner von Braun, was arrested by the Gestapo; he was accused of making the remark that the ultimate goal of the rocket program was space travel, a remark not consistent with the required all-out war effort. It took Hitler's personal intervention to get him out of jail.)

Fig. 24.1 The recovery operation of Jules Verne's spaceship, as portrayed in a contemporary drawing, very much resembles the present procedure.

The process by which these early efforts turned into the contemporary space program was quite complicated. In the beginning of 1945, before the Russians captured the rocket laboratory at Peenemünde, von Braun and his co-workers moved to the south of Germany. When he then wanted to surrender his group to the American army he was at first turned down; since there was the rule that German forces were to surrender where they had last been stationed, he was expected to surrender to the Russians. In the end, the rocket group came to the United States in "Operation Paperclip." But in spite of all this captured knowledge about rocketry, it took a shock to finally start a serious U.S. space program. For example, in 1949 an advisory report by the National Advisory Committee on Aeronautics (NACA, the forerunner of NASA) to the Air Force included only one sentence referring to a "satellite being a definite possibility." As the director of NACA, Dr. Hugh Dryden, admitted: "We were rather conservative engineers . . . in 1953 I proposed . . . that we may reasonably suppose that a satellite vehicle is entirely practicable now and that travel to the moon is attainable in the next 50 years." Dr. Theodore von Karman said: ". . . serious attempts to build a space ship should await the advent of the nuclear rocket." So the U.S. planned the scientific Vanguard satellite series for the International Geophysical Year of 1958.

Then came Sputnik I on October 4, 1957. The first U.S. reactions were disparaging, as Chief of Naval Operations Admiral Arleigh Burke said: "Hunk of iron almost anybody could launch," and Presidential Advisor Clarence Randall said: "Silly bauble." However, under potent public pressure, the Eisenhower administration had to do something; one step taken was the appointment of Dr. James R. Killian, then President of MIT, as the first official Presidential Science Advisor. Under Senator Lyndon B. Johnson, the Senate Preparedness Subcommittee suggested an independent civilian space agency. Although the scientific community as a whole did not want a very large space effort for fear that this would cut into support for other basic efforts, they also did not want the military to preempt a civilian space program. So the National Academy of Sciences in January of 1958 came out in favor of a unified space establishment to undertake scientific exploration of space. As Dr. Dryden put it:

> . . . the basic reason underlying these proposals for a new civilian agency is plain. The scientific community, understandably, is

worried about the possibility that the extremely important non-military aspects of space technology should be submerged or perhaps even lost if included as a mere adjunct to a military program. (As quoted in Ref. 24.1, p. 55.)

The bill establishing NASA to carry out this scientific research was quickly written to forestall military-congressional interference. Yet the military was able to retain a share of the space effort through its Advanced Research Projects Agency, and complete scientific control of NASA was prevented by establishing as part of this legislative package a National Aeronautics and Space Council, which would advise the President on the space program and which included the Secretary of Defense. The scientists lost even further control of NASA when their low-key Vanguard effort failed to get a satellite up quickly enough, and when they failed to recognize all of the political implications of the space program.

The space program for some time remained a low-level effort even after the establishment of NASA, as President Eisenhower wanted to restrict it to a modest budget. There was only a commitment to build the Saturn launcher and to proceed with the Mercury one-man orbiting program. Then came President Kennedy. He, too, did not want to push the manned space program. He had seen poverty in West Virginia and kept asking, "Can't you fellows invent some other race here on earth that will do some good?" But Vice-President Johnson was for an all-out space effort. "Are you in favor of the U.S. being a second-rate nation?" he supposedly kept asking members of the NASA council. He urged the landing on the moon as a national goal; the alternative goals of a space station or of a manned flight around the moon did not seem big enough, as the Russians were expected to accomplish those first. And then came the Bay of Pigs, and finally Yuri Gagarin's 89-minute orbital flight.

THE APOLLO MOON PROGRAM

So on May 25 of 1961, President Kennedy announced the lunar goal to the Congress:

If we are to win the battle that is now going on around the world between freedom and tyranny, recent dramatic achievements in space should have made clear to us all, as did the sputnik in

1957, the impact of this adventure on the minds of men every-where. . . .

It is time now to take longer strides—time for a great new Ameri-can enterprise—time for this nation to take a clearly leading role in space achievement, which in many ways may hold the key to our future on earth. . . .

Recognizing the head start obtained by the Soviets with their large rocket engines . . . and recognizing the likelihood that they will exploit this lead for some time to come in still more im-pressive successes, we nevertheless are required to make new efforts on our own. For while we cannot guarantee that we shall one day be first, we can guarantee that any failure to make this effort will make us last. . . .

But this is not merely a race. Space is open to us now; and our eagerness to share its meaning is not governed by the efforts of others. We go into space because whatever mankind must under-take, free men must fully share. . . .

I believe that this nation should commit itself to achieving the goal, before this decade is out, of landing a man on the moon and returning him safely to the earth. No single space project in this period will be more impressive to mankind, or more important for the long-range exploration of space; and none will be so dif-ficult or expensive to accomplish. . . .

Let it be clear . . . that I am asking the Congress and the country to accept a firm commitment to a new course of action—a course which will last for many years and carry very heavy costs. . . . If we are to go only halfway, or reduce our sights in the face of difficulty, in my judgment it would be better not to go at all.

I believe we should go to the moon. But I think every citizen of this country, as well as the members of the Congress, should con-sider the matter carefully in making their judgment, to which we have given attention over many weeks and months; because it is a heavy burden, and there is no sense in agreeing or desiring that the United States take an affirmative position in outer space unless we are prepared to do the work and bear the burdens to make it successful. . . .

The amount of money spent on space since then has been quite large: about $40 billion by 1970 on NASA, plus probably a comparable amount for the military aspects of space (spy satellites, etc.). The Apollo moon shots alone have cost on the order of $25 billion. Since the beginning in 1958, the NASA budget hit a maximum of $5.2 billion in 1965, and from then on the appropriations have been steadily decreasing, as the primary objective of the moon has been reached. This much money is, of course, a modern version of a pork barrel, insofar as it has helped various areas of the country. At its peak, the Apollo program involved 300,000 people. In Florida 23,000 employees at Cape Kennedy earned one-half billion dollars annually, making this the third largest industry after tourism and citrus fruit; the Michoud Saturn rocket-assembly facility in Louisiana employed about 11,000; there is the Bay Saint Louis test facility in Mississippi, the Manned Spacecraft Center outside Houston, employing 13,000, and the Marshall Space Flight Center in Huntsville, Alabama.

And after all that money and all that effort, man has indeed walked on the moon. In his book *The Mouse on the Moon*, Leonard Wibberly summarized this accomplishment very nicely (as he told in 1965 of the moon-landing of the rocket of the Duchy of Grand Fenwick, propelled by last year's wine):

"God Save the Dutchess Gloriana XII. May she live forever." With that Vincent raised the flag, thrusting the staff into the pumice-like stone of the escarpment. He had no sooner done this than he was smothered in a shower of tin cans which floated down out of the heavens about him, as if the earth, having listened to his speech, had thrown all its garbage at him. Empty cans of barbecued beans, of frankfurters, sauerkraut, condensed milk, beer, Coca-Cola, together with glass jars that had once contained peanut butter, pickled herrings and grape jelly—in fact, all the garbage which he had thrust out of the rocket during their nine-day journey from earth, now clattered around in a pile which buried both him and the flag.

"Damnation!" roared Vincent, fighting his way out of this pile. "Who did that?" "You did," said Kokintz. "That's all the garbage you threw out of the rocket." He surveyed the odious pile sadly. "Even without a flag" he said, "it would be plain that people from earth were here." (Ref. 24.10, p.112.)

THE JUSTIFICATION OF THE SPACE PROGRAM

Now that all that money has been spent, now that President Kennedy's goal has been fulfilled and man has reached the moon, there remains the question: why did we go to the moon and what did we actually accomplish by the trip? In discussing the question, one has to be very careful to distinguish between the benefits from the unmanned and the manned parts of the space program.

The unmanned space program can be discussed in a fairly rational way. It has sizable scientific benefits because

a) through satellites we get a new view of the earth from the outside,
b) satellite telescopes and the lunar, Mars, and Venus probes give closeup views of other parts of the solar system,
c) we get information about space itself, and
d) we can investigate the inherent aspects of spaceflight through the physiological reactions of animals.

The technological and economic benefits can also be assessed. There are communications satellites. There is improved weather predicting. (The National Aeronautics and Space Council claims to have estimates that the present-day crude weather satellites are already saving the U.S. annually $6 billion in agriculture, water resources management, and surface transportation.) And there is much technological spin-off, as NASA encourages the industrial use of its developments, such as high-low temperature resisting coatings, fireproof materials, nuclear batteries, and super-miniaturized electronic components. The military satellite program is doing very well; the need for U-2 reconnaissance overflights has been eliminated. A photographic satellite is launched every few weeks; it takes pictures of the area under inspection, then drops the film toward the earth where it is caught by high-flying airplanes. The resolution in this spying is now approaching the ultimate limit of distinguishing two objects four inches apart.

But the justifications for the manned space program are much more subtle. The decision to start the Apollo program clearly had many reasons behind it. A very superficial one was the scientific exploration of the moon; and such experiments as the bouncing of laser beams off astronaut-planted mirrors indeed have great potential for giving information both about the origin of the moon and about the earth's surface. But the Apollo program has by necessity been far too concerned with the safety of the astronauts to leave much room for interest in science; scientific expertise on the part of the astronauts has had to be sacrificed in exchange for test-pilot levels of flying skills. On the whole, the scientific community would much prefer an upgrading of the unmanned space program, a program which could probably perform as well or better than astronauts and at far less cost and risk.

Economically, the Apollo program has given certain areas of the country financial, educational, and industrial boosts. But these benefits could have been equally well given by some other technological effort, and therefore such a justification is not enough. Militarily, the U.S. has also attained its objectives with the moon shot; it can do in space whatever is necessary to avoid military surprises, and the moon is now an off-limits area for military purposes, but such an agreement on that could probably have been achieved without the moon landings.

Perhaps the biggest objective of the Apollo program was related to the matter of international prestige and national self-confidence; President Kennedy wanted to propose some national goal which would counteract the pessimism induced by the Russian successes in space and by the military-political debacle of the Bay of Pigs invasion of Cuba. Internationally this goal has indeed been accomplished. It must have been impressive to the world to see such a goal announced in a public way and then met in such a technologically efficient and competent manner. The internal pressure to achieve a technological masterpiece has certainly been relieved. But the goal to unite the country by this challenge has seemingly not worked. Instead of the inspiration of success, there has been a questioning of the appropriateness of spending such large sums of money on such a technological and dehumanized endeavor, particularly when the social needs of the country are so overwhelming. The contrast of the astronauts' book, *First on the Moon*, with Norman Mailer's *Of a Fire on the Moon* is almost unbelievable. So much has changed in the United States since 1961 that this accomplishment does not seem like an adventure to the majority of Americans.

THE FUTURE OF SPACE FLIGHT

Where do we go from here? What is the next step in the space program? On economic-political grounds we must do something further, but on budgetary-sociological grounds we are not totally free in the

directions we can go. A special task force under Vice-President Spiro
T. Agnew has outlined three possible alternatives for the future programs of NASA, with 10-year budgetary estimates ranging from $70
billion to $105 billion. (Actual appropriations are more likely to be
$3 billion per year.) These three major alternatives are a Mars shot,
a moon base, and a large earth orbital station. The first would probably have to be propelled by a nuclear-powered rocket, and such a
rocket is taking a long time to develop. The moon station is somewhat
uncertain and expensive. The orbital station is the most likely (and
the cheapest) alternative. It could be operational by the mid-1970s
for $5 billion; it would be designed for 12 men, but could ultimately
be expanded to take care of 100 men. But this would soon require
a reduction in the cost of transportation into orbit, so an additional
$7 billion would be required to perfect a reusable booster and space-
craft ferry.

What are the steps after that? What can we do in the far-off
future? We can, or course, explore all the planets in the solar system.
But after than we run into a seemingly insurmountable barrier imposed
by the theory of relativity. It appears that it will take us too long to
explore any significant distance into outer space, simply because the
speed of light is the upper limit to any physical motion. There are
really only two star systems promising for planets within a distance of
15 light years: Epsilon Eridani and Tau Ceti, where the latter is 10.8
light years away. Even if we could go there at close to the speed of
light, it would still take 21.6 years for the round trip. And, as pointed
out in Chapter 13, the speed of light is indeed a real upper limit to
such space travel.

Other than this relativistic limit, there is of course a practical
limit; how close can we actually get to the speed of light? Chemical
rockets are relatively ineffective for long-time accelerations; the pro-
pulsion per unit fuel is too low. Nuclear-heat-transfer engines are
proposed for travel within the solar system, but even those are not
good enough for interstellar travel; some sort of fusion drive is necessary. One very far-out proposal of this type was the Orion Project
(now cancelled, see Ref. 24.11). In this project, hydrogen fusion bombs
were to be continuously exploded behind a spaceship to propel it with
a continuously increasing velocity. The estimate was that for $100
billion we could right now accelerate a 100,000-ton spaceship to a
speed of 6000 mi/sec (which is three percent of the speed of light).

Then the nearest star could be reached in about 300 years. If one could extrapolate the growth of our present GNP at four percent a year 200 years into the future, then by the year 2170 the cost of this project would seem like the cost of one Saturn V rocket now. But such an extrapolation is purely a game; besides, who wants to spend 300 years to get to the nearest star?

SUMMARY

The most interesting question about the NASA space programs is not what they are and what they have accomplished, but rather why they were undertaken. Most of them were started as a response to a Russian challenge, and that has colored much of the resulting activity in space. If NASA was intended to be a scientific venture, then it should probably have gone at a slower and more deliberate pace and should, so far, have restricted itself primarily to unmanned explorations. But since the goal of a moon landing was set to ensure a U.S. first, scientists and scientific goals have in the past been definitely secondary in most of NASA's activities.

The actual reasons for going to the moon instead included such subtle goals as spurring economic activity, producing an outstanding technological accomplishment, and achieving prestige. And these have been fulfilled. Since 1961 there has however been a gradual shift in national social priorities, so that these goals seem no longer as important as they once did. As a consequence, NASA is losing its national support at the very moment of its greatest successes, and the space program is leading to polarization rather than to unity. In retrospect, there was probably not a clear enough analysis of the reasons for going to the moon, and we are only now discovering that perhaps we really did not want to go in the first place.

REFERENCES

Prime reference

24.1 D. W. Cox, *America's New Policy Makers: The Scientists Rise to Power*, New York: Chilton Books, 1964; Chapter 5, "Sputnik Spurs the Space Scientists," pp. 49–66, Chapter 6, "Dr.

Hagen's Nightmare," pp. 67–73, Chapter 10, "Scientists Can Be Indecisive Too," pp. 106–120, Chapter 11, "The Starfish That Wouldn't Die," pp. 121–137.

Interesting reading

24.2 J. Strong, *Flight to the Stars*, New York: Hart Publishing Co., 1965.

24.3 L. Levy, Ed., *Space: Its Impact on Man and Society*, New York: W. W. Norton, 1965.

24.4 F. M. Banley, *Exploration of the Moon*, Garden City, New York: Natural History Press, 1964.

24.5 H. Bondi, *The Universe at Large*, Garden City, New York: Anchor Books, 1960.

24.6 M. H. Nicolson, *Voyages to the Moon*, New York: Macmillan Co., 1945; how Galileo's observations of the moon led to thoughts of space flight.

24.7 H. Wright and S. Rapport, Eds., *To the Moon!*, New York: Meredith Press, 1968; old moonlore, etc.

24.8 E. Rostand, *Cyrano de Bergerac* (translated by B. Hooker), New York: Bantam Books JC136, 1959.

24.9 J. Verne, *From the Earth to the Moon and Round the Moon*, New York: Dodd, Mead and Co., 1962.

24.10 L. Wibberly, *The Mouse on the Moon*, New York: Bantam Books FP104, 1965.

24.11 F. Dyson, "Interstellar Transport," *Physics Today*, Oct. 1968, pp. 41–45.

24.12 A. C. Clarke, *2001: A Space Odyssey*, New York: New American Library, 1968.

24.13 N. Mailer, *Of a Fire on the Moon*, Boston: Little, Brown & Co., 1970.

24.14 N. Armstrong, M. Collins, and E. E. Aldrin, Jr., written with G. Farmer and D. J. Hamblin, *First on the Moon*, Boston: Little, Brown & Co., 1970.

QUESTIONS FOR DISCUSSION

1. Why has man always wanted to go to the moon? Were the reasons consistent with such a purely technological and unprosaic way of reaching it?

2. Von Braun worked for the military in order to go to the moon. Was there any other way open to him?

3. Use the Weinberg criteria to evaluate the merits of the space program, and specifically of the Apollo moon shots.

4. Was the moon shot an inevitable technological program?

5. Is it proper to set a national goal on a crash basis without considering the economic and social consequences of the subsequent phasing out of the program?

25 | THE ABM: THE ROLE OF SCIENCE ADVISORS

[McNamara] finds invariably [in the 1968 posture statement] that the offense, by spending considerably less money than the defense, can restore casualties and destruction to the original level before defenses were installed.

Richard L. Garwin and Hans A. Bethe

To raise the level of fatalities back up to the undefended level . . . would require an incremental Soviet expenditure on their offensive forces that would exceed the cost of the defense.

Robert S. McNamara, posture statement of 1967

The history and the public scientific facts concerning the antiballistic missile are presented. Using the scientists involved in the ABM as illustrations, an attempt is made to separate the consensus scientific aspects from the nonscientific political decisions which are involved in this case.

INTRODUCTION

One of the most controversial recent public debates involving science and technology has been about the antiballistic missile (ABM). Scientists in general, and physicists in particular, have provided not only most of the publicly known technical information and data concerning the ABM, but have also carried out much of the public nontechnical debate. Whenever this issue is considered, the thoughts of such scientists as Wiesner, Bethe, Eugene P. Wigner, physics Nobel prize winner from Princeton University, and Donald G. Brennan, mathematician from the Hudson Institute, are sure to be included. This is perhaps the most visible example of scientific involvement in a technical-political problem.

This chapter will do two things. First it will review the history of the present nuclear stalemate leading up to the ABM and summarize the scientific-technological aspects of it. Secondly, it will point out the various levels involved in the debate, levels which continuously get further removed from the consensus scientific aspects toward the nonconsensus political aspects. These levels will then be used to suggest that the involvement of scientists in the nontechnical aspects of the debate has had a doubly bad effect. This involvement harmed consensus science by introducing nonconsensus politics into it; and it harmed the ABM debate by transferring some of the aura of consensus from science into a discussion which basically was not amenable to a consensus. The ABM debate is an excellent illustration of how hard it is for scientists to draw the line between scientific fact and political advocacy.

HISTORY LEADING TO THE ABM

In a sense, the ABM is a symbol of failure; namely, of the failure to achieve any significant nuclear disarmament. Any history of the ABM must therefore begin by looking at past attempts at disarmament. The question of nuclear disarmament is interesting in its own right because it contains all the conflicts induced when scientists attempt to achieve a consensus on a question which is basically political.

From the very beginning of the nuclear age, there had been the desire that nuclear armament be as limited as possible. But until there was something resembling nuclear parity between the U.S. and Russia, no such armament agreements were possible. Late in 1957, when both sides had developed the fusion bomb, Russia proposed a testing moratorium for nuclear weapons, and soon after, President Eisenhower agreed to a conference on this issue. The scientific experts at this conference agreed quite quickly that both above-ground and under-water nuclear tests were easily detectable. The feasibility of detecting underground tests was not so clear-cut. Everyone had been too busy with arms development in the past to have bothered with any disarmament-related studies of seismic detection systems.

Jerome Wiesner for example in 1960 suggested an increase in the arms control staff:

> ... A major effort, compared to past efforts, would be twenty people working full-time, though a much bigger operation can easily be justified. ... why [was] this work not begun a long time ago? ... Probably because sensitive seismic detectors are not needed in the development of nuclear weapons ... (Ref. 25.13, pp. 176–177.)

But in August of 1958, this conference of experts agreed that an inspection system of 180 control stations spread over the earth's surface could police any agreement about weapons as small as 5 kilotons. There was not political commitment, but this technical agreement led to voluntary test cessations at the end of 1958. But then Teller stated that new test data indicated that it would be impossible to reliably detect all underground nuclear explosions below 20 kilotons without many more detecting stations. This argument was based on the concept that even a single illegal nuclear test would have a significant effect on the nuclear balance, so that any inspection system would have to be 100% reliable. In addition, the argument involved secret data which could not be challenged in public, some of which, in fact, turned out to be erroneous. For example, the Air Force was wrong in its estimates of seismic activity in Russia, and it was symptomatic that this error was revealed only after nuclear testing had once again been resumed.

With the breakdown of the technical consensus, the moratorium inevitably broke down in 1961. One specific reason for the breakdown at that point was the fact that the U-2 overflights and the Samos satellites embarrassed the Soviet Union by showing that its military strength was actually much weaker than generally believed. It was only after the public showed great concern about the enormous fallout from these bombs, particularly about the very dirty 58-megaton Russian bomb, and only after the Cuban missile crisis, that the public was able to force support of the limited above-ground test-ban treaty of 1963. Here scientists could agree on the feasibility of detection, and the passage of the treaty was assured because voting against it was like voting for fallout. However, in spite of this test-ban, the nuclear nonproliferation treaty, and the SALT talks, the net result since 1945 has been a continuous arms race. And the ABM is a defensive response to this race.

THE NIKE-ZEUS SYSTEM

The history of the ABM as part of a post-1945 continental air defense system is both long and typical of complicated weapons systems. Initially no effective defense against atomic weapons was thought possible; however, when Russia acquired atomic capabilities, such a defense was reconsidered. And by the end of the 1950s, over $17 billion had been invested in a continental air defense system against bombers. Unfortunately, just as this system neared completion, the Soviet Union developed ballistic missiles, against which this defense was useless.

Consequently, in 1958, just after Sputnik, the Nike-Zeus system of the Army was chosen to be the next generation in air defense. Since the Army had lost almost one-third of its divisions in the budget cuts from 1954 to 1959, it immediately laid heavy stress on the deterrent value of air defense, and considered this to be its "second-primary function." And in 1957, Lt. General James Gavin, Chief of Army R&D, declared that a 100% effective air defense was the nation's need and was in fact "attainable." So the Army began pushing for ABM deployment just as soon as its development was completed. However, the Department of Defense (DoD) was not too happy with the system and refused to deploy it, allocating instead an average of $300-$400 million annually for development. This was in part because the Zeus radar had trouble discriminating between warheads and decoys, involved mechanically moving scanners which made it very vulnerable to damage, and had a range so short that deployment would have required a large civil-defense expenditure to protect against fallout.

The pressure toward deployment of this system was so great that in 1959 and 1960 Congress allocated $137 million for long lead time "pre-production" items for it. However, the Secretary of Defense refused to spend this money, even though the pressure continued into the Kennedy administration. In 1961 the military-industrial complex tried to force the Nike-Zeus issue by such techniques as publishing in the *Army* magazine ads by contractors and even a map showing the national distribution of the resulting economic benefits of the procurements for the system. Congress pushed for further funding, and Speaker of the House John McCormack demanded that:

> . . . we muzzle the mad-dog missile threat of the Soviet Union [and] loose the Zeus through America's magnificent production lines now. (As quoted in Ref. 25.4, p. 1583.)

In fact, the resumption of U.S. nuclear testing in 1962, and the continuation of underground testing after 1963, was to a large extent for checking ABM warheads.

THE NIKE-X SYSTEM

The Nike-Zeus system was replaced after 1963 with the Nike-X system. Even ABM opponents admit that this is indeed a significant improvement; as the physicist Freeman Dyson put it in 1964:

> Problems that ten years ago seemed unapproachably difficult are now either solved or close to being solved. The builders of anti-missile systems ... can now justifiably claim to be able to provide a partial defense, a defense which would make some significant difference to the strategic balance .... (Ref. 25.5, p.13.)

The big improvement is that the radar no longer involves any mechanical motion. This system was also amply supported for R&D; supposedly Kennedy's Secretary of Defense Robert McNamara said to his R&D chief that as far as priorities were concerned:

> Number one: R&D for Vietnam. Number two: assured penetration. Number three: ABM, *but don't precommit me*. (As quoted in Ref. 25.6, p.31.)

As a result of the large R&D funding, the Nike-X is a much improved system.

THE PHYSICS OF THE ABM

Here might be an appropriate point to examine the ABM system in a little detail. The best scientific discussion is probably by Richard L. Garwin and Hans A. Bethe in the March 1968 issue of *Scientific American* (Ref. 25.2). The first thing to ask is how do these ABM systems work? There are two missiles involved in the Nike-X system: the short range, but rapidly accelerating Sprint missile with a range of about 25 miles, and the longer range Spartan missile with a range of more than 150 miles. These are to be deployed in groups called "farms" and guided to their targets by radar. This radar includes a Perimeter Acquisition Radar system (PAR), which guides the Spartan for faraway interception, and a Missile Site Radar (MSR), which helps guide the Spartan and controls the Sprint. The Spartan is to carry out the interception above the atmosphere, while the Sprint will intercept in the atmosphere itself. The destruction of the incoming intercontinental ballistic missile (ICBM) will be accomplished by thermonuclear warheads; conventional explosives have too small a kill-range to be useful.

There are three primary kill interactions.

1. If the interception takes place in the atmosphere, then the blast from the thermonuclear explosion near the ICBM will subject the missile reentry vehicle (RV) to very large accelerations, which will disable the warhead. This effect will occur only for the Sprint; for the Spartan there is no atmosphere to transmit a blast. One difficulty with this is that it is hard to tell whether the RV has indeed been disabled until the warhead either goes off or does not go off. And the structural rigidity of the warhead can fairly easily be increased.

2. The neutron emission from the nuclear bomb can also be used as a kill interaction. Neutrons have the ability to penetrate through the weapon; they can then produce some fission in the warhead. This releases heat which can distort the weapon enough so it no longer can go off. It is difficult to harden a warhead against neutrons; note, for example, how much shielding is necessary for a nuclear reactor to keep the neutrons in.

3. X-rays from the nuclear processes are particularly effective in large megaton warheads which explode above the atmosphere. Larger weapons emit a larger fraction of their energy as x-rays, and the absence of the atmosphere lets the x-rays travel unimpeded to the incoming warhead. The x-rays heat the surface layer of the RV, causing it to vaporize. This sends a shock wave through the heat shield, which may destroy either the heat shield or the underlying structure. Because they are used above the atmosphere, these defensive warheads can be very large in megatons without endangering cities; in this way they can have a very large "kill" radius and thus reduce the necessary aiming accuracy. This feature allows interception at long distances, which is the key to the Safeguard system. However, the heat shield damage will only become apparent on reentry into the atmosphere, so a backup (or mop-up) short-range defense system is required in addition. Hardening against x-rays is possible.

ON OVERCOMING THE ABM

These scientific and technological facts about the ABM are not usually the subject in an ABM debate, although the percent reliability of the various components can be debated. Somewhat less certain is the ease with which such a defensive ABM system may be overcome, and at what cost. If the defense invests $10 billion in an ABM system, how much will it cost the offense to offset this advantage? The scientific capability of analysis already starts to break down in this most basic question of the cost effectiveness of offense versus defense. Estimates in the ratio of defensive costs to offsetting offensive costs range from typically 10:1 to 4:1 (by the opponents of the ABM) to 1:1 or better (by the proponents). In other words, the opponents of the ABM use the numbers to show that it is cheap to overcome the ABM, while the proponents argue the opposite.

What can be done to overcome the ABM system? Obviously one can send in enough missiles to saturate the defense. If one could shoot down one enemy ICBM at $7 million with one Sprint or Spartan which costs about $8 million, then one would break about even with the defense. But there are more complicated maneuvers available for the offense to overcome the defense. One way would be to send the offensive missile not along a normal trajectory with a height of about 800 miles, but in a fractional-orbiting trajectory with a maximum height of about 100 miles. At the cost of about half the payload, the warning time to the defense could then be reduced from 10 minutes down to 3 minutes; this would largely negate any ABM benefits.

One class of offensive devices is called penetration aids. With these aids, the incoming ICBM attempts to confuse the defensive radar by multiplying the number of apparent warheads to be shot at. (a) The booster rocket may be broken up deliberately into fragments resembling the warhead. (b) Fine wires or chaff of the right length to simulate a warhead may be distributed by the millions. For a one-meter-wavelength radar, a million wires of one mil diameter would require only about 440 pounds of copper. (c) A simple decoy is a balloon of the same shape as the reentry vehicle; it is so light that many can be included in the missile. Most of these decoys would be very fragile and easily destroyed by an explosion, or if the defense can wait long enough, the fakes will be slowed down by the atmosphere much more than the real warhead, so that a secondary Sprint defense would not have to go after them all. (d) The warhead may have incorporated into it electronic jamming equipment to confuse the radar. (e) Finally, nuclear bombs may be used to ionize the air in the area of the incoming missiles; this would also confuse the radar and prevent guidance of the ABM missiles.

The ultimate offensive confusion is to subdivide the warhead into smaller units. For example, the 25-megaton warhead in a missile could be replaced by three 4-megaton warheads, and after reentry these could be sent on to three separate targets. This is the MIRV, the multiple independently targetable reentry vehicle. In that way the defense has more warheads to shoot at; or else fewer rockets must survive an initial attack (a first strike) to allow sufficient retaliation (a second strike).

Table 25.1
Estimated numbers of fatalities in an all-out strategic exchange, mid-1970s (in millions). (As quoted, for example, in Ref. 25.8, p. 250.)

U.S. program	Soviet response	Soviets strike first against military and city targets; United States retaliates against cities.		United States strikes first at military targets; Soviets retaliate against U.S. cities; United States retaliates against Soviet cities.	
		U.S. fatalities	Soviet fatalities	U.S. fatalities	Soviet fatalities
No ABM	None	120	120	120	80
Sentinel	None	100	120	90	80
($5 billion)	Pen-Aids	120	120	110	80
Posture A	None	40	120	10	80
($13 billion)	MIRV, Pen-Aids	110	120	60	80
	Plus mobile ICBM's	110	120	90	80
Posture B	None	20	120	10	80
($22 billion)	MIRV, Pen-Aids	70	120	40	80
	Plus 550 mobile ICBM's . .	100	120	90	80

Table 25.1 shows several scenarios for ABM systems of differing costs, presented by McNamara in his 1968 posture statement. From this table Wiesner reached the conclusion that:

> Secretary McNamara ... concede[s] that an anti-Soviet ABM defense would not be worth the huge expense, because the Russians could nullify its effectiveness at considerably lower cost to themselves. (Ref. 25.1, p. 26.)

This conclusion is similar to that of Garwin and Bethe quoted at the beginning of this chapter. They may all have been referring to the fact that the $13 billion Posture A can be almost completely offset by a MIRV system coupled with relatively inexpensive penetration aids. Since $3.2 billion will convert 600 warheads for Polaris submarines into 4000 MIRV warheads, the cost exchange ratio here is essentially four to one ($13 billion: $3.2 billion = 4:1) in favor of the offense. A year earlier, McNamara had reached the different conclusion cited at the beginning of this chapter by looking at a somewhat different hypothetical scenario.

THE GOALS OF THE ABM SYSTEM

Even more hazy are the goals of the ABM. They seem to be very flexible and responsive to the political opinion of the voters. When McNamara finally acceded to the deployment of the Sentinel system in 1967, it was to primarily defend U.S. cities against a potential Chinese missile attack, with secondary goals being a partial protection of our ICBMs against Soviet attacks and a protection of the cities against a possible accidental ICBM launching by one of the nuclear powers. The expansion of that system to protect the population against an all-out missile attack by Russia was characterized by the more expensive Postures A and B in Table 25.1.

In June of 1968, the Senate voted one-quarter billion dollars toward the Sentinel system (and some talk began about its uses against large-scale Russian attacks as well). However, popular protests against the installations of the missiles began to be heard, as the inhabitants of the cities which were to be defended became aware that they might as a result become targets for nuclear attacks above and beyond the "normal" course of events. So in the spring of 1969, President Nixon announced his Safeguard version of the Nike-X, with a considerable shift of the goals. The system was then to be primarily a protection of ICBM bases against an all-out Russian attack rather than an area defense against the Chinese or an area defense against an accidental missile launch. The ABM sites were now to be moved away from any major cities except for Washington, D.C. Interestingly enough, the overall nationwide distribution of the missile sites for the Safeguard system is not greatly different from that of the Sentinel system, in spite of the changes in objectives.

POSSIBLE RUSSIAN RESPONSES

Even less certain are game theories involving possible responses to an American ABM system by the Russians. This area is replete with past miscalculations. How many missiles does Russia have? In 1961 Kennedy talked about a missile gap when there was none, when we were in fact way ahead. The U.S. seems still way ahead in separate warheads that can be delivered, while Russia can deliver a larger total megatonnage. And it is typical of this game that any extrapolations into the future are proven wrong just as soon as they are made. What is the status of the Russian ABM program? We started our MIRV program in part in response to their Galosh system around Moscow (a system which resembles the Nike-Zeus mechanical radar) and in response to the Leningrad Tallin defense system, which has turned out to be not an ABM system but rather a defense against our B-70 bomber, which we never built.

POLITICAL AND SOCIAL CONCERNS

If we want to get even further away from remotely consensible questions, then we can examine political objectives and responses.

a) Our goal is to have left, after even a first strike by Russia, 400 retaliatory missiles to kill at least 40% of the Russians and destroy at least 76% of their industrial capacity. What determined this goal?

b) What are the uses of these missiles in a local power confrontation, as during the Cuban missile crisis?

c) Do we blast the Chinese with nuclear weapons if their troops invade South Vietnam?

d) Will our possessing an ABM system reassure the countries under our nuclear umbrella so that they will not demand a nuclear capability of their own?

And, finally, there are the social and ethical considerations.

a) What is it worth to reduce the potential American casualties in a nuclear war from 100 million to 60 million? Might a sufficiently low casualty prediction tempt some military planners to consider a nuclear war feasible after all?

b) Does the ABM technology create itself? That is, since the ABM is like shooting at a needle in the dark with another needle, isn't it too technically sweet to resist?

c) Since civil defense appears a necessary adjunct to any people-oriented ABM defense, and since we refuse the concept of civil defense because it might "harden" our population, can we ever have a real ABM defense?

d) How much military can we afford?

e) Do we want to spent the Russians to death by forcing them to keep pace with our military expenditures?

f) What does this nuclear tension do to the American "way of life"?

CONCLUSIONS

Most of these questions do not have even a remote connection with science, and hence do not really belong here—except to show the extremes to which this ABM debate can and must go, and to show how small a contribution science can make to resolving this problem. Consensus science stops at the very edge of the debate. Yet scientists have carried out a disproportionate amount of the debating on this question. It is clearly too tempting to use the expertise on the scientific aspects of the topic as a justification for considering the non-scientific aspects as well. And the aura of the "white lab coat" does transfer to some extent, lending extra weight to the scientists' political opinion. But this weighting is not justified; in the political aspects the scientists are no more competent than any other citizen.

To me it seems that the final result of undue scientific involvement in this question can only be a net decrease in the correctness of the final decision on the ABM. Furthermore, scientific involvement in an extremely nonconsensible topic ultimately can only lead to a decrease in the credibility of scientists, even on topics where they do have competence. Consensus science and politics seem incompatible; therefore, if a scientist becomes involved in a scientific-political question, he should be very careful to distinguish when he is talking on some aspects with expertise and when he is speaking as an average citizen with personal concerns.

REFERENCES

Prime references

25.1 Wm. O. Douglas, L. Johnson, G. S. McGovern, J. B. Wiesner, "ABM: Yes or No," Santa Barbara, Calif.: Center for the Study of Democratic Institutions, *A Center Occasional Paper*, Vo. II,#2, 1969.

25.2 R. L. Garwin and H. A. Bethe, "Anti-Ballistic-Missile Systems," *Scientific American* **218** (#3), 21–31 (March 1968).

Interesting reading

25.3 Fulbright, Rathjens, Bethe, Sternglass, Dyson, and York, "Missiles and Antimissiles, Six Views," *Bulletin of the Atomic Scientists* **25** (#6), 20–28 (June 1969).

25.4 *Congressional Quarterly*, "Congress and the Nation, 1945–1964," Washington, D.C.: 1965.

25.5 F. Dyson, "Defense Against Ballistic Missiles," *Bulletin of the Atomic Scientists* **20**, 13 (June 1964).

25.6 S. Alsop, "His business is War," *Saturday Evening Post*, May 21, 1966, p. 31.

25.7 W. B. Bader, *The United States and the Spread of Nuclear Weapons*, New York: Pegasus Original, 1968.

25.8 A. Chayes and J. B. Wiesner, Eds., *ABM*, New York: Signet Broadside, New American Library, 1969; anti-ABM articles.

25.9   W. R. Kintner, *Safeguard: Why the ABM Makes Sense*, New York: Hawthorn Books, Inc., 1969; pro-ABM.

25.10 H. Kahn, *Thinking About the Unthinkable*, New York: Avon Discus Book W135, 1968; grim scenarios of nuclear war.

25.11 J. J. Stone, *Containing the Arms Race*, Cambridge, Mass.: The M.I.T Press, 1966.

25.12 R. E. Lapp, *The Weapons Culture*, Baltimore: Penguin Books Inc., 1969.

25.13 J. B. Wiesner, *Where Science and Politics Meet*, (Ref. 4.9); "Learning About Disarmament," pp. 165–296.

QUESTIONS FOR DISCUSSION

1. What are the contributions which science and scientists can make to the ABM question, particularly to the political questions?

2. Is there any sense in which scientists are better qualified to debate the ABM issue?

3. If you are a scientist, and feel very strongly about the ABM, should you use your consensus aura to see that the right decision is reached?

4. Do scientists have any social responsibility for creating this ABM problem?

26 | CYBERNETICS

*I went to the University of Wisconsin's Computing Center and said,
"I want to use your machines to analyze fictional prose style." ...
The answer was, "Fine, we think we can help you; but first you'll
have to tell us that you mean by style."*

Karl Kroeber

The scientific and technological reasons for the sudden development of the computer are discussed. The social aspects of computers are examined; and the nature (and limitation) of artificial intelligence is illustrated through computer applications in the humanities.

INTRODUCTION

Just as "pollution" seems to be the technological concern of the 1970s, "automation" was perhaps the concern of the 1960s. This concern reflected the fact that computers began to play a very visible role in our national life during that time. Cybernetics began to have contact not only with economics through automation, but also with the social structure itself through personal surveillance via computerized accounting, with education through computer teaching, and with thoughts about the very nature of man through the possibilities of artificial intelligence. The advent of a large-scale computer technology and capability forced the critical analysis of many traditional viewpoints in these fields.

This chapter will review the physics and the technology of the computer in order to show why the computer revolution took place when it did. This will be followed by an outline of some of the interactions of computers with society, and by an examination of the validity of some of the concerns which made computers objects of fear. Finally we will look at some applications of computers in humanistic studies. These will illustrate the limitations of computers, particularly with respect to intelligence—limitations which illuminate the differences between the two cultures.

WHY COMPUTERS NOW?

What do computers have to do with physics? Why bring them up in the context of this book? The answer will show why computers are a contemporary phenomenon. The idea of a computer is, in fact, quite old. Edgar Allen Poe wrote about a chess-playing robot named Maezel (which actually had a midget inside it); and in the middle of the 19th century, Charles Babbage proposed and partially constructed a complicated mechanical device which would carry out long sequences of calculations without human intervention. Yet the computer has come of age only since World War II.

The answer lies in the actual operations performed by a computer. The large modern computers do computations by manipulating and storing digital numbers. That is to say, all their operations involve numbers that are precisely fixed, with no range of uncertainty. In fact, these numbers are ultimately reduced to the binary system, which uses only the two symbols 0 and 1. The beginning decimal numbers are then expressible as $1 = 1, 2 = 10, 3 = 11, 4 = 100, 5 = 101, 6 = 110, 7 = 111, 8 = 1000$, etc. This mode of expression is very convenient for a computer, since all the elements of the computer then need only two distinct states, such as on and off. It is then very easy to represent the limited number of letters in the alphabet by some specific number. If there is a somewhat more complicated input, such as an analog voltage (e.g., that of a continuously variable voltmeter reading), then the input must first be converted into the limited (but more precisely fixed) digital form.

The computer performs various operations on these binary numbers. It adds them or compares them through various logic functions performed by simple combinations of on-off elements. At various points, the information may be stored in the computer memory, again by elements which have only two states. The need for large numbers of these elements was a basic factor in the development of computers.

The original designs of Babbage tried to perform these functions with mechanical wheels and cams; this was an impossibly clumsy system. The Mark I computer of the Second World War was built out of a huge number of relays. A relay obviously has two states—open or closed—and therefore is suitable as a binary device. The ENIAC and MANIAC computers of the postwar period operated with electron-tube diodes, in which either a lot of current flowed or no current flowed at all. And, finally, the contemporary computers use transistors as binary operating devices (with a current off or on). And the memory is made up of a magnetic core in which the magnetization of the ferrite elements is flipped up or down by means of currents passing through them (like reversing the magnetization of the needle in a compass by passing it through a wire coil with a current flowing through it).

It is now easy to see why computers are necessarily a modern product. (1) To be useful, the computer must have many components, both in its large memory and for the many logic circuits. Therefore the components must be small. The mechanical relays were huge, the electronic tubes were large; so it is only since the transistor was developed after 1948 that computers could become complex enough (see Fig. 26.1). Of course, very high-purity material is required for the transistor crystals; this made an earlier development of solid-state devices technologically impossible, and hence fixed the starting date for the large-scale development of the computer. (2) To be useful, a computer must be fast; it must be able to carry out many computations in a very short time. The mechanical models could not do this, since the operation of cams or relays involved the movement of physical components. In the electron tubes and transistors, the moving components are electrons; these are much easier to accelerate and stop. Small transistors promise much higher speeds than the electron tubes. Improvements in the speed of the memory processes are also a technological problem. (3) To be useful and economical, the computer must be reliable; i.e., its components must be reliable. The mechanical monsters were very bad because their operation was a matter of physical contact. And the electron tubes were not much better. The current flow in an electronic tube consists of electrons boiled off a

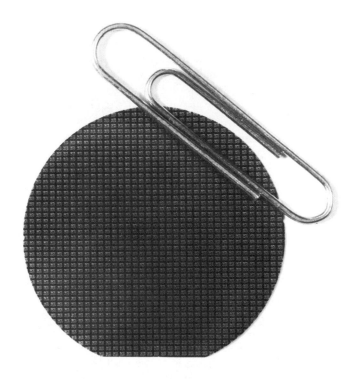

Fig. 26.1   A one-inch slice of silicon, containing some 1000 integrated circuits. The paper clip in the photograph is included to give an idea of size.

metal plate by heating it to a very high temperature. These high temperatures mean wear and tear on the tubes so that they age very quickly. Consequently, they are not only bulky and expensive but are also short-lived. In addition, the heating process consumes expensive electrical energy and requires an enormous amount of cooling to carry away the generated heat.

From all this it is clear that computers are a recent development because the essential technology became available only after the discovery of the transistor. There is, however, the additional factor that the need for the computer has become particularly acute only since World War II, when extensive calculations were required to determine the parameters of the hydrogen bomb and when the radar communications of the various bomber and missile detection systems became a problem.

THE IMPACT OF COMPUTERS THROUGH AUTOMATION

Has the computer age actually arrived? The answer seems to be yes, as the size of the computer industry alone forces that conclusion. Whereas only 10 to 15 computers existed in the U.S. in 1950, in 1975 there will be about 85,000. By then investments in them will be more than $30 billion. There are now over one-half million people employed in the computer business as systems analysts and programmers. This represents a significant fraction of the economy and of the population. The computer characterizes the tendency toward automation, toward the Second Industrial Revolution, as Norbert Wiener likes to call it. Complete factories can be put under machine control, with feedback circuits allowing instantaneous adjustments to keep the end-product constant. And it is this technological interaction through automation, with its resultant labor displacements and other adjustment problems, which really makes the computer a feared antagonist to many people. Just one example of this impact: President Kennedy was reluctant to fund the Apollo moon-shot program because he had seen the poverty in Appalachia resulting from the displacement of coal miners by automation; 85,000 men out of 125,000 lost their jobs in West Virginia during a time interval when the coal production decreased by only 25%. Then there is the displacement of 30,000 elevator operators, not to mention an even larger number of unemployed bowling-alley pinboys.

The question whether the fears of automation are indeed justified is as yet unresolved. Certainly adjustments are necessary as automation increases; some people must find different jobs. But there is disagreement as to whether automation has an overall harmful effect on the labor market. There are net losses in occupations involving physical labor, but not too much in sales and among clerical and service workers. The data is simply hard to analyze; presumably as long as the economy keeps expanding there are no real problems. An even more difficult question is whether or not workers and jobs are becoming mismatched. Are educational requirements for jobs rising because more education is required to perform them? Or is it simply that so many more educated workers are available that a lack of education is a handicap on appearance alone?

SOCIAL ASPECTS OF COMPUTERS

In talking about the societal aspects of the development of computers, we must mention the effect on education. Schools have now over one-half billion dollars invested in computing facilities; the annual educational computing budget in the universities exceeds $300 million; and computing skills are now frequently allowed in graduate schools as alternatives to a second foreign language. There have long been promises that computers would make feasible a private tutor for every individual schoolchild. Equally interesting is the fact that the educational use of computers illustrates a mode of operation of modern technology. Many of the new uses of computers were first explored at universities; these explorations indicated a large need for computers. Now the universities have been forced to institutionalize this need through the teaching of programming; this, in turn, has forced the universities to purchase (or rent) very advanced computers. So the universities to some extent have pioneered both the possibilities of, and the needs for computers, which leads to a rather circular and hence somewhat artificial growth in computer technology.

Another social aspect is related to information storage and retrieval. This is certainly one of the more "computerlike" uses of a computer. Yet not much of what has been promised has been accomplished. We do not have instant access to all the volumes in the Library of Congress (in fact, the computer still cannot read books without human intervention); much of the communicating in science is still carried out by typewritten preprints, handwritten letters, and by private conversations, etc. However, information storage in another sense does pose a major threat. Since individuals in the U.S. have become totally identifiable by their social security numbers, it is now possible not only to store large quantities of information about individuals in computer memories but also to exchange these between the Internal Revenue service, the state-government auto-licensing bureaus, and the local banks. This raises the specter of complete loss of privacy.

COMPUTERS AND THE HUMANITIES

But perhaps the most revealing of the social implications of the computer lies in its uses in the humanities because they clearly demonstrate its capabilities and limitations. Particularly significant are computers' uses in analyses of literature and music simply because in these cases the basic data is presented in limited and readily quantifiable notation. There are basically two things a computer can do in these fields: it can organize or index a work, or it can look for patterns in it. In either case the work must first be fed into the computer memory, and since computers still can't read arbitrarily printed material, this "feeding" process is still laborious and makes this type of research hard work. (Actually this may be almost a benefit, because it encourages careful planning and defining of the project.)

The first type of computer use is in indexing, such as in the making of literary concordances. These concordances are simply alphabetical listings of all words in the text; each time they occur they are printed, together with their context. This KWIC (Key Word in Context) approach is used, for example, by the journal *Chemical Abstracts* to provide an index to help people search for articles in their favorite topic in current and past chemistry journals. The time savings in this computer usage can be enormous. For example, it took one person 44 years to prepare by hand the letters A through H of a Chaucer lexicon. A similar concordance of the works of Matthew Arnold took an IBM 7090 computer $2\frac{1}{2}$ hours, including the printout. And the program to do this is generally available.

In music a similar use of computers is the setting up of a thematic index. Here the idea is to somehow index the themes presented in the first 7 to 12 notes of a work. However, music is somewhat more complicated than literature, since not only are there more possible notes, but these notes have various possible durations as well. When, in addition, possible key changes due to transcriptions must also be considered and when orchestral works with all the volume indications and tempi are to be analyzed, then even this simple problem becomes difficult. So indexing has been satisfactorily accomplished only for the simpler works of some early composers like Palestrina.

Such indexing seems worthwhile enough, but the next step is of far more interest. In both these fields, the ultimate question is one of

Table 26.1

Comparisons of the occurrence of certain words in *Persuasion*, by Jane Austen, and in *Jacob's Room*, by Virginia Woolf. (Data taken from Ref. 26.8, pp. 139–140.)

	Austen	Woolf
Average sentence length	25	16
Ratio of subordinate to main clauses	1.0	0.36
Percent complex narration	69	27
Ratio of concrete to abstract nouns	0.75	1.7
Percent adverbs: manner	46	34
time	14	23
place	17	29
Percent nouns: parts of body	13	32
parts of house	8	26
time	28	27
sound	1	9
emotion	31	4
mental action	19	2
Percent adjectives: color	1	48
emotion	43	21
value	56	31

style: what makes one work different from another, and hence what makes one great and one a disaster. In literature, this question might be: what makes Jane Austen different from Virginia Woolf? Of course, literary critics have answered such questions by saying so-and-so's writing is flabby or luminous. But what answer does the computer give? As the introductory quotation indicates, the question must be very precisely defined before the computer can answer it. One attempt to answer the question is to let the computer count various types of words and structures in representative works of the two authors. The typical results of such a counting are shown in Table 26.1. Obviously a reading of the two books would also have revealed this opposition of concrete concerns in Woolf versus the emotions and thoughts of Austen. But these computer counts have forced a clearer understanding of the meaning of style, and have put some quantitative and objective criteria into the discussion.

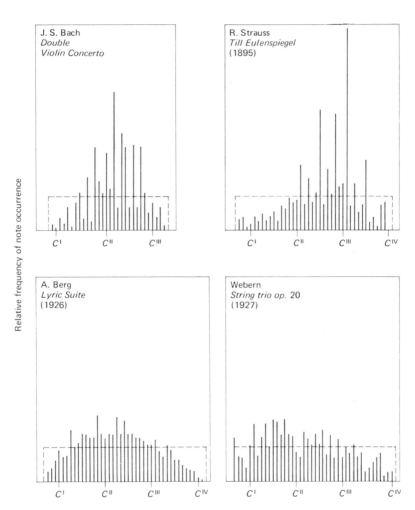

Fig. 26.2 Distribution of note occurrence in the violin parts of music composed at various dates. (Data taken from Ref. 26.9.)

In music analysis there are, of course, similar problems. For example, such modern composers as Alban Berg and Anton Webern sound much more disorganized than Johann Sebastian Bach. Is it possible to develop an objective criterion for this subjective feeling? Using a computer, it is indeed possible to analyze the musical scores for this information. Figure 26.2 shows the relative frequency of occurrence of the various notes in certain works of Bach, Richard Strauss, Berg, and Webern. And the note distribution for the work by Bach clearly shows the spikes corresponding to staying with the original key, as well as a fairly narrow range. In contrast, the works of Berg and Webern have a very flat and broad note distribution, as these composers do not feel so restricted to any specified key. The interesting point is that Strauss, whom many would consider to be a modern composer, has a note distribution much closer to Bach than to either Berg or Webern. Apparently the date of composition is not sufficient to make a work modern. Here is a contribution made by the computer to the understanding of style simply through forcing an analysis of the meaning of that word.

ARTIFICIAL INTELLIGENCE

One of the great fears concerning computers has always been that they might someday become so intelligent that they will surpass man's thinking abilities and take over the world. There even exist considerations of how to program a robot in such a way as to avoid its harming human beings, while still allowing it maximum leeway in the performance of its assigned tasks (e.g., Ref. 26.12). There is the apocryphal story about a highly developed computer who is asked by his programmer the ultimate question: "Is there a God?" And after making sure that he could not be turned off, the computer answers: "*Now* there is."

However, this fear has now greatly decreased, mainly because it has been found hard to get computers to act intelligently. To program a computer to do such simple things as carrying out the form associations in Fig. 26.3, or of playing championship-class chess, or of translating a foreign language, has turned out to be unexpectedly difficult. Computers are not as intelligent as we expected them to be, which is a reflection perhaps on our lack of understanding the nature

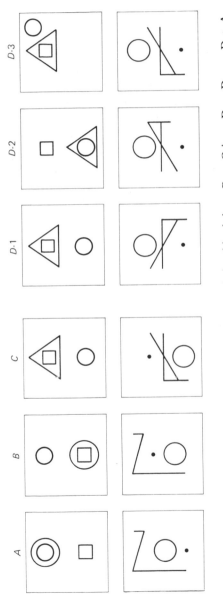

Fig. 26.3 In these figures the problem is to solve the relationship A is to B as C is to D-1, D-2 or D-3. A program by Thomas Evans at M.I.T allowed a computer to solve the upper, but not the lower problem. (From "Information and Computers." Copyright © 1966 by *Scientific American*, Inc. All rights reserved.

of intelligence. And again it is the fact that we are forced to consider the nature of intelligence, which is turning out to be the most important aspect of this concern.

SUMMARY

Due to the fact that solid-state electronic devices are necessary to make computers with useful capabilities, computers are necessarily a modern development. Their development has indeed had a significant impact on the social order. Not only is automation modifying the economic scene, but there have been changes induced in a wide range of social activities such as education and literary analysis. Actually computers are somewhat more limited than expected; they are not yet able to approximate thinking. As a consequence, most of the problems arising from their use, such as the invasion of privacy, are simply due to improper use, not due to any unpredictable computer behavior.

In fact, the most significant benefits derived from computers may be the consequent need to examine some of our attitudes. It is not so much that computers are useful in teaching; it is more that the purposes and meanings of education, learning, and knowledge must be more clearly understood in order to program computers to teach. It is not so much that computers are very adept at analyzing literary styles; it is more that they force an analysis of the meaning of style. Ultimately even a definition of intelligence may develop out of the use of computers. In a sense, this is a joining of the two cultures; here this new imagination derived from technology leads to a new insight in the arts; and this new way of analyzing quantitative data leads to new scientific insights.

REFERENCES

Prime references

26.1 "Information and Computers," a whole issue on this topic in *Scientific American* **215** (#3) (September 1966); see particularly J. McCarthy "Information," pp. 65–73, and D. C. Evans "Computer Logic and Memory," pp. 75–85.

Interesting reading

26.2 W. Buckingham, *Automation*, New York: Harper and Row, 1961.

26.3 W. Francois, *Automation: Industrialization Comes of Age*, New York: Collier Books, 1964.

26.4 G. Burck, Ed., *The Computer Age*, New York: Harper and Row, 1965.

26.5 J. Pfeiffer, *The Thinking Machine*, New York: J. B. Lippincott, 1962.

26.6 A. G. Oettinger, *Run, Computer, Run*, Cambridge, Mass.: Harvard University Press, 1969; computers in education.

26.7 D. G. Fink, *Computers and the Human Mind*, Garden City, N.J.: Anchor Books, 1966.

26.8 E. A. Bowles, Ed., *Computers in Humanistic Research*, Englewood Cliffs, N.J.: Prentice Hall, 1967; has the introductory quotation.

26.9 W. Fuchs, "Mathematische Analyze von Formalstrukturen von Werken der Musik," *Arbeitsgemeinschaft Rheinland-Westfalen*, **124**, 39 (1963).

26.10 N. Wiener, *God and Golem, Inc.: A Comment on Certain Points where Cybernetics Impinges on Religion*, Cambridge, Mass.: The MIT Press, 1964.

26.11 N. Wiener, *The Human Uses of Human Beings*, New York: Avon W114, 1967.

26.12 I. Asimov, *I, Robot*, Garden City, N.Y.: Doubleday, 1950; has the equivalent of the Ten Commandments for robots.

QUESTIONS FOR DISCUSSION

1. Is there conclusive evidence whether or not computers are leading to automation unemployment?

2. Would you prefer a robot to drive your car?

3. Is the quality of life decreased or increased by automation and computerization? Will not automation further destroy the simple way of life? Is there such a thing as too much leisure?

4. It may be possible to have a computer design a cheap violin which has the tone quality of a Stradivarius. Would music be the better for this mass-produced quality?

5. How might one define intelligence with respect to a computer? The Turing test suggests you talk with it via a teletype system, and if its answers to your questions don't reveal that it is a computer, then it is defined as possessing intelligence. Is this a reasonable definition?

27 | PHYSICS AND THE FUTURE: ENERGY POLLUTION

In Köln, a town of monks and bones
And pavements fang'd with murderous stones
And rags, and hags, and hideous wenches,
I counted two and seventy stenches,
All well defined, and several stinks!

Ye nymphs that reign o'er sewers and sinks,
The river Rhine, it is well known,
Doth wash your city of Cologne;
But tell me, Nymphs, what power divine
Shall henceforth wash the river Rhine.

Samuel Coleridge

A review is presented of the various sources of energy available to man, and future energy requirements are examined. Energy release appears to be the source of ultimate nonreversible pollution of the earth. For example: If all the energy utilized by man were to go into melting the polar icecap, then by the year 2030 the ocean level may have risen by about one foot.

INTRODUCTION

Whereas cybernetics through automation was the social-technological concern of the 1960s, pollution appears to be the concern of the 1970s. Inspired perhaps by the space program, man has finally begun to think in global terms about his "spaceship earth." Having seen the earth hanging so isolated in space, man is beginning to realize that he is part of a self-contained system and that he has to conserve what the system has to offer, since no significant fraction of the earth's population will ever be able to emigrate from it.

Pollution is the end result of processes which take raw materials from the earth, convert them into less usable forms, and at the same time give off wastes into the atmosphere and into the water supply. There is nothing specifically new about the concern with pollution. Thomas R. Malthus long ago worried that there would not be enough food to feed an exponentially increasing population. The romanticists of the early 19th century complained bitterly about the pollution of the air and water by industry, as did Coleridge in the introductory quotation. And the London fog of Sherlock Holmes in the 19th century was mostly smog produced by the burning of impure coal to heat homes, a practice which has now been corrected, with the result that London is cleaner than it has been for centuries. The biggest change in pollution has been simply an increase in the magnitude of the problem—just as the magnitude of virtually every other human problem seems to have increased. However, many conservationists feel that now there is even a qualitative difference in this problem, that the degradation of the environment is inevitably going to have uncontrollable sociological consequences.

There may be further problems in pollution arising sometime in the future which will be qualitatively different in the sense of being *not* soluble even in the most utopian society. Most of the pollution of the past, present, and near future is potentially reversible if only enough energy is available to do the reversing. For example, if we are willing to settle for lower horsepower in our automobile engines, then most of the gasoline pollution problems can be solved; if we have enough energy available, we can reprocess much of our scrap metals: if we have enough energy available, we can easily purify our rivers and even desalinate ocean water. In the near future the only problem seems to be to get enough cheap energy to reverse our pollution. But sometime in the not-so-distant future this fight against pollution will itself produce a thermal pollution which is ultimately not reversible.

In this chapter we will briefly discuss the total available supplies of various sources of energy including fossil and fission fuels. A separate section will be devoted to the possibilities and present status of controlled fusion as an energy source. Then the magnitudes of the rising demands for usable energy will be reviewed. Finally there will be some pessimistic extrapolations which suggest that the resulting overall energy pollution may lead in the not-too-distant future to noticeable increases in global temperatures and in the ocean water level.

AVAILABLE ENERGY SUPPLIES

We might begin by taking a look at the various sources of energy available on and in the earth, the relative ease of extracting this energy, and the ultimate limits of their availability. There are essentially three major classifications of available stored energy.

1. There are the energy sources in which the physical configuration of a substance is important, as in winding a spring, and in the motion of wind and water. Typical amounts of energy available from such sources are about one large Calorie per pound of material (1 Cal/lb), where one Calorie is that energy which will heat one pound of water by 1°F. The relevant fact to remember here is that the average human energy consumption from food is about 2000 Cal per day, which is equivalent to the energy released by a constantly burning 100-watt light bulb.

2. There are the chemical sources, in which a chemical rearrangement of the substance takes place through the motion of electrons from one atom to another, as in the burning of various substances. These sources contain typically 5000 Cal/lb.

3. Finally there are the nuclear power sources, which release energy by the fission or fusion of nuclei. These release on the order of 8 and 70 billion Cal/lb, respectively.

Since these forms of energy can be transformed into electrical or mechanical energy and can then be used to do work in the home for cooking or in the factory for turning machinery, the critical question is how big is our available supply of energy in each of these categories? The convention seems to be to use units of billion-billions (10^{18}) when discussing such large quantities of energy; the British, for example, use a Q unit, which is 10^{18} btu. I will use multiples of large Calories, simply because man is a ready measure of this unit. Q is then about $1/4$ of 10^{18} Cal. Our present world-wide energy consumption of about

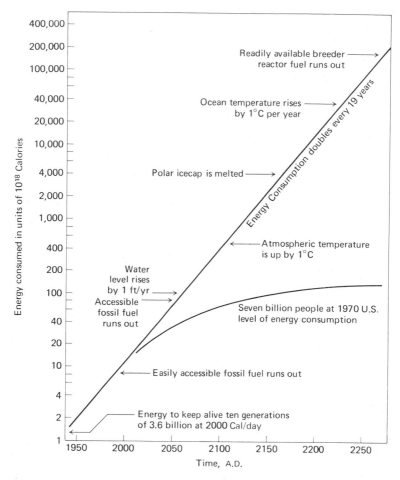

Fig. 27.1 Energy consumption extrapolation assuming that this consumption continues to double every 19 years.

4×10^{16} Cal per year will provide a comparison point for these numbers. (See Fig. 27.1 for an extrapolation of how rapidly this demand is increasing and how long these supplies may be expected to last.)

1. In energy due to flowing streams, for example, there is available annually an absolute maximum of exactly the present demand; in actuality only about 4×10^{14} Cal (i.e., one percent) of that amount is turned into usable hydroelectric energy (Ref. 27.4, p. 66). This is, however, a constantly renewed energy reserve.

2. Chemical (fossil) fuels, on the other hand, are exhaustible since they were produced by storage of solar energy over many millions of years. Any estimates of such supplies tend to be very time-dependent. What we are basically interested in is the ultimately usable supply, but what is known at any given time is only the readily available supply. As better prospecting and recovery techniques are developed, these available supplies increase. For example, in 1952 the world's fossil fuel supplies were estimated at about 10×10^{18} Cal (Ref. 27.5, p. 65), while in 1967 the world's usable coal reserves alone were estimated at 7.6 trillion tons or 76×10^{18} Cal (Ref. 27.1, p. 414). Then again in 1971 the known fossil fuel was estimated at 5.7×10^{18} Cal, with potential reserves at 120×10^{18} Cal (Ref. 27.2, p. 53).

3. In the nuclear fuels the supplies are of several kinds; in particular, there are fusion sources, which will be discussed below, and there are fission sources. In fission one must distinguish between the use of the 0.7% of U^{235} which occurs in natural uranium, and the use of Pu^{239} or thorium-233 (Th^{233}) which is produced in a special "breeder" nuclear reactor by neutron irradiation of naturally plentiful U^{238} and Th^{232}. In addition, we must distinguish whether or not these ore supplies are readily available. The readily accessible uranium ore could yield through U^{235} 2.8×10^{18} Cal, while the potential (but difficult to mine) ore supply could be as much as 7500×10^{18} Cal (Ref. 27.2, p. 53). If, however, we begin to use all of the uranium and thorium ores to provide energy through breeder reactors, then the readily available energy might be 2000×10^{18} Cal, while the potential supply could go as high as $10,000,000 \times 10^{18}$ Cal (Ref. 27.2, p. 53).

ENERGY FROM FUSION

That leaves the potential energy supply of the fusion process. We saw in Chapter 20 that in the fusion process some light nuclei like those of hydrogen, deuterium, or tritium are heated to sunlike temperatures so that they collide with speeds high enough to fuse together and release up to 0.7% of their mass as energy. This process is not only seven times as efficient as the fission process in converting mass into energy, but furthermore the raw materials for the reaction are potentially inexhaustible. If this process is so desirable, why have we not already built controlled fusion reactors?

The difficulty lies, of course, in starting these reactions. This can only be done by pushing together tritium, deuterium, or hydrogen gases at very high temperatures. The easiest of these reactions to start is the D-T reaction in which a deuterium and a tritium nucleus fuse together. This reaction has a critical temperature of 45 million degrees centigrade, which compares with 100 million degrees for the D-D (deuteron-deuteron) reaction, or several hundred million degrees for a H-H (hydrogen-hydrogen) reaction. This D-T reaction also requires a density of about 10^{15} particles per cubic centimeter (which is about 1/10,000 times the density of our atmosphere), and the gas must be held together for about a second (the confinement time). In the fusion bomb the high temperature was provided by the fission-bomb trigger, and since the fusion bomb was made out of a solid, the particle density was so high that the confinement time could be quite short. But controlled fusion presents formidable difficulties.

The concept of controlled fusion dates back to World War II. At that time the program was placed under military secrecy control, as it seemed closely related to the development of the fusion bomb itself. However, once it became obvious that this controlled-fusion program, called Project Sherwood, was not responding to crash conditions, the investigations were made public in 1958. (Actually the Russians were the first to give up their secrecy about controlled fusion.) This branch of physics, called plasma physics, since then has been gradually progressing toward the control of fusion. In the middle of the 1960s, theory seemed to suggest that there was no possible solution to the problem; but now the scientists are reasonably confident, enough so that they are even holding conferences on possible designs of energy-producing fusion reactors. The latest Russian machine, called

Tokomak, in 1969 reached a temperature of tens of millions of degrees centigrade; i.e., less than a factor of ten to go. It achieved a particle density of tens of million-millions per cubic centimeter (10^{13} per cm³); i.e., less than a factor of 100 to go. And it obtained a confinement time of 1/30 of a second, which can be increased simply by increasing the size of the machine. In the past, improvements of factors of 10 in one or the other of these parameters has come about every two years; this would suggest that the first laboratory reaction might occur by about 1975. Predictions of a power-producing fusion reactor by the end of the century can be heard from realistic experts; although this would only be a working model rather than an economical one.

At these very high temperatures the gases become a plasma, in which the electrons and the positively charged nuclei separate completely. And it is the containment of this plasma which presents the problems; there is no way to make a physical container for the gas, after all, solids vaporize at less than 6000°C. So the fusion reactor will be a magnetic "bottle" of one form or another. In such a device a magnetic field is used to keep the plasma from striking the walls. One takes, for example, a ring-shaped evacuated tube and wraps wire around it through which a current is passed. This produces a magnetic field inside the tube. If a plasma is then injected into the tube, it is forced to circulate inside the tube since the charged particles of the plasma will spiral around the magnetic field. By increasing the current, and hence the magnetic field, it is possible to squeeze this hot plasma to attain the required density.

Unfortunately a squeezed (or "pinched") plasma tends to become unstable and abruptly expand. Much of the fusion-control work up to now has consisted of attempts to control these instabilities through ever more fancy configurations of the tube. Plasma physicists have obtained a lot of pleasure from dreaming up exotic names for these devices. There are the Perhapsatron, the Columbus model, the Stablized Toroidal Pinch, and the Triaxial Pinch (where the plasma current produces its own magnetic field to pinch itself into a small volume). There are the Stellarator, or Astron, series, where the magnetic field is provided externally. And then there are Albedo, Table Top, Toy Top, Scylla, Ixion, Felix, and Orion, each of which is a progressively more advanced model of a magnetic bottle with magnetic mirrors at the end to reflect the plasma and thus keep it contained. And gradually the conditions necessary for controlled fusion are being approached.

There are many advantages to using fusion processes to supply energy. As indicated before, the raw materials for this source are essentially inexhaustible, even if we consider only the easier process of fusing heavy hydrogen in a D-D reaction. If we could use for this the deuterium which occurs naturally in all water, we would have the situation where each gallon of sea water is equivalent to 350 gallons of gasoline. Can you picture driving your car into a gas station and saying: "Fill'er up with water"? You get 10 gallons, equivalent to 3500 gallons of gasoline, drive 70,000 miles, and then fill'er up again. That is a silly example, but it gives an idea of the energy supply available. Another way of putting it is to say that if we were to fuse all the heavy hydrogen in ordinary water, the released energy would be enough to heat all water by over 3 million degrees centigrade, or the whole earth by about 5000°C.

In addition to the inexhaustibility of the fuel, the fusion reactors would offer some additional attractions. There are, for example, no inherent dangers in the fusion process per se. If there is any threat of explosion, the expanding plasma would touch the physical walls of the reactor vessel, and this would immediately quench the fusion reaction. In addition, there is relatively little radioactivity produced in the fusion process, with the exception of some radioactive tritium, which can hopefully be recycled to continue the fusion reaction.

FUTURE ENERGY CONSUMPTION

But the vastness of these energy supplies leads to the potential pollution of the earth by the resultant released energy. A look at the foreseeable future energy-demands seems to suggest that there may be more than just local thermal pollution in the not-to-distant future. Table 27.1 shows the distribution of energy consumption in the world as of 1964. The most interesting aspect of this table is the fact that the per capita energy consumption in India is only about twice the energy consumed just for subsistence (at 2000 Cal per day per person).

We can play games with these numbers in an attempt to illustrate their magnitudes. Specifically, let us assume that the demand for energy keeps rising by a factor of two every 19 years, just as it has been doing in the recent past. Then we will further assume that all the.

Table 27.1
Annual per capita energy consumption in units of one million large Calories, as of 1964. (Data taken from Ref. 27.4, p. 33.)

Country	Annual per capita consumption ($\times 10^6$ Cal)
U.S.	61.5
Canada	49.9
U.K.	35.0
Germany	29.6
U.S.S.R.	24.0
France	20.5
Japan	11.6
Italy	11.5
Brazil	2.6
India	1.1
World Average	10.7

energy we consume, as it is converted into heat, goes primarily into heating the ocean and/or melting the polar icecap. Figure 27.1 shows some of the highlights of the resultant projection. The energy that we have used to the present time is sufficient to have melted enough ice to raise the ocean water level by about one-half inch. By the year 2050 this could amount to one foot each year. By the year 2170 all the icecaps could be melted; the ocean water level would then be up by as much as 400 feet, enough to cover New York, London, and Tokyo. By the year 2220 we could have an annual ocean temperature rise of 1°C.

Is the future really that grim? Hopefully not; these extrapolations are only supposed to be a game. Unfortunately some of these assumptions are really not that far-fetched. For example, what about the projected exponential rise in the world's energy consumption? There is every reason to expect that this consumption will indeed continue to double roughly every 19 years for some time into the future. Even if the U.S. would suddenly stop increasing its demand for energy, some of the have-not countries like India and China will presumably come up to the U.S. level of consumption before they would be prepared to become conservation minded. One might be optimistic and hope that the population explosion will soon come under control. But the exponential rise in the population actually contributes only a relatively small amount to the increase in energy demand, it is really the per capita demand that is exploding.

In creating these scare figures, it was assumed that all of the released energy goes into either heating the ocean or icecap. This is intended only to illustrate the quantities of energy involved. But it may, in fact, not be an unreasonable assumption. At the present time we already dump most of this energy either into the air or into water; and in the future, the large power stations will probably have to be located in the ocean in order to release the energy directly into ocean water. The circulation of both the atmosphere and the oceans is such that the energy will probably remain in the combined reservoir of water and ice. A prediction of a similar type was made by Alvin Weinberg (Ref. 27.1, p. 416), when he estimated that an annual energy consumption of 1.6×10^{19} Cal will raise the temperature of the atmosphere by one degree centigrade. According to the calculations in Fig. 27.1, this will happen in the year 2130. So, while the precise details of the results of the energy pollution may not be very well defined, the magnitude of the concern is clear. Within 100 years this may indeed have become a major problem.

DISCUSSION

So in global energy pollution we have a potential problem which seems insoluble, even in theory. There are no visible ways of ejecting from the earth the energy released in our ever-more-mechanized way of life. Even building an enormous refrigerator would not work, since a refrigerator always gives off more heat than it removes. Note that we are not talking about local hotspots near a power plant, but rather about global temperature increases. The hotspot problem can usually be solved by a judicious combination of science, technology, and some economic and political concessions. But the global thermal pollution may ultimately be solvable only by abstinence from energy consumption.

If we take these calculations at all seriously, we may someday have to start asking, "Is it energetically better to run 40 automobiles or one bus?" As well as "Which chemically pollutes the air more?" rather than, "Which is cheaper?" Instead of asking about the technological merits (i.e., the economic benefits) of a new way of consuming energy, we must then ask about the broader, long-term social implications of thermal pollution.

However, we may never really face this problem, as the rising population and technological dependence may lead to other social problems long before global thermal pollution becomes a problem. In his articles Weinberg projected an energy need for the future of two times the present U.S. average for up to 20 billion people. Much of his life has, in fact, been devoted to ensuring a decent life for that many people by providing such quantities of energy through fission breeding reactors. As he puts it:

> No one questions that the population must be stabilized, but so far no one has found a workable, humane, and politically feasible means of doing so .... Energy, we believe, is a possible key to ensuring a rational outcome and to buying the time needed to enforce fertility control. (Ref. 27.1, p. 412.)

Weinberg feels that planning for 20 billion people is humanitarian, since they will be there in the year 2100. This philosophy, however, has come under considerable attack by such conservationists as Lincoln P. Brower:

> ... the technological solutions ... to sustain a world population of 20 billion people are far more immoral than were the decisions to use the A-bomb and H-bomb. Other superbombs are *scientifically possible*; a world of 20 billion people may be *scientifically possible*. But the decision to gear our scientific research and technological effort toward making these possibilities a reality is to me a dismal solution to our problems. (Ref. 27.9, p. 618.)

The point is that many people believe that the social, ecological, and even genetic consequences of such a beehive of people would be disastrous. In their view it is then immoral to even suggest that it is technically feasible, because that encourages delays in deciding on immediate control of population and of energy consumption. And if the social fears of these conservationists are right, then global energy pollution is an irrelevant concern, because the world as we know it will never get to the point where it becomes a problem.

REFERENCES

Prime references

27.1 A. M. Weinberg and R. P. Hammond, "Limits to the Use of Energy," *The American Scientist* **58**, 412–418 (July-August 1970).

27.2 W. C. Gough and B. J. Eastland, "The Prospects of Fusion Power," *Scientific American* **224** (#2), 50–64 (February 1971).

Interesting reading

27.3 T. K. Fowler and R. F. Post, "Progress Toward Fusion Power," *Scientific American* **215** (#6), 21–31 (December 1966).

27.4 G. R. Harrison, *The Conquest of Energy*, New York: Wm. Morrow and Co., 1968.

27.5 A. R. Ubbelohde, *Man and Energy*, Baltimore: Penguin Books Inc., 1963.

27.6 A. S. Bishop, *Project Sherwood: The U.S. Program in Controlled Fusion*, Reading, Mass.: Addison-Wesley Publishing Co., 1958.

27.7 A. M. Weinberg, "Nuclear Energy and the Environment," *Bulletin of the Atomic-Scientists* **25**, 69–74 (June 1970).

27.8 D. J. Rose, "Controlled Nuclear Fusion: Status and Outlook," *Science* **172**, 797–807 (May 1971).

27.9 Various letters by Brower, Clendon, Conta, and Strong (to the editor of *The American Scientist* in response to Ref. 27.1) in *The American Scientist* **58**, 618–620 (November-December 1970).

27.10 P. R. Ehrlich and A. H. Ehrlich, *Population, Resources, and Environment: Issues in Human Ecology*, (Ref. 3.9); summary of the population and resources problem.

QUESTIONS FOR DISCUSSION

1. Should we worry at this point about global thermal pollution compared to nuclear war, DDT pollution, etc.?

2. Whose responsibility is it to worry about the problem of thermal pollution?

3. Who should do the population and energy allocation, if we decide to limit these?

4. If we cannot come to a social agreement about how to control the population and the energy consumption, should we then stop fusion research to force a "Malthusian" collision; i.e., let people starve to save the environment?

CONCLUSIONS

As indicated at the beginning of this book, it is too much to expect an answer to the question "Is science a Sacred Cow?" But one can at least try to understand the question. In that sense one can ask whether the proposed four ways of categorizing the science-society interaction are significant and useful. Their significance can perhaps best be measured by how well they serve in analyzing the past; and in that respect they seem quite satisfactory. They form a thread which runs through all of history, and they provide tiepoints which hold together much of the fabric of the present. But to what extent can they be used to guide and direct the future? That is a question that has no clear-cut answer.

In speaking about the *cultural* impact of science, we saw that there have been two cultures in one form or another for a long time. A more useful description of them is in terms of their modes of thought: the scientific culture views the universe as something mechanistic, while the humanistic culture sees it as an organic whole. The mechanistic approach has brought many protests against science as a soul-deadening influence, protests dating as far back as Aristotle. And these protests will continue to arise as long as there are men's souls which rebel against being no different from the rest of matter. The hope is that these protests will lead to something productive—that the humanistic imagination will combine with the scientific love of detail to produce a new synthesis.

A similar hope must be expressed about the *technological* impact of science on society. Here the question is how technology has modified life, and what the origins and consequences of this modification are. This technological interaction has frequently lead to protests about the seeming destruction of the "good life." Once we separate the effects of science on the quantity of life from the effects on the quality of life, then we see that the protests are usually about the latter. These complaints also have an ancient tradition; there seems not to have been a sudden change in the amount of technology—only a continuous (though exponential) growth. Furthermore, the protests about the quality of life are a matter of subjective judgment, and this judgment, at least in the past, has usually been made by people who already had the full quantity of life—like the aristocrats. Because of this matter of history and of subjective judgment, there must be some skepticism toward anyone who predicts the "end of the world as we know it" as a consequence of technology; too often in the past the end of the world has been averted by this same technology. The real problem is that technological solutions have the tendency to generate new problems, and it may be that the contemporary dilemma lies in the rapidity of this replacement process.

If there is to occur some ultimate *social* disaster for the world due to technology, then it will come because of the exponential growth of scientific and technological capabilities in energy consumption and in pollution. If we want to do something about this exponential growth, then some criteria must be developed for making choices between activities that society as a whole engages in; that is, a system of social priorities must be developed. The Weinberg criteria seem to have some validity for this purpose; we can at least show that ignoring them in the past has led to some major crises. These crises suggest that one may no longer claim a self-justifying rationale for science. Instead of the previous question "How much money can science reasonably use?," we must now ask "How much money does science need and deserve?" Science cannot, as in the past, refuse to be judged from the outside in the same way as are other activities of society.

Finally, it would seem that current demands for a social responsibility of scientists make for some difficulties for science as a *discipline*. Most of the problems which society appears to have with science are actually problems with technology. Once a distinction is made between science and technology on the public-knowledge basis, then it becomes clear that science perhaps does not have the primary responsibility for solving these problems. However, in exchange for relinquishing this responsibility, science must also give up all credit for the technological benefits derived from its discoveries. It must then justify its existence on grounds other than possible future technological benefits accruing to mankind. At the same time, in order to preserve its consensus nature, science must also give up its pretense to expertise in nonscientific areas. Scientists should draw a very strong distinction between scientific activities and the activities of scientists as citizens and as human beings. Some of the present difficulties occuring in the interaction of science and politics become clearer on considering this definition of science as an attempt at a consensus; both scientists and society must be careful not to demand that scientists act as political individuals at the same time that they are acting as scientific experts. Only in this way can science retain its uniqueness as a consensus discipline.

INDEX

INDEX